In Tandem

Cricket's Great Pace Pairs

By Patrick Ferriday

"I myself am best
When least in company."
Orsino to Viola, Twelfth Night 1.4.37-8

First published in Great Britain by
VON KRUMM PUBLISHING
31 Highcroft Villas
Brighton BN1 5PS
www.vonkrummpublishing.co.uk

A CIP record of this book is available from the British Library.

Cover and all interior graphic design by Lottie Warren

Printed and Bound in the United Kingdom

ISBN 978-0-9567321-6-3

Contents

Introduction

Tune in to any cricket commentary or read any match report in the English-speaking world and the phrase 'hunting in pairs', or even in 'packs', will make an appearance sooner rather than later. The quarry is the batsman and the hunter the fast bowler. If circumstances dictate, there may be the death by a thousand cuts and the mesmerising slow torture of the cruel and artful spinner. All very neat and metaphorical. While cricket is not a bloodsport, Philip Hughes was a tragic and stark reminder of what can happen.

It now seems barely credible that such an appalling incident hadn't occurred before in Test cricket. Nari Contractor and Ewen Chatfield were dire warnings as were Rick McCosker, Denis Compton, Bruce Mitchell, Bertie Oldfield, Mike Gatting and any number of other highly-skilled practitioners of their profession who have been felled by a cricket ball to the head. Most were back in the middle within hours or days and Gatting could make rueful jokes at the expense of a hapless journalist asking a stupid question. But all could have been killed.

So, why then the enduring fascination with the danger of fast bowling? And why is the fascination doubled when that threat is coming from both ends? Is this the ultimate test of both the skill and the nerve of the batsman? And if we are posing questions there is another: why did it take half a century from the appearance of the first really quick bowlers to introduce protective headgear? Players had long worn protection on their legs, hands and genitalia but saw fit to leave their heads bare to the elements.

Certainly, the unrestrained speed battalions of the Packer era and beyond made the game more dangerous than ever but it's not as if Harold Larwood in the '30s; Ray Lindwall, Peter Heine or Frank Tyson in the '50s; or Wes Hall and Charlie Griffith in the '60s hadn't presented a clear and present danger. Perhaps the turning point was watching Colin Cowdrey facing up to Dennis Lillee and Jeff Thomson in 1974 before they, in turn, traded blows with Andy Roberts and Michael Holding. Mr Packer certainly saw something visceral that he could package and sell to a new generation. Raw pace was to be his key marketing tool and for two decades it dominated international cricket until Abdul Qadir and Shane Warne, amongst others, turned the clock back.

In pre-television days fast bowling was quite simply thrilling in a way that no other method could be. From the boundary edge you could see exactly what the bowler was doing – there were no dark arts of googlies, late away swing and befuddled batsmen, just searing pace and batsmen groping for absent milliseconds. For live spectators this still holds true even if the audience at home can now count revs, and super slow mo's untangle the skills of the spinners. The presence of potential danger has always been a draw-card and tested the mettle and heart of any batsman faced with a possible life-changing incident every minute. It's a dangerous game and always will be and that, ultimately, has always been a part of the appeal. A small part maybe but Shoaib Akhtar, Mitchell Johnson and Dale Steyn have kept the tradition alive this century and they won't be the last. Or will they?

Test cricket has reached a crossroads that quite simply can't be ignored. Financially it is, with a few exceptions, unsustainable. Against this, English county cricket has been in this position for half a century yet every April several hundred hardy souls re-appear to the backdrop of light drizzle and massed hand wringing. The real money for both cricket boards and players all over the world is in the limited-overs format with T20 the jewel in the crown. Test cricket may be the 'ultimate examination' but T20 is the magic money tree and the temptation for any young cricketer to put cash first is enormous.

The shortest form of cricket is many things to many people but even its most strident advocate can hardly find room for the patient accumulator of runs or the fiery but sometimes-wayward pace bowler. The key skills are to score runs as quickly as possible and to pitch the ball on exactly the required spot, both of which are extremely difficult to master. The question here is where does this leave the genuine pace bowler? How would a Wes Hall or Andy Roberts have responded to the peculiar demands of T20? It's a hypothetical question of course but less so if one considers what happens to a young, aspiring fast bowler with the embryonic skills of these past masters.

It's probably safe to say that we will never see another pair to match those highlighted in this book. If we do, it will not last any great length of time. Increasingly the equation is simple – pace is for show but taking pace off is for dough. The financial imperatives of the IPL or Big Bash require new priorities from players, coaches and cricket authorities. Common sense now says that rest is required at the sign of a niggle, not a series of injections. If the problem increases then drop the slog of Test cricket and in extreme cases restrict yourself to just 24 balls. If those 24 balls are good enough there's a fat pay packet to collect without incurring long-term damage. Where it seemed long ago that limited-overs cricket would be the death of the spinner it now seems that it is the genuinely fast bowler who is becoming redundant. High-speed bowling is high risk and is unlikely to be economic in either runs per over or dollars per annum. In Tests it still has a place but as Tests become less and less relevant to the calendar of world cricket so the fast bowler must follow this decline.

Cricket has often been described as a team game where the individual can excel and virtually win a game single-handedly at any level. Ian Botham, Keith Miller, Kapil Dev and Imran Khan have shown this to be true – Don Bradman found it a bit harder but certainly made innumerable Tests unlosable for his side. Also within the team we sometimes find the pair that seems to have a special bond that binds them to one another even if this bond is more imagination than reality.

For example there is the greatest ever opening pair of Jack Hobbs and Herbert Sutcliffe. One amassed more first-class runs and centuries than anyone ever will and the other averaged over 60 in Test matches. Together for England they were a formidable combination on shirt-fronts, sticky dogs and all points between but in what sense were they really a pair beyond the fact that they opened for their country 25 times and had a partnership average of 67.8? There was the famed running between the wickets, the intuition and understanding of when and when not to go without a call. This drove opposing captains to distraction and certainly added to already impressive totals. But fundamentally it was a story of two exceptionally talented batsmen scoring lots of runs, something they also did when not playing together. Gordon Greenidge did not disappear into his shell when Desmond Haynes was sidelined, Justin Langer was a fine compliment to Matthew Hayden in many respects but both scored abundantly without one another.

The supporters of any country, not to mention the padded-up middle order of the team, love to see a settled and reliable top two returning year after year to see the shine off and then put up a three-figure partnership. The value to the team is enormous and the familiarity is endearing – there they are again, maybe slightly thicker round the waist but just as reliable as five years ago. The reason they do keep returning to represent their country is that they are the best openers available and not because they magically bring out the best in one another. They may enjoy batting together but to a large degree batting is a solitary occupation and if both are experienced it matters little if Vlad the Impaler is the non-striker as long as he goes when called and averages upwards of 40.

The same may or may not be the case with bowlers operating in tandem but the equations are more complicated. There is the same feeling of security when the ball is thrown to Robin Ashwin and Ravi Jadeja or JJ Ferris and Charlie Turner year in year out. Familiarity does not breed contempt in this context, quite the opposite. When the new ball invited the attentions of Curtly Ambrose and Courtney Walsh or Allan Donald and Shaun Pollock there was the likelihood, bordering on certainty, that the batsmen would have to work to stay at the wicket let alone score runs. Was the threat lessened if Makhaya Ntini replaced Donald or Ian Bishop partnered Ambrose? The answer must be 'yes', but was it by any more than the superiority of Donald over Ntini and Walsh over Bishop? This is fundamental to the question of the special appeal of pace pairs – does their combined potency amount to more than their individual talents?

Statistics will show a variety of answers and remain open to interpretation for the most part. Is it really surprising that in the case of Brian Statham his best performance came without Fred Trueman taking wickets at the other end? This was the 'problem' for Malcolm Marshall – how to get more than a handful of wickets before his partners had taken their share. Surely no bowler in history is so associated with 4-42-type figures. A total of just four 10-wicket hauls in 81 Tests is absurdly small for a man who can be considered amongst the greatest ever to mark a run. Lillee and Richard Hadlee were both twice as successful by this measurement and certainly weren't twice the bowlers.

There are other psychological factors to consider. Is there inspiration and momentum to be gleaned from watching a rival (and often good friend) performing better than yourself? Perhaps the loss of this partner to injury might be an inspiration in itself as the remaining fit opening bowler is now the lone spearhead – Stuart Broad and Keith Miller are just two examples of bowlers who have experienced this and excelled when shorn of their long-standing partners. But it would be wrong to analyse this only from the bowler's perspective – the batsman will certainly have an opinion.

The most famous pace attack of all was relentless. In 1981 when Roberts and Holding had finished their opening assault they could rest up, to be replaced by Joel Garner and Colin Croft – the fast attack kept coming but it wasn't just a fast attack, it was a rare quartet of four top-class bowlers who were all fast and offered differing threats. Is the pressure any less when having seen off Brett Lee the man who joins Glenn McGrath in the attack is Warne? The physical threat may have been removed but the threat to the precious wicket has been increased. A very good bowler has been replaced by a genius. McGrath and Warne were a great pair, they were also great bowlers. A partnership will only flower if both components are top-class and their proximity to one another can only influence that in limited ways. Lindwall and Miller, Trueman and Statham, Ambrose and Walsh; none were significant factors in the development of the other. Each had already reached a high level of ability before becoming international team-mates and each had very contrasting methods. With Waqar Younis and Wasim Akram or Allan Donald and Shaun Pollock the position is perhaps more complex.

Some names just belong together and no book or set of statistics will change that. Certain pairs of fast bowlers just roll off the tongue: was there really a Griffith without a Hall or a Miller without his Lindwall? As we shall see, there was.

Mike Selvey was covering the England tour of South Africa in 1999 and saw enough of Donald and Pollock to cast his mind onto the concept of fast-bowling combinations. His conclusions, eloquently expressed, followed the generally accepted line:

> 'The most resonant names are not batsmen but fast bowlers, pacemen who hunt together. Their names trip from the tongue conjuring pictures of sweat, toil and blood as well: Larwood and Voce terrorising the Aussies with Bodyline, Lillee and Thomson returning the compliment with interest 40 years later, Lindwall and Miller, Hall and Griffith, Trueman and Statham, Wasim and Waqar, right through to Ambrose and Walsh. Stupendous all of them, each bringing out the best in the other, each pairing offering no respite, each greater than the sum of its constituent parts. How many wickets did Brian Statham's nagging, whippy accuracy get for Fiery Fred, ferocious and confrontational at the other end? Or Keith Miller's devil-take-the-hindmost attitude for the sleek Lindwall? See one off and the other was still there.'

It's impossible to verify the accuracy of Selvey's thesis but in view of the following studies of the great pairs it holds a lot less water than is usually considered to be the case. One could plausibly argue that it is, in fact, palpably untrue. How many *did* Statham and Miller get for Trueman and Lindwall? It's impossible to estimate, but both the Yorkshireman and the New South Welshman would certainly have been great bowlers, but maybe lesser men, without those partners.

Nonetheless, the link remains and not just from the hindsight afforded by history but in the collective imagination of the time. Whether a construct coined by journalists, mythical or not, the coupling had a currency not just with contemporary cricket followers but with the captains and batsmen of the time. The paired bowlers themselves could hardly fail to feel part of this whether the link was born of mutual friendship, a grudging sharing of experience and expertise or sometimes even bitter rivalry.

Lillee and Thomson (Lilian Thomson) were a potent mix that dazed many an English or West Indian batsman but many of their greatest deeds were achieved outside this coupling. In fact, of all the great fast-bowling pairs only one can really be seen as a truly career commitment – Ambrose and Walsh played together 95 times (mostly sharing the new ball), Ambrose appeared in only three Tests without his partner. Anderson and Broad will, in due course, join the illustrious West Indians.

But these names have been pulled together in the same way that great opening batting pairs are relished; more so. Sometimes the connection seems tenuous but Hall and Griffith or Adcock and Heine seem conjoined in perpetuity for any lover of cricket history and the habit has not died. Donald and Pollock, Wasim and Waqar, Imran and Sarfraz – nothing excites supporters like a pair of quicks to rattle stumps early and put the fear of god into the opposition.

But this may simply be poor judgement – an emotional heuristic, to paraphrase psychologists Daniel Kahneman and Amos Tversky, whereby we see something because we like the idea of it. This is, in turn, fed by journalists and commentators because we like to hear it and have our ideas echoed.

The best way to establish any truth or falsehoods in the 'hunting in pairs' concept is to look at the careers of some pairs who are generally considered to have hunted together. How did they perform together and apart, how did they influence one another, what did they achieve and was the sum total greater than that of the two parts?

Measuring the speed of bowlers is a necessary adjunct to this study and both measurements are used.

70 mph = 112.7 kph
80 mph = 128.7 kph
85 mph = 136.8 kph

90 mph = 144.8 kph
95 mph = 152.9 kph
100 mph = 160.9 kph

YouTube highlights are included on the statistics pages of each pair of bowlers but virtually all, and many others, can be seen in action by watching David Frith's documentary *Great Bowlers*, also on YouTube.

Before The Lights Went Out

Fast bowling was a relatively late development in cricket. Test matches, county, and state cricket were well established before a quick bowler, as we would recognise him, first arrived. The main reason is relatively straightforward – there was no real need. Pitches were unreliable enough to rely on accuracy above all else with perhaps a bit of break and spin for a rare flat deck. Furthermore batsmen outside the select few in each team were easy pickings.

As pitch preparation and batsmanship became more scientific arts in both England and Australia and money breathed a professional air into the game, those easy pickings disappeared from the lower branches and bowlers were required to climb higher for their fruit. Arms moved higher and run-ups became longer as a quest for greater miles per hour began. Even SF Barnes recalled his early ambitions amounting to little more than using all his height to bowl as fast as possible. It wasn't, however, until Ernie Jones of Australia made an appearance and the Doctor's beard was parted that all-out fast bowling became a reality.

It's easy to be fooled by accounts of Golden Age cricket and believe that pace bowling was part of it. By and large it wasn't. The first great Ashes bowler, Fred 'The Demon' Spofforth, was not possessed of demonic pace. He was essentially a medium pacer as we would now recognise it with some very, very clever tricks. Tom Richardson is generally regarded as England's first top-class fast bowler but all the evidence points to him being fast-medium at most. Again, this is not to decry his skill (or phenomenal stamina) but rather to get a sense of what was considered fast bowling before 1914. Bill Lockwood, Richardson's Surrey and England team-mate, was also quick for his time but any suggestion that he and Richardson formed the first fast pair in Test cricket is simply not true. They played together for England just five times, never took the new ball in tandem and Lockwood managed just five wickets in these games although he did take 38 in the seven Tests he played without Richardson. Against this it should be mentioned that wicket-keepers invariably stood back to this pair, an indication that they were quicker than all bar a few contemporaries.

There were some that we might consider genuinely fast but even that is open to doubt. Stories abound of the thunderous pace of Charles Kortright, Neville Knox and Walter Brearley and Pelham Warner considered the 'stream of fast bowlers at flood level' in 1895. Yet none of the three aforementioned enjoyed any success in Test cricket.

Outside England three names merit consideration as fast. JJ Kotze of South Africa (his wicket-keeper 'Barburton' Halliwell stood up), Jones (whose action was dubious to say the least and whose tearaway speed was soon curtailed) and Tibby Cotter (with a Thommo-like sling). Yet none of these enjoyed any consistent success. Jones took a mere 15 wickets in his first seven and last eight Tests combined; his reputation rests on a burst of four consecutive matches in 1898 and 1899 where his 32 wickets cost just 17 each. Cotter's record was more impressive over 21 Tests but 89 wickets at 28.5 does not smack of destructive pace especially when compared to near contemporary Monty Noble, an allrounder with a better bowling record. Kotze barely registers as a Test bowler despite his fearsome reputation and desire to 'shiver the timbers' of opposing batsmen.

The mainstays of the bowling attacks of the three Test-playing nations remained seamers, swervers and, above all, spinners. South Africa had a battery of leggies, Australia looked mainly to cut and swerve with some leg break while England had variety incorporating left-arm spin and right-arm swerve. The greatest of all was Barnes who spun the ball both ways at medium pace from a great height with relentless accuracy. He himself considered Bill O'Reilly to be of similar pace – as a wrist spinner O'Reilly was barely faster than 70 mph despite his aggressive approach. Yet in 1952 Lionel Tennyson referred to Barnes as 'fast', a clue indeed as to what 'fast' actually meant before 1914.

Stanley Jackson called Charlie Turner 'medium-paced', another clue. Even *Cricinfo* lists Turner as medium-fast. Yet his speed was accurately measured at 55 mph and he bowled finger spin – he had an alarming change of pace but he was a spinner bowling at a conventional spinner's pace. It is with such classifications that the confusion begins – if Turner was 'medium-paced' then what were George Hirst, Bart King or Noble? Medium-fast is about right, so probably between 70 and 75 mph. Arthur Fielder of Kent was described as 'right-arm fast' but relied on swing and break to a 'keeper standing up – not fast then, maybe in the upper seventies or lower eighties mph. It may be conjecture but that leaves the accepted 'fast' bowlers of the pre-1914 era in the low eighties with perhaps the odd one sometimes touching 85 mph. This is not genuine fast bowling as we have understood it for nearly 100 years. We would expect a Michael Holding or Shoaib Akhtar in their pomp to be averaging around 90mph with the effort balls hitting 95.

All this association and informed guesswork may seem beside the point in a study of great pace pairs but it is relevant to what we mean by 'pace'.

Before 1914 there were bowlers considered fast (maybe a Jimmy Anderson or Ishant Sharma), by 1932 there was a real fast bowler for the ages in Harold Larwood and thereafter genuine fast bowlers, with the odd short hiatus, were a fixture in Test cricket. Even India abandoned a spin-only attack as soon as an alternative appeared.

Between The Wars

With the success of Jack **Gregory** and Ted **McDonald** and the new fangled idea of opening with speed from both ends it seemed that maybe the clock couldn't be turned back and in some senses it never was. A problem, however, soon became apparent; how to find two bowlers to fill the role so masterfully occupied by the two Australians for 10 glorious months in 1921?

Realistically the odds were stacked against a repetition even if the effectiveness was obvious as England were knocked aside in two successive series. In 30 years of Test cricket England had yet to produce even one genuinely quick bowler, neither had South Africa. Australia had enjoyed the brief luxury of Ernie Jones and Tibby Cotter before 1914 but there was no store of powerful young men waiting to take over as Gregory's partner once McDonald had moved to Lancashire. Instead Australia relied on wrist spinners – first Arthur Mailey then Clarrie Grimmett and finally Bill O'Reilly – supported by a mish-mash of whoever was available, very often a batsman who could bowl a bit such as Jack Ryder, Stork Hendry or Stan McCabe. Bert Ironmonger and Arthur Chipperfield had turns as spinning support but the chief weapon Australia possessed on the inter-war pitches of over-prepared marl was its run machines with Don Bradman pulling stroke, aided and abetted by Bill Ponsford, McCabe, Bill Woodfull and a host of others revelling in timeless Tests. Eventually the limitless patience and stamina of the leggies would prevail even if they had to get through 100-plus overs. Two pace bowlers did appear but not together and neither lasted long. Tim Wall was fast but lacked accuracy and Ernie McCormick's lumbago held him back from establishing any lasting place in the national side. There might have been a third but a dubious action and Aboriginal heritage were obstacles too large for Eddie Gilbert to surmount.

It was never really likely that South Africa could or would subscribe to the new order. With such a small pool of players to draw from, courtesy of black and coloured exclusion and Afrikaner indifference, and a strictly amateur structure the likelihood of pace in Africa was virtually nil. An additional factor was that any young white man with pretensions to bowling fast would soon have his heart broken by matting wickets that only started being replaced in the 1930s. South Africa spent the entire inter-war years without one top-class bowler. Bob Crisp, Sandy Bell and Chud Langton had their moments but in general there was no pace or spin – just medium-quick and a reliance on good fortune such as the plague of leatherjackets at Lord's in 1935.

The two decades of peace did at least see the Test club double in size as new members New Zealand, India and West Indies were accepted by the Imperial Cricket Conference. Jack Cowie was quick for New Zealand but his team was poor. Astonishingly, in view of the next 50 years, India brought a more than respectable new-ball pairing to England for their first tour. Amar Singh and Mohammad Nissar collected 22 wickets in the three-Test series in 1936 though both disappeared from the game soon afterwards. Neither was truly fast but they remained probably India's best new-ball pairing for 50 years until Kapil Dev and Javagal Srinath began to change the face of the subcontinental approach.

West Indies arrived on the Test scene favouring speed over spin. On their first tour Herman Griffith was the outstanding performer but it is Learie Constantine and Manny Martindale who are best remembered, and with good reason. In the seven games they played together they took 47 wickets and at Manchester in 1933 they went after Douglas Jardine with a bodyline attack. But Old Trafford was not Adelaide and they weren't Harold Larwood and he of the harlequin cap hit a century. They might be remembered as a pair but in fact Constantine was only fast when the fancy took him (he could do *anything* when the fancy took him) and was often not the preferred new-ball bowler.

West Indies (apart from George Headley), like India and New Zealand, found the going tough at the outset but unlike the others they acclimatized quickly and by 1939 would have been a fair match for South Africa if such a meeting had been possible. Quick bowling and the black Bradman lay behind their relative strength – when they won 2-1 at home to England in 1934-35, Headley averaged 97 and the three quicks took three-quarters of the wickets.

That left England, with a large pool of professionals, as always the most likely to find one or more fast bowlers. The first master of the period was Maurice Tate, the man with the huge feet and the heart of lion and temperament of a pussy cat. Like Alec Bedser two decades later he was deceptively quick off the pitch but rarely was the wicket-keeper forced to stand back to either man.

While Tate was stirring England with his deeds both at home and abroad a new phenomenon was emerging from the Nottinghamshire coalfields – Larwood, the first real fast bowler to represent his country, who could bowl at 85 mph and above for 20 overs in a day. Not only was he fast, he was accurate too and he had a partner in left-armer and county team-mate Bill Voce. These two names are so often bracketed together that they seem like a foretaste of Wasim Akram and Waqar Younis yet they only wore England caps together four times and on all four occasions they were the purveyors of Bodyline. Voce was strictly the foil to Larwood's rapier on that controversial tour of Australia. Reaching a measured speed of 96 mph Larwood was too hot to handle with his Jardine field and Jardine instructions.

The tale hardly needs re-telling of how Bradman was laid low before MCC discarded Larwood, before Voce then went on to greater deeds without his partner four years later at Brisbane and Sydney and before a strained back then counted him out and the series was lost. After Larwood came Bill Bowes and Ken Farnes – both quick but relatively brief in an attack that changed around the spin of Hedley Verity. Nothing here to match Gregory and McDonald.

Two decades of batting domination on largely dead wickets did little for the bowler's craft in Test matches. In 1927 the size of the ball was reduced and four years later the size of the wickets increased but still Bradman, Wally Hammond, Headley and the others made hay except on the rare occasions when the sun didn't shine and the rain fell on an uncovered wicket. Then it was a field day for the finger spinners.

Gregory
and
McDonald

Jack Gregory

You couldn't take your eyes off him. He took a long run, with tremendous hops, finishing with a nine-foot bound as he reached the stumps and let the ball go. There was a frightfulness in the action of this giant of some six feet four inches, who hurled the ball down from an awkward angle and made the ball bounce fast and high. – Johnnie Moyes

Ted McDonald

Whence does McDonald draw his terrible strength and velocity? His run to the wicket is so easy, so silent. He does not thunder over the earth like Gregory – like a bull at a gate. No; he runs along a sinister curve, lithe as a panther, his whole body moving like visible, dangerous music. The man's whole being tells of the sinister destructive forces of nature – he is a satanic bowler, menacing but princely. – Neville Cardus

On the face of it the combination of Jack Gregory and Ted McDonald barely deserves a place amongst the great pace pairs of cricket history. Just 11 Test matches in 10 months over three series with a combined total of 86 wickets at an average of around 30. And if that leaves an underwhelming impression there is the presence of leg spinner Arthur Mailey in nine of those Tests in which he scooped 55 wickets. Those are the figures, but the names of Gregory and McDonald are inextricably linked because they were the first, and one of the best, of their kind, even if longevity is lacking.

Their captain during the 10 months of 1921 was Warwick Armstrong, 'The Big Ship'. In many ways this sobriquet and the attached images of the 120kg behemoth do the man an injustice. He was a mighty batsman, a niggly and effective leg spinner and a clever thinker once handed the captaincy. It is this latter quality that was to be so influential on the careers of Gregory, McDonald and the history of the game. His chosen method of rotating his bowlers seems obvious now but it wasn't back then. His bowling attack consisted of two fast bowlers, a leg spinner (Mailey), an allrounder leg spinner (himself), two allrounder medium pacers (Jack Ryder and Charles Kelleway) and an allrounder left-arm spinner (Charlie Macartney). His tactic was to open with his two quicks and then rotate the pair at the most favourable end while using Mailey and the others in support. It's hardly rocket science but the appearance of serious fast bowling at both ends while the shine was still on the ball was a shock to opening batsmen.

Neither Gregory nor McDonald had made any great waves before the outbreak of war in 1914. Gregory was part of the great dynasty that included cousin Syd, captain of Australia in 1912, and Uncles Dave and Ned who both represented their country. He had, however, shown no great interest in cricket as a youth and any growing aptitude in North Sydney CC was soon cut off by hostilities when he was 19. Gregory signed up for the forces and served with great distinction in France, rising through the ranks from artillery gunner to lieutenant.

McDonald, born four years before Gregory, had a considerably more colourful life prior to 1914. A highly promising cricketer and Aussie Rules footballer in his native Tasmania, he left for Melbourne under a cloud after 'accounting irregularities' were found at his place of work in Launceston. Avoiding prosecution and given a second chance he quickly forced his way into the Victoria side and was given reason to believe that he would be included in the Australian party for the 1912 Triangular Tournament in

England. In truth his performances hardly merited such elevation but it was a patchwork side as six of the leading players became embroiled in a stand-off with the Board of Control and refused to tour. The selectors certainly erred – their selection as fast bowler, John McLaren, barely played a match and disappeared without trace from the game.

McDonald, beset by injury, made more progress in his football career during the war years but when Sheffield Shield fixtures were reinstated for the 1918-19 season he was quick to strike and his efforts did not go unnoticed. Victoria's captain warned Clem Hill, out of retirement to captain South Australia, "We have one of the best bowlers you've ever seen." McDonald took 12 wickets in the match. Vic Richardson, making his debut for SA, never forgot this display and always considered McDonald the best fast bowler he saw – and he saw Harold Larwood, Ray Lindwall, and Wes Hall. Little wonder then that Armstrong had pencilled in McDonald for the national side that he would probably be leading against the MCC tourists two years hence.

Gregory's career was escalating even more dramatically on the other side of the world. The cessation of hostilities in November 1918 had brought a brief moment of euphoria in the victorious nations but within weeks the reality had sunk in. Ruined lives, families and economies cast a pall over societies in Europe – no victory could replace the crippling losses amassed over four years of unimaginable bloodshed. A return to relative normality was sought and sport was expected to play its part. In England the County Championship was hastily convened for the summer of 1919 with all games lasting two exceptionally long days in order to facilitate travel in a country stumbling back to reality. A touch of glamour was added to the season by the efforts of the Australian Imperial Forces (AIF) team and no more glamorous figure was to be found than Gregory.

At nearly six feet four (an exceptional height at the time and a dangerous one too in the trenches of Northern France) he was a formidable figure and he used his physical advantages in all facets of his game. His long arms and huge hands made him an exceptional slip fielder, his reach and strength allowed him to be a mighty left-handed striker of the ball and his height presented a fearsome right-arm prospect to any batsman as he bounded, unfettered, towards the bowling crease. The image was backed by deeds over the course of the season. The AIF side travelled the length and breadth of the country recording victory after victory and at the centre of it all was the new supreme allrounder. Beyond other future Test players Herby Collins, Johnny Taylor, Bert Oldfield and Nip Pellew it was not an exceptional side but the vim, brio and boundless talent and energy of Gregory made them formidable opposition as they recorded 12 wins, 12 draws and only four defeats. The best example of Gregory's influence came at Sheffield in the match against Yorkshire: having taken 13 wickets he arrived at the crease with AIF at 111-8 chasing 170 for victory. Gregory scored an unbeaten 41 in a one-wicket win. Back in Sydney, Dr Leslie Poidevin recorded that reports from the Old Country of Gregory's deeds were met at first with surprise, then incredulity before wonder and anticipation.

At the end of the season the team travelled to South Africa to record more victories where Gregory averaged 40 with the bat and 12 with the ball. Then to home – and it was a country agog at his achievements and slavering at the prospect of seeing him make his first-class debut in the land of his birth. He didn't disappoint. In the opening game against Victoria, captained by Armstrong, he took 7-22; his subsequent partner McDonald managed five wickets including Collins in both innings. Against New South Wales he took eight and scored a century in each innings. The reports from England and South Africa had not been exaggerated and the watching Warwick Armstrong could happily plan building a team around this force of nature for the following season.

In that same season McDonald, by contrast, seemed to take a step backwards. Having started well enough with 12 wickets in the first two Shield matches and then five more against AIF he missed the remaining first-class season through injury. Scribes sharpened their pencils and in the inevitable comparisons between the bowling of Gregory and McDonald the latter did not prosper. He was quick for sure but stamina seemed to be a short suit and this did not go down well in the media. Could it be that he was a bit of a shirker, not really prepared to throw himself body and soul into the fight? 'Moody' was another adjective employed. This was an accusation that could never be levelled at Gregory. Frank Iredale summed up the general feeling of the time.

> 'McDonald is at present Australia's second fast bowler. It is hard to gauge his real merit…At his best he has good pace but he does not appear to be able to keep it up. He does not appear to be physically fit for much strenuous work as a fast bowler.'

But it wasn't that simple. McDonald was slender and taciturn but a fine record in Rules football did not indicate a man without attitude and his beautifully rhythmic action could only help any perceived lack of strength.

That's the way Warwick Armstrong saw it and notwithstanding the various factions and infighting within Australian cricket he would be the man to lead his country when England arrived the following year.

Armstrong did captain the side, but only just. He had made many enemies during the pre-1914 'Big Six' dispute and was not a man of flowering diplomacy who could, or wanted to, let bygones be bygones. He would lead Australia because he was the best man for the job on the field, not off it. For those anti-Armstrongers, Collins was a very respectable alternative after his successes leading the AIF side. Armstrong won the day but initially his wings were clipped – appointed only for the first Test he was also denied a position as selector in favour of his vice-captain Collins. A bizarre muddle to say the least.

There was, inevitably, huge interest and enthusiasm for the tourists. After the horrors and bloodshed here was a return to normality that sport was ideally placed to provide. Jack Hobbs, Wilfred Rhodes, Jack Hearne and Frank Woolley would be back, Macartney, Warren Bardsley and Armstrong too. Just like old times – almost.

Gregory and McDonald were in different positions. The former a certainty, the latter on the fringes and seemingly reliant on early-season form and the influence of his skipper. Despite some encouraging spells and a display of the longed-for stamina, McDonald did not make the cut. Gregory would be supported by the medium pace of Kelleway and Ryder who, crucially in timeless Tests, were more than capable batsmen.

MCC had performed well in the lead-up to the series opener at Sydney and if their bowling was nothing special they at least boasted an impressive top six. The reality was soon apparent – honours even after the opening day and subsequently one-way traffic as Australia triumphed by 377 runs. Gregory's Test debut was not a great triumph but he played his part – six wickets and three catches. Having curiously moved into the slips due to a finger injury, he was now showing himself to be the best.

Throughout his career his work in this position was a thing of wonder. Blessed with great reactions and an uncanny knack of prediction allied to athleticism and reach, he was a one-man circus in the cordon. High chances were flicked upwards and caught on the drop, huge hands clasped balls that by rights should be crashing into the pickets, and catches were taken one-handed with both legs flailing in the air. There had never been anything like it and probably never has been since. But he did drop sitters, as if they were beneath contempt and lacking in challenge. In many ways this is how Gregory played the game. He loved the challenge, to pit his physical prowess against the opposition. He batted without gloves and almost without technique but the reactions, reach and anticipation that made him such a slipper could be used in batting. That, allied to his sheer, unadulterated strength made him a fearsome opponent. He would never be reliable or score regularly but he was, in modern parlance, a man who could take the game away from you in an hour. Always in the game, the eyes of the spectators could not but be drawn to his figure – tall and full of vigour. One can only guess at the effect on team-mates.

After such a crushing victory it was inevitable that Australia would stick with the same XI at Melbourne. McDonald had made hay in a Shield match but his services would not be required for his country – at least not yet.

If Gregory had had a quiet, by his standards, debut his second Test was a cacophony of brilliance. England were unfortunate with the weather but Gregory, batting at nine, hit 100 in 115 minutes with the game in the balance and then blew the visitors away with 7-69. The game was over in just over three days. His hitting was heavy and his bowling, conserved in short bursts by his skipper, was everything that any Australian could have hoped for. Bounding in with that now familiar 'kangaroo hop' he showed the ability to mix great pace with skilled guile – too much for all bar Hobbs.

Despite the overwhelming victory the Australian selectors (presumably leant on by Armstrong) now dropped a batsman for a bowler and the Gregory and McDonald partnership was born. Armstrong had long admired McDonald and could see the opportunities opened up by having two genuinely quick bowlers, both during the rest of this series and subsequently in the next English summer. He also knew exactly how he wanted to use his pacemen.

Not an especially innovative captain, Armstrong was doubtless astute and vastly experienced and it was his use of the tools at his disposal as much as the tools themselves that made Gregory and McDonald the first international pace pair. The template was simple – Gregory would take the end with the wind or slope and McDonald the other. This in itself was an oddity – most captains tended to open with a fast/slow combination. After an opening burst the two men would be used in short spells at the more favourable end while the others, led by Armstrong himself and Mailey, would occupy the other. Of course there were variations but he was determined not to exhaust his quicks as others had done. Tom Richardson had been bowled into the ground by a succession of desperate captains. Gregory later recalled 'that we were to give him the wink when we were feeling the slightest bit tired. He always told us that we could recover from tiredness quicker than strain.'

The beginning was hardly dramatic but 15 January 1921 must go down as a date of great significance in the development of Test cricket. The Adelaide pitch was made for batting and a run fest eventually finished on day six with Australia comfortably enough in front. Here though, on day two, was the chance at last to enjoy these great bowlers and compare and contrast. Plenty of eye-witness reports remain. Percy Fender thought McDonald the quicker but found Gregory's bounce made him harder to score from. Bert Oldfield had the prime spot behind the stumps:

> 'Gregory always swung the new ball more effectively than his teammate and he was, if anything, slightly faster while the sheen remained on the ball. Once the newness was worn off he relied wholly on pace whereas McDonald was able to turn the ball back from the off even at his fastest speed, and with this ball he could be most destructive. The spin that McDonald imparted added speed to his delivery in a most deceptive manner, after the ball made contact with the pitch. On the other hand, Gregory's delivery did not gain pace from the pitch, rather did it lose impetus, particularly on a lifeless wicket…[Gregory's] high deliveries, bounding run and controlled accuracy made him a dangerous and effective bowler. Using the new ball he swung it more disconcertingly than any other fast bowler to whom I ever kept wicket. His good length deliveries lifted awkwardly, as though they were short pitched, and so proved extremely troublesome to all types of batsmen… [McDonald] bowled with such rhythm that his action seemed to flow as smoothly as a river. All his energy went into flinging the ball down and none into superfluous pounding of the earth or waving of the arms.'

Echoes of Courtney Walsh and Curtly Ambrose perhaps.

Three wickets for 173 runs was hardly a dream debut for McDonald but in a high-scoring match he successfully sidelined proponents of the theory that he lacked stamina, rarely dropping his pace over a gruelling 48 overs. It was the attritional Mailey with 10-302 who led the grind to victory. Not that Gregory didn't do his bit – five wickets, all front-line batsmen, a half-century and a couple of catches were about par for a man who had made his first-class debut less than two years earlier and was now the most exciting player in the world.

The fourth Test was a similar story. England had a squeak of a chance but the relentless Mailey (13 wickets in 76 overs) and a brilliant hundred by the captain saw Australia home once again and 4-0 up in the series. Armstrong was careful not to flog his quick bowlers, preferring to support Mailey with the gentle medium pace of Kelleway and Ryder with an eye to the fifth Test and then an arduous tour of England two months later. One wicket apiece but another half-century and three catches kept Gregory's name in the limelight while McDonald waited patiently for a pitch on which to prosper.

The final Test continued the pattern. Mailey moved to a record 36 wickets for the series, a humbled England blundered to defeat, a superb century to order (this time from Macartney), a big half-century and six catches for Gregory (giving him a still-standing record of 15 for the series) and another quiet match for McDonald. For Armstrong it was mission accomplished both in terms of results and preparation for the next test. His team was fit and well and they would need to be with the absurdly convoluted schedule they faced in England from April to September 1921.

It seems madness now that a touring side should depart Australian shores to face 38 matches in England followed by a handful in South Africa with only four front-line bowlers – two quicks and two leggies – supported by a few batting allrounders. There was a political element to at least one selection – Edgar Mayne, a Board man through and through whom Armstrong treated with disdain.

Armstrong himself, one of the four bowlers, was now pushing 42 and with a capacious waistline. He was certainly aware that an injury or two to his bowlers would have made his team very vulnerable. With this in mind he enlisted the companionship of McDonald for daily stoking shifts in the bowels of the *Osterly*. He would sweat off his excess weight (unsuccessfully as it turned out) and Mac would banish any doubts about stamina for once and for all. Gregory just needed a bit of a rest – just a little work would get him back to full fitness.

After their rollicking success at home the 15th Australian touring side attracted enormous interest on their arrival in England but continued dominance was not expected back on softer wickets. Could Mailey possibly find such assistance as he had at home? Would those selfsame pitches not blunt the natural pace of the opening pair even given Gregory's performances for the AIF team two years previously? And what to make of McDonald with just six wickets at 65 in three Tests but still carrying the confidence of his captain?

The first minutes of first-class action in England have been described before but need doing so again; the symbolism of the exchange between McDonald and Harry Whitehead of Leicestershire was to prove an accurate barometer of the pressure of the summer's proceedings. A seasoned professional, Whitehead was now 36 years old and one ball from Gregory was quite enough. This was what the war had done to English cricket; the men who would have replaced Whitehead and his generation had been decimated mentally, physically and even financially. Little wonder that all county sides were forced to call back players well past their sell-by date.

After Whitehead's departure it was the turn of McDonald on his first outing on an English wicket. His 8-41 was a precursor to a decade of trouble for English county batsmen. The remaining seven 'warm-up' games before the first Test posed few problems and the opening pair were rarely asked to work together or really exert themselves for any length of time but there was plenty of indication that they would be a formidable combination and that McDonald had taken to English conditions as to the manor born.

The Nottingham Test, much anticipated, was a disaster for England and presaged a summer of torment. Within 20 minutes Gregory had ripped out the top order with 'very fast and somewhat intimidating' bowling. Armstrong shed his big sweater to remove English skipper Johnny Douglas, McDonald swept away the middle order and Gregory came back to pull the tail. All done in just over two hours and without Mailey, left out because of the pitch. Next day, with Australia leading by 120 on first innings, the process was repeated albeit not so frenetically. The England batsmen had no answer to cricket's first pace pair. True enough that without Hobbs the English batting was not the strongest despite the presence of Woolley and Patsy Hendren but it was a shellacking worthy of any dished out in Ashes history.

The home press, as they are wont to do, concentrated on the failings of their batsmen rather than the achievement of the tourists' bowling. Pelham Warner in *The Cricketer* did eventually turn to the men who had collected 16 wickets between them and like most others was enamoured of the artistry of McDonald. His stealthy approach to the crease, economy and beauty of action, genuine pace, variety and intense accuracy was a model for the purists. It is doubtful that anyone bar Gregory had previously bowled faster than McDonald in Test history and those such as Ernie Jones or Tibby Cotter who had approached his pace had nothing like the skill he displayed at Trent Bridge. Above all McDonald was the revelation – Gregory's fire-and-brimstone approach was known and feared and wickets would inevitably come his way. But now there was 'the silk express' as well. Plenty for the English selectors to ponder as they attempted the conjuror's trick of tinkering their way to parity at Lord's.

Multiple changes made a minimal difference as England were again cast aside on a pitch 'in perfect order'. A pair of nineties from Woolley at least gave the game a semblance of a contest but by mid-afternoon on day one McDonald had clean bowled four of the top order and the home side were reeling. Gregory had a rare off day but soon made amends by striking a half-century and taking four second-innings wickets. Armstrong continued to take care of his prime assets but this was the home of cricket and if he couldn't give them free rein here then where could he?

And so the summer continued – crowds flocked to Northampton, Sheffield and Southend to see the local matadors trampled by the rampant kangaroo. It was done with such zest that there was only joy to be had in the sight of Macartney at the crease or Mailey marking his run. And above them all strode the new-fangled pace attack and the master of ceremonies, Warwick Armstrong.

The series was won at Leeds in early July and then the energy began to recede under the weight of an impossible schedule. The fourth Test was lost to the weather and Armstrong was happy to play out a comfortable draw at the Oval. Even the cherished unbeaten record was punctured by Archie MacLaren's famous side of invited amateurs at Eastbourne.

By the time the tour ground to a halt in mid-September a record of 22 wins and 14 draws had been established from 38 games and with that a place in the annals. Armstrong felt the side couldn't hold a candle to the 1902 vintage of Victor Trumper, Monty Noble and Hugh Trumble and he was probably right. Certainly they can't be considered close to Bradman's Invincibles, who could boast everything the 1921 side had and a lot more besides. But a fine side they were against unlucky and poorly-managed opponents and the two fast bowlers became the symbol of their progress through the shires. Both men undertook tremendous amounts of work and 270 wickets between them, including 46 in Tests, was their reward. In addition Gregory hit 1100 runs. There were certainly no more mentions of McDonald's stamina but there were plenty of rumours attached to his name and they centred on his future and the Lancashire League.

Ronald Mason's account of the tour, *Warwick Armstrong's Australians*, leaves the reader in little doubt as to which players were both the most watchable and the most influential during the five Tests.

> 'It was Gregory and McDonald who shot away the tenuous foundations of any English courage and consistency that may have been there at the start; and in the serene recollections of half a century it is still the demonic image of this great pair of fast bowlers that rises instantly to the memory and rekindles the undying sense of apprehension. It is difficult to find words to express the demoralizing efficacy of this superb partnership.'

There was a living to be earned in cricket and McDonald was keen to see where this would take him. For Australian cricketers the rewards were minimal beyond the fee for touring as part of the national team and that was not an annual event. After initial overtures from Cecil Parkin during the series in Australia, McDonald was courted by Lancashire League side Nelson with an offer of £500 per season. Rumours speckled the newspapers throughout the summer of 1921 and through the subsequent tour of South Africa until confirmation was eventually announced that an offer worth £1650 over three years had been accepted. This in contrast to nominal or no earnings in Australia and a sum approaching £500 for touring Britain once every four years. He couldn't know he'd still be fit or in form for 1926. It's clear enough that McDonald had acted less than transparently – not only was he now lost to the national team but he'd left a parting bite on the hand that had fed him. His skipper Armstrong was strongly supportive, at least privately, of his move. "Go for your life, Mac, and I'm with you!" was his response to an inquiry as to his thoughts.

It's not hard to understand the reasoning, however. McDonald's day job with the Victorian Producers Co-op was not satisfying and once it became apparent that a much better wage was on offer for playing cricket then the deal was done and the young family would move to England.

So the trip to South Africa following the tour of England would be McDonald's Test swansong. Not so Gregory who hit the ground running and never stopped. The series was finally won 1-0 after two stultifying draws punctuated by one of the most violent Test centuries ever seen as Gregory hammered 119 in 85 minutes at Johannesburg – still the fastest Test century by minutes (just 70) and now the fifth by balls bowled (67). His 15 wickets at 18.9 in the three Tests are an indication of a man still brimming with vigour and relishing the lift from the matting wickets even if his pace was compromised.

McDonald was quieter but still proved a constant threat even on wickets doing him no favours. And with that they were done – at least as an international strike force.

McDonald prospered in North-West England. It was hardly surprising that League batsmen would be unequal to the challenge and equally unsurprising that the county side would soon come calling once his residency had been established. In seven seasons sporting the red rose he took over 1000 wickets at a miserly average and was the pivot on which Lancashire claimed four titles. Other counties looked enviously at this golden signing and Lord Hawke of Yorkshire was in the forefront of criticism: 'I heartily hope that no county will ever again be strengthened by overseas importations which savour of the long purse and keep home-born cricketers out of the side'. Despite being 33 years old when making his Championship debut, McDonald was considered the fastest bowler in the country during his first two seasons. Even as his pace dropped over subsequent years he was more than able to compensate – he had always been a bowler of rare skill who could utilise brute pace when needed but was far from reliant on any one method. In 1931 it all fell apart as injury and loss of form led to a return to the leagues after a glorious stay, in some ways reminiscent of Mushtaq Ahmed's years at Sussex. Sadly he was killed in a traffic accident in 1937, knocked down by a passing car while waiting for police to attend an accident from which he had emerged unscathed. Old Trafford had good cause to fondly remember his 'saturnine and mahogany-grim features'.

Jack Gregory still had plenty to offer both his state and country after the defection of his pace partner but he never again achieved the dizzying heights of his first three years of first-class cricket. Injury and work commitments kept him out of the game for two seasons but he was back for the Ashes series in 1924-25 and even at reduced pace he was the fastest bowler on either side and still a magnificent athlete and inspirational team-mate. His 22 wickets in these timeless and attritional Tests were of huge importance even if he was thoroughly outshone by England's Maurice Tate. One more visit to England beckoned, in 1926, but by now he was a stock bowler and no longer a batsman to be feared. England regained the Ashes and, in truth, it was only the lack of alternatives that kept Gregory in the side. Selected for the opener of the 1928-29 series against England he sent down 41 overs in removing Wally Hammond, Herbert Sutcliffe and Percy Chapman before, ironically, Harold Larwood proved his undoing. He fell heavily on a previously damaged knee while attempting to catch England's new pace sensation and knew instantly that his career was over.

In 1972 the tenacious David Frith tracked Gregory down to his reclusive retirement house in Narooma and was able to pen one of his wonderful 'encounters'. He had avoided all contact with the media since being wilfully misconstrued in print in 1926. He died the following year.

Surely no pair of fast bowlers has left such an imprint on the history of the game based on such a short time span together. The timing was significant but the manner was paramount over anything, even statistics. Lionel Tennyson, writing in 1952, recalled the effect of the pair on the English batsmen in 1921.

> 'These two great Australians created an absolute panic, and later McDonald, with the exception of Sydney Barnes, I considered then to be the finest fast bowler I had ever seen. I still stick to that opinion, after seeing several of them, including Lindwall and Miller...Gregory was also better than the present Australian fast bowlers.'

Tennyson may not have been the most reliable witness (Sydney Barnes, fast?) but his observations have been amply amplified. Percy Holmes was observed to have backed away during the first Test in 1921 – watching selector Harry Foster saw this as retreat: "So long as I have influence, that man bats not in another Test for England." In the second Test, Johnny Evans was drafted in. It was his only Test; one team-mate observed that he was 'so nervous that he could hardly hold his bat and his knees were literally knocking together' and this was a man decorated with the MC and bar and who had organised various dashing escapes from prisoner-of-war camps.

Any number of contemporary testimonies come tumbling from the history cupboard: Woolley considered McDonald faster than Larwood ever was, Percy Fender was solidly in the McDonald camp as regards pace and length while Don Bradman (who played with one and against the other) opined:

> 'If ever a player could be termed vital and vehement it was Gregory. His bowling in the early days was positively violent in its intensity...[On McDonald] It was hard to visualise a more beautiful action which, coupled with splendid control and real pace, made him the most feared bowler in England at that time [1930].'

Larwood tilted the other way:

> 'Jack Gregory I nominate as the greatest among the Australian fast bowlers. There was little to choose between him and Ted McDonald in regard to speed but I think Gregory was just a little ahead of his great opening partner because he was a man of more terrifying appearance.'

Frank Foster was less interested in comparing and contrasting than evaluating the pair as a whole, while emphasising Armstrong as the genius puppet master.

> '...the man who introduced post-war fast bowling to England, and the man who had the confounded cheek to commence his attack with two fast bowlers! No wonder England gasped and quailed, shuddered and fell and then expired.'

The great Australian journalist and almost Test player Johnnie Moyes saw both men at close quarters. He spoke of Gregory in reverential terms and the sadness of his final injury. A huge presence and sense of *joie de vivre* had left the game. Rare are the all-action allrounders who thrill the world with their exploits – Learie Constantine, Keith Miller, Garry Sobers, Mike Procter, Ian Botham, Imran Khan and Kapil Dev. The list is not a long one. 'No figures could adequately measure Jack Gregory's value to the game.'

Moyes' appreciation of McDonald was more technical. He was a more thoughtful bowler, allying swing, movement off the seam and masterly pace changes with relentless accuracy and length. Maybe Gregory was quicker and certainly more awe-inspiring but writing in 1950 Moyes was categorical that McDonald was the best fast bowler he had seen.

The comparisons between the two may be inevitable because they bowled together and were both purveyors of pace but those same comparisons are also an irrelevance. These were two vastly contrasting bowlers who, when taken together, were a perfect combined force.

Gregory and McDonald

Results

	Total	Won	Drawn	Lost
Gregory	24	13	8	3
McDonald	11	7	4	0
Gregory and McDonald	11	7	4	0

Test Bowling Overall

	Mat	Balls	Runs	Wkts	Ave	SR	ER	5W1/10WM
Gregory	24	5582	2648	85	31.15	65.6	2.84	4/0
McDonald	11	2885	1431	43	33.27	67.0	2.97	2/0

Test Bowling Together

	Mat	Balls	Runs	Wkts	Ave	SR	ER	5W1/10WM
Gregory	11	2509	1165	43	27.09	58.3	2.78	2/0
McDonald	11	2885	1431	43	33.27	67.0	2.97	2/0

Test Bowling Apart

	Mat	Balls	Runs	Wkts	Ave	SR	ER	5W1/10WM
Gregory	13	3073	1483	42	35.31	73.2	2.89	2/0
McDonald	NA							

Best Series Together - England 1921

	Mat	Balls	Runs	Wkts	Ave	SR	ER	5W1/10WM
Gregory	5	1094	552	19	29.05	57.5	3.02	1/0
McDonald	5	1230	668	27	24.74	45.7	3.24	2/0

Best Test Figures - Innings/Match

Gregory (with McDonald)	6-58 vs England, Nottingham – 1921
Gregory (with McDonald)	8-103 vs England, Nottingham – 1921
Gregory (without McDonald)	7-69 vs England, Melbourne – 1920
Gregory (without McDonald)	8-103 vs England, Melbourne – 1920
McDonald (with Gregory)	5-32 vs England, Nottingham – 1921
McDonald (with Gregory)	8-74 vs England, Nottingham – 1921
McDonald (without Gregory)	N/A
McDonald (without Gregory)	N/A

YouTube Bowling Highlights

Search Phrases (sic)

The Fight For The Ashes AKA The Australians Are Here! (1926) – at 2.55

Good Luck With Bat And Ball (1921)

Australians' First Match (1921)

The Fifties and Sixties

When Test cricket resumed after the world war it soon became apparent that Australia had found a startling equivalent to the Gregory and McDonald partnership that had carried all before them for 12 months in 1921. Ray **Lindwall** and Keith **Miller** were the envy of all other teams. The fact that Australia also possessed the talents of Don Bradman, Arthur Morris, Lindsay Hassett and Bill Johnston perhaps tended to disguise their importance for the first few years of peace, but as they knocked over all opposition the other countries cast around for an equivalent pairing, or even just a singleton.

England had the redoubtable Alec Bedser but no quicks. West Indies found a pair, but they were spinners. South Africa briefly held high hopes for Cuan McCarthy. India could barely produce a medium-pace bowler but spinners proliferated. When Pakistan was formed and joined the Test club Fazal Mahmood was a force on his home matting and also on damp English wickets but fast he was not. Overall it seemed as if the 1950s might be as bereft as the '30s had been.

Then suddenly England had Fred **Trueman**, Brian **Statham** and Frank Tyson. The latter blazed fiercely over a short period and then England came to terms with the eccentricities of Trueman and settled into enjoyment of his partnership with Statham. Alan Davidson never found a partner in Australia, the appearance of Graham McKenzie was too late for the pair to combine. McKenzie then carried the new-ball duties, as Davidson had done, with a variety of partners who were not his equal. The Asian countries continued to be prisoners of their own pitches but in South Africa and then the West Indies something was stirring.

The first 50 years of South African cricket had produced all manner of wrist spinners, cutters, seamers and swingers but never a finger spinner or genuine fast bowler. Suddenly in the mid-fifties it had both. The relentless accuracy of Hugh Tayfield was joined by the aggression of Neil **Adcock** and Peter **Heine** and never again would a South African attack lack pace, even if they are still searching for spin. Adcock and Heine were replaced by Peter Pollock who formed a partnership with Mike Procter for one memorable series against Australia, the last before isolation. Pollock had been fading fast but Proctor's appearance seemed to galvanize him for one last burst before injury ended his career before apartheid could.

The great spinning pair of Alf Valentine and Sonny Ramadhin had carried West Indies' bowling for almost a decade before age and pad-play caught up with them. Their replacements could hardly have been a greater contrast. Wes **Hall** combined with Roy Gilchrist and Chester Watson before his most famous partner, Charlie **Griffith**, appeared in the early sixties. Just as cricket was recovering from years of controversy over dragging and chucking, Griffith reignited the debate and his career was dogged by a giant question mark hanging over his fastest ball.

New Zealand enjoyed the services of two fine medium-quick bowlers in Dick Motz and Richard Collinge but would have to wait for Richard Hadlee to transform their standing in world cricket. After the retirement of Trueman and Statham, England were able to call on the depth of county cricket to provide acceptable attacks but it was only with the appearance of John Snow that real pace was allied with real quality.

Lindwall

and

Miller

Ray Lindwall

Lindwall approaches the crease with the poise, balance and increasing impetus of a champion broad jumper. In the yard or two from the umpire to the wicket lies the secret of his ability. He hurls every ounce of strength into his delivery at this point, and follows through with such purpose that pace from the pitch is "natural".
– Ginty Lush

Keith Miller

He was a magnificent sight, using his height to full advantage and with his back arched like a bow with the arrow on the point of release. His arm turned full circle, except when his quixotic spirit moved him to try round arm. He seldom bowled off the same mark, which meant that if he suddenly turned round and ran off a few paces the batsman might not be mentally ready. The trouble was he could be just as quick off a short run. – Denis Compton

The cricketing years following the peace of 1918 had been dominated by Warwick Armstrong's mighty Australian side spearheaded by the first pace duo, Jack Gregory and Ted McDonald. As we have seen, the rest of the twenties and all of the thirties threw up some promising combinations and some worthy fast bowlers but none of the enlarged band of Test-playing nations could really lay claim to having discovered the next great pair. This situation lasted until another world war had been fought before, from the ashes of Europe, another Australian pair appeared, bearing an uncanny resemblance to the first.

Keith Miller was the all-action allrounder, appearing in England as part of a forces side and bowling over crowds and opposition with energy and charisma to spare. Ray Lindwall was the quieter, more calculating one – equally, if not more, devastating than his partner. Together they would prove to be as effective as Gregory and McDonald as well as being considerably longer lasting.

For nearly a decade after the 1945 peace the Australians were the dominant force in world cricket by some margin, initially under Don Bradman and then led by Lindsay Hassett. Stronger than the post-1918 vintage they had a mighty batting line-up supported by a hugely talented bowling side. Speed was very much in the ascendant with only the short career spans of spinners such as Jack Iverson and Ernie Toshack to add any significant variety. Fortunately neither Lindwall nor Miller were lost to the Lancashire League as McDonald had been and both had better luck with injuries than Gregory.

Both Lindwall and Miller had been promising young cricketers before 1939 but nobody could possibly have imagined that they would ever share the new ball for their country for the simple reason that both were batsmen. Lindwall's first visit to a Test match was memorable for seeing Harold Larwood, but despite being more than taken with what he saw he remained primarily a batsman in club and grade cricket – ironically his contemporary Arthur Morris was progressing through the ranks as a bowler. Being a cricket fanatic, Lindwall had always fancied bowling as well, reasoning that being a useful change swing bowler couldn't do his prospects any harm. His captain at St George, Bill O'Reilly, had seen enough in the nets:

'This young fellow had tremendous ability in getting to the crease and delivering the ball and looking hostile enough to make the batsman sorry that he was about. He had a beautifully smooth, rhythmic action – I'd say the Boss Upstairs gave it to him the morning he was born.'

So when O'Reilly chucked Lindwall the new ball one afternoon and said "You're bowling fast. Lengthen your run a couple of yards. Bowl fast", the die was cast. Lindwall was a capable batsman but over the next few seasons as he grew in strength so his ability and reputation grew as a bowler. And he learnt everything he could – Stan McCabe stepped in one afternoon with some simple but crucial advice; don't look at the batsman or the stumps, just at where you want to pitch the ball. If his progress hadn't been meteoric it had at least been steady and before war intervened O'Reilly was predicting "He's a great fast bowler in the making." Soon afterwards he joined up and saw action in New Guinea.

While Lindwall was making his way as a multi-talented sportsman in Sydney, another young man, two years his senior, was treading a similar path in Melbourne. It seems astonishing now that Miller's ambition up to the age of 16 had been to ride professionally, with the Melbourne Cup as his ultimate goal. Then he grew one foot in 12 months – his dreams of donning jockey's silks had gone but he was developing into a formidable cricketer and Rules footballer with size and strength to match his natural ability. Suddenly he was twirling a full-size bat instead of the cut-off version and his performances improved rapidly culminating in a big century on first-class debut. He could hit the ball mightily and scored fast but was essentially a correct player (his early heroes were the Bills, Ponsford and Woodfull) and still there was no sign of the bowler within him. A war-benefit match in 1940 gave a indication of things to come. Playing for Stan McCabe's XI he was summoned by Clarrie Grimmet on the basis of his physique to replace the two injured opening bowlers. Having never bowled 'seriously' before he went for sheer speed, took a wicket and had Bradman dropped in the slips. Hmm, interesting.

A dramatic spell in the RAAF, flying mosquitos over Europe, left Miller a modified man. Pressure was shaking a Messerschmitt off your tail or landing with an incendiary bomb still attached to a wing, not playing cricket. A back injury was one legacy, 'survivor guilt' another and then the mindset described by John Arlott of 'living life in case he ran out of it'. And live it he did through the war years and into the 'Victory Tests' of 1945 where he almost carried a makeshift Australian team against a near full-strength English side. His batting was the best on either side both in figures and manner and his bowling began to emerge despite persistent back problems.

Real Test cricket resumed in 1946 and with Lindwall's pre-war promise now flowering abundantly the stage was set if Miller would play ball – but he wanted to play bat. On one hand Hassett was telling everyone that Lindwall was faster and more accurate than anybody in England, a view shared by Herbert Sutcliffe and passed on to Len Hutton, and on the other Herby Collins was predicting Miller's use as a shock bowler while Miller himself was downplaying his bowling at every opportunity.

Both men were a shoe-in for the home series against England but how they would be utilised and how Lindwall would fare against Hutton or Wally Hammond was open to conjecture. The records show that Australia won enormously at Brisbane. The most famous incident was Bradman's reprieve from a contested catch which possibly extended his career by three famous years.

For Lindwall and Miller the contrasts could hardly have been starker. Lindwall succumbed to chicken pox and left wicketless; Miller was handed the poison chalice of the new ball and proceeded to take 9-77 including Hutton twice. But on the rain-ruined pitch it was off breaks not pace that proved successful for Miller. Almost equally significant was a short passage of play before the rain came. On the same lifeless pitch on which Australia had just accumulated 645 Hutton was reduced to ducking and weaving under a fearsome assault not totally dissimilar to that experienced by Bradman back in 1932-33. In just 20 minutes Lindwall and Miller gave England a taster of how the next decade might just pan out.

That taster did not, however, extend to this series. Miller took just seven more wickets (although he did average 77 with the bat) while Lindwall established his position as the world's best fast bowler in the space of three games culminating in a 7-63 which had judges from Cardus to Woodfull speaking of Gregory, McDonald and Larwood. With the praise and attention his action came under the microscope. Lindwall's method was essentially one of low trajectory. His majestic approach to the wicket was no real indication of what was to come but it was 'sheer poetry' to the eyes of Pelham Warner. The delivery arm was actually dropped and this was accentuated by a left leg bent at the knee at the point of delivery. All this sounds unpromising for a purveyor of bouncers and he certainly couldn't use height to get lift but when he dropped the ball short enough the result was a skimmer at the throat that demanded immediate attention. Then suddenly would come the full delivery at the stumps with the batsman already weighted to play back not forward.

Of his seven victims in the first innings at Sydney four were clean bowled and only Compton fell to the short ball when treading on his wicket.

Another element of Lindwall's bowling to come under scrutiny, mostly from English pressmen, was his 'drag'. As subsequent footage would show, he was able to place his front foot over the crease and drag his rear foot through – the umpire could scarcely be expected to establish the exact position of the back foot at the exact point of delivery and therein lay the fundamental flaw in the back-foot law. But the naked eye in the press box could detect a bowler pushing the limits, and tongues began to wag.

A one-sided series against India did little for the reputation of either man. Miller was a largely detached figure – moments of brilliance punctuating periods of sleepwalking as the tourists were knocked back and forth. The challenge was lacking. For Lindwall the summer was a battle for fitness and legality as he was no-balled for dragging in a Shield game. The omens were now less bright. Could Lindwall sustain himself for a long English summer and had the dual demands now placed on Miller taken the sheen off him in both disciplines? Ray Robinson certainly thought so:

> 'The flame of his batsmanship is not burning with the same purity...[He is] far too precious to be tarnished and squandered in the dust and pot holes of the bowling crease.'

The man who would ultimately decide how best to employ Miller was his captain, Don Bradman.

The year of the Invincibles, 1948, has always stood boldly in English cricket history. Bradman's final foray to English shores was as etched with triumph as Armstrong's had been in 1921. But the Don's vintage side took care not to let their concentration slip and remained unbeaten which was clearly the aim from day one and before. With a batting line-up headed by Arthur Morris, Sid Barnes, Bradman and Hassett (young Neil Harvey in reserve), runs wouldn't be a problem. The bowling was slightly thinner and with Hutton, Compton, Cyril Washbrook and Bill Edrich leading the line for England a summer of runs and stalemate was widely predicted. Against this stood uncovered pitches and a trial of making a new ball available every 55 overs. For Australia it was clear where Miller was needed most. His record shows that he fell between two stools – 13 wickets at 23 and 184 runs at 26 was hardly a disaster but the moments of brilliance only served to highlight the run-of-the-mill sessions. And brilliant they were; Jack Fingleton recalled his innings at Leeds (when

Australia were, for once, struggling) – 'I cannot believe it is possible for a cricket brain to conceive of any innings which could be greater'.

Bowling-wise, the great pair in waiting were not having the best of it. A groin strain saw Lindwall laid low in the first Test, Miller took the strain and crocked his back and couldn't bowl in the second or third matches. But Lindwall was back with 13 wickets and Bill Johnston and Ernie Toshack were proving more then able supporters. The fourth, played on a batting paradise, saw Miller and Lindwall re-united as a new-ball pairing but they fared no better or worse than any of their sweat-drenched and footsore fellow trundlers. Then in Bradman's final Test on the sawdust festooned Oval square the three quick bowlers put out England twice for 240, Hollies bowled Bradman and the series was won 4-0. Had the Lindwall and Miller partnership prospered? Scarcely. Lindwall was now the most feared quick bowler in the world as 27 wickets at 19.6 would attest. Not only had he outbowled Miller but he had even outscored him, and could lay claim to an allrounder's place.

Despite the relative lack of success, Miller was still the great draw bar Bradman. His athletic frame, thick mop of hair and abundant good looks were more than a match for the more lounge-lizard appeal of Denis Compton. You never knew what Miller might do and therein lay another enduring appeal – he might grab a used ball and proceed to cut out three batsman in a trice or smash a quick 70 where others could barely find the middle of the bat. He was still far from an enthusiastic bowler but he was a team man and as such had done his duty even if there had been a public spat when he appeared to refuse Bradman's request to bowl.

It was another run-in with Bradman the following year that could have cost him his career. In a farewell match for the champion, Miller had the temerity to try a bouncer and then another and then a third which took the master's wicket. A few days later the Australian side to tour South Africa was announced and Miller's name was missing. It was an unaccountable omission. Jack Fingleton wrote, 'I thought it was the ugliest blot that had splashed from the pen of the selectors on to the pages of Test history'. The South African authorities, with an eye on gate money, were hardly more pleased and petitioned for him to join the squad when Johnston was hurt in a car crash.

Fortunately Miller was not a man to harbour grudges and his career was saved. Another series was won 4-0 and another series passed without any addition to the legend of Lindwall and Miller. This time the weak link was Lindwall who arrived overweight and struggled for fitness throughout – 12 wickets at 20.6 including many tailenders and he was omitted for the final

Test. But talk of his demise was surely premature. Jack Cheetham thought him the fastest he had ever seen and was captivated by his ability to bowl a perfect yorker almost at will where the margin of error was so tiny. Miller still shone in fits and starts although his 5-40 in the first game was a match-winning contribution and set the tone for the series. As in England he delighted the crowds but Johnston had been the success of the series with Lindwall and Miller his able assistants. This is not how we remember the Australian team of the early fifties.

The second post-war English tourists boasted the two outstanding players of the series – Hutton and Alec Bedser rose head and shoulders above all others and yet their team was trounced. Miller was the leading batsman for the home side and also a serious bowler as the tour progressed. But by the time the series was decided at 3-0 with two to play it was Bill Johnston and Jack Iverson who had dominated proceedings with 35 wickets; Lindwall and Miller had just 18. That said, Miller had been seen to great advantage at Sydney when his side were in danger – a masterful century considering the state of the game followed by a decisive burst with the old ball to remove Hutton, Compton and Reg Simpson in four overs. Somehow he conjured pace where there had been none. The fire still burnt. Lindwall had struggled on the slow pitches and wisely reined himself in with little to gain from bending his back. But as the wickets got better so his form improved, culminating in his best bowling of the series in the final Test where he shared seven wickets with Miller. But Simpson played an astonishing innings and England won.

The pair had now been together for six years as team-mates, room-mates and friends. They had toured and travelled together, shared concerns over injuries and form and formed a bond that was to last two lifetimes. But it's worthwhile, at this halfway stage, stepping back and looking at what they had achieved as a fast-bowling pair. They had played five full series together and shared the field 24 times. If Lindwall's record in the previous two series had been below his best he had shown enough to still be regarded as the world's best, albeit at a time when genuine fast bowlers were a rarity. He still had the lightening pace when required but he had also learnt to conserve his strength and, at 29, was sure he had many fruitful years in front of him whatever anyone might say. Miller was perceived as a new man. EW Swanton detected a calmness in his demeanour while Johnnie Moyes wrote of him as a 'mellowed, mature master'. Not that his crowd-pleasing antics or crackling bursts of energy with bat or ball were gone.

Wherever he played, wherever he went, all eyes were drawn to the energy and bravado of his every move.

Statistically Miller's runs were backed by 66 wickets. Lindwall had 92, a total of 158, or less than seven a game. Furthermore they had frequently not shared the new ball and on only three occasions had they shared more than 10 wickets and each time Miller was very much the foil for Lindwall rather than an equal partner. There was little or no evidence of them as a genuine double threat yet singly they remained a fearsome proposition. They had become fixtures in the Australian side but Miller's role chopped and changed according to the demands of the team and pitch. He was certainly not the new-ball partner for Lindwall that history tends to recall – or at least only very occasionally.

Australia had dominated world cricket for six years but one more victory was now required as West Indies emerged as a world force having beaten England home and away. They proved to be brittle opponents – in some ways only half a team with the three Ws receiving only meek support and a pace attack with little more ambition than to remove the shine for Sonny Ramadhin and Alf Valentine. Once Miller and Hassett had solved the mystery of Ramadhin and batted him out of the series the outcome was only briefly in doubt although there remained the obstacle of Weekes, Worrell and Walcott and at 2-1 with two to play a solution needed to be found and that solution was bumper-orientated. It was the contest between Lindwall and Weekes in the final Test that encapsulated the argument.

Up to this point the short-pitched delivery had been used judiciously in the most part with some effect. This time, with Weekes well set, Lindwall sent down four in a row to a compulsive hooker. To add to the drama West Indian skipper and non-striker Jeff Stollmeyer came down the wicket beseeching Weekes to resist temptation. On commentary Alan McGilvray railed against what he was watching and in the press box O'Reilly was apoplectic. It wasn't bodyline but it brought back some bitter memories and perhaps even smacked of bullying. O'Reilly even made the pertinent point that one day the 'same stuff' would come back down the track the other way. For Lindwall it was a question of removing the danger man. He could see Weekes caught in two minds, a fact Weekes himself corroborated when calling the spell 'beautiful psychology'. The fourth of the bouncers had Weekes caught behind, hooking.

The incident is revealing of the mindset and abilities of Lindwall. He was ruthless, fast and accurate. But the ruthlessness extended only to taking wickets. He was inviting Weekes to hook, not trying to send him to hospital. The bouncer was as legitimate as the yorker, the slower ball or the away-swinger and given the batsman at the other end it was the right weapon at the right time. But it re-ignited the question that had first appeared in 1921 (or even before) and still rumbles on today and will probably flare into life again in the not-too-distant future. Lindwall and Miller were, at that time, the only effective purveyors of this dark art but others were coming.

Australia were now champions in all senses and it was a question of retaining that status at home to South Africa, home and away to England and then in the West Indies over the next three years. With Hassett, Morris and Harvey still in fine fettle; new men such as Richie Benaud and Alan Davidson making giant strides and Lindwall and Miller seemingly fit and raring to go there were great causes for optimism that the run of success could continue.

As it transpired a rude awakening was round the corner. A limited but inspired South Africa held Australia to a draw against all predictions. Then England regained the Ashes at home in 1953 and sent Frank Tyson to retain them before Australia comprehensively won their first away series against West Indies who fielded one of the weakest bowling sides ever seen. Not only had the balance of power changed but the balance of pace was changing too. England had found a bundle of quick bowlers and South Africa and West Indies were desperately trying to unearth their own Lindwall or Tyson. If the Australian speedsters had done anything since the war it was to show that long-term success on a variety of wickets needs fast bowlers.

Lindwall and Miller were a mixed bag over these four series. Against South Africa a variety of injuries meant they only shared the new ball twice but 25 wickets in those two matches showed the pair to be as good as ever against tenacious and cautious batting. When both men were forced to miss the final Test the result did not bode well for the long-term future of the side.

Only a month later and it was off to England. Doubts about the pair's fitness were understandable but proved to be only partly accurate. Any weaknesses were likely to be exposed as their long-term ally, understudy and sometime leading man Bill Johnston injured a knee and was never match-fit again. There had been no doubt about the new-ball pairing but this was likely to add significantly to Miller's workload. As in 1948 his batting would have to play second fiddle.

The return of the Australians, and particularly those who were on their second or third trip, was a major event in a Britain still locked into post-war austerity. They would be in homes up and down the country for the best part of five months and if there was less opportunity to see them on television than nowadays there was the knowledge that they could be seen in the flesh in a town not far away. There were familiar figures, how would they compare to their 1948 selves? The impish Hassett, the princely Harvey, the coil of elegance and strength that was Lindwall and the Millerman that was 'Nugget'. Simultaneously friends and enemies, rivals to be feared, respected and admired and a chunk of summer to be relished with all its associations of warmth and beauty.

The series stood at 0-0 but could have been 2-2, or 3-1 or 1-3, going into the final Test. England won, and again it was Hutton and Bedser who stood supreme both on the field and in the record books. Although unable to bowl in the first Test and with concerns about both his back and knee, Miller still sent down 186 overs – he just couldn't be used as a shock bowler only, the back-up was too threadbare. Lindwall delivered 240 overs and rarely wavered in line or length but the workload took its toll on both men. At Lord's England needed to survive a whole day with three men out overnight. The resistance of Willie Watson and Trevor Bailey was nigh on heroic but the Australian spinners performed poorly on a helpful wicket and most judges considered that the Lindwall and Miller of 1948 would have broken the deadlock.

Lindwall's 26 wickets at 18.8 may have paled in comparison to Bedser's 39 at 17.4 but he was a man alone – only Miller of the rest managed double figures. If Lindwall had lost something of his youthful vigour he had gained the inswinger, the legacy of a season at Lancashire League Nelson. Little wonder then that Lindwall and Bedser were expected to be the key bowlers the following year in the return leg. And if Miller's body would hold up, well then.

England, flying on the shoulders of Tyson, came from behind to win 3-1 in Australia to retain the Ashes. Lindwall and Miller both missed a match and finished fourth and fifth in the averages. This was a brutal regression even given Miller's brilliant assaults at Melbourne (which removed Hutton, Edrich and Compton) and Adelaide (which removed Hutton, Edrich and Cowdrey and brought the England captain's famous dressing-room lament "The so-and-so's going to do us again") and the monumental achievement of a 100th Ashes wicket for Lindwall which was gift wrapped in admiration from Trevor Bailey.

Seemingly there could be no way back. Both men were down on speed and fitness and the press were down on their generation – it was time for change. Change, however, requires new blood and the bank was foundering.

Davidson and Benaud had progressed more slowly than expected and Ron Archer was many things but not a new Lindwall. Only one month later the boat was leaving for the Caribbean and the selectors stuck to the same group of players and the same captain, Ian Johnson, who had pipped Miller for the position. Like Shane Warne 60 years later there was perceived to be just a little too much baggage and in both cases the spectators were robbed of a fascinating interaction.

Expectation was low back home with Arthur Mailey offering to dine on a stump if Australia could win even one match on the slow, grassless wickets against the three Ws. Mailey could gorge on a full set as Australia won a run-fest 3-0. Walcott and Weekes apart, West Indies were a poor side even given young Garry Sobers and Collie Smith but there was a real ebullience and flair in the Australian old boys as well as it being the breakthrough series for Benaud.

For Lindwall and Miller the whole tour was a treasure. At the outset there had been calls for their heads but once away they were treated with reverence, respect and even awe by spectators. They loved the batting – Miller hit three Test centuries and Lindwall one – and put in the hard yards on unresponsive pitches rarely resorting to full speed or bouncers. True, both had fitness concerns as befits a quick bowler in his mid-30s but they got through 364 overs and took 40 wickets. They couldn't go on forever but neither was ready for pasture and this series guaranteed them at least one more crack at the Ashes in England.

The final chapter hardly needs retelling. A liberal application of marl at Leeds and Manchester gave Laker and Lock game, set and match. No wonder the Australians were sour. Miller already knew that this was his swansong with a move into journalism in the offing and had had high hopes of a sun-filled summer, wielding the willow and offering occasional support with the ball to his old mucker and the new supporting crew. Captaincy would have been the icing on the cake but Johnson was retained after the West Indian successes. Miller's reputation for impulsiveness and a lack of attention to detail coupled with a very cool relationship with the *eminence gris* that was Bradman were insurmountable obstacles.

Lindwall had been weakened by hepatitis and was then further restricted by a groin strain and unsuitable footwear and finished the series with just seven wickets. Miller stepped into the breach, bowling Australia to victory at Lord's. With Lindwall absent, he collected 10 wickets for the only time in his Test career, outbowling Trueman and Statham with a masterful display of fast-medium bowling in thoroughly English conditions. The English cricket authorities took note and spinner's pitches duly followed. Try as he might Miller could do little more although his final total of 21 wickets at 22.2 was comfortably the best in his side. His batting suffered and he looked a shadow of his former self as ungainly lunge and vain swish followed one another in response to Laker's withering spin.

The pair were now done bar a single Test on the way home in Karachi where Fazal Mahmood offered a lesson in matting bowling. Lindwall continued for another four years but the glory days were gone even if he was capable of bowling Benaud one of the fastest overs he ever faced at the age of 36 – he was cross at some dubious umpiring decisions!

This priceless pair had been at the heart of Australian cricket for over a decade. Lindwall was the first fast bowler to 100 and 200 wickets and if Miller was slightly less prolific with the ball he could still boast nearly 3000 Test runs at an average of 37. Dig deeper into the records of both men and their achievements only grow. Of Miller's 170 Test victims exactly 100 were batting in the top five. Lindwall's average was also rarely boosted by mopping up of tails – both men were at their best when challenged by the best be it Hutton, Compton or Weekes. Lindwall's methods are amply illustrated by his record of 56 per cent of dismissals requiring no assistance from fielders. Miller's batting followed the same pattern as his bowling – almost all his best work was done when the chips were down and the pressure was on – but not the pressure of an enemy fighter trying to shoot you out of the sky.

Any reasonably appointed cricket library will have masses of literature describing the pair both individually and together and, gratifyingly, a coherent picture emerges. And that picture is one of dramatic contrasts in personality, persona, cricketing philosophy and most anything else one cares to name. Yet at the same time the best of friends – the attraction of opposites.

Ray Lindwall was quite simply 'the greatest bowler of my time' according to Hutton, a view seconded by Compton. It is true that the late '40s and early '50s were not a great period for fast bowling but neither man specified fast bowling and both played long enough to experience a resurgence of the pace bowler. So this puts Lindwall in front of O'Reilly, Bedser, Ramadhin, Tyson, Trueman, Laker and Tayfield – the accepted masters of their age.

He combined a beautiful action with body strength and the mind of a spinner in detecting a batsman's weaknesses. The low, round arm would bring the ball from the line of the umpire at an unpredictable pace. Without any detectable alteration in action it might be the late or early away-swinger, the viciously fast leg-stump yorker or the skimming bouncer all delivered with relentless accuracy. If he didn't always bowl at top pace there was always the threat that he *might*. After giving up Rugby League his fitness suffered to the degree that he was described as a 'portly ghost of a fast bowler' in South Africa in 1950. He immediately set about remedying the situation and as a result was still a capable fast bowler almost a decade later. He took his cricket seriously both physically and mentally. When Benaud was considering how he might win the Ashes at Old Trafford in 1961 it was the advice of his vice-captain Harvey and his one time team-mate Lindwall that he sought.

If Lindwall was the quiet and unassuming deadly destroyer then Miller must go down as the man who wore his huge heart right where everyone could see it. He was not a man for the morning run, he was forced to nurse persistent back and knee injuries and in many senses he was a throwback to the older idiom of 'the game's the thing'. Not for Miller subtle disguise or plotting and planning – he barely knew what he was going to bowl when he began his run up and that run up might start from 15 paces, three paces or even at mid-off where he had just fielded the ball. The seam was often held vertically for the fun of seeing which way it might move. The bouncer was virtually telegraphed by a toss of the mane, a look skywards and a galloping approach to the crease. Hutton said that of all the bowlers who hit him over the course of his career Miller was the only one who he felt was impossible to avoid. His pace and control could be stupefying and his career is littered with five-over cameos in which he removed the heart of the opposition batting and turned a game on its head; very often with an old ball on an unhelpful wicket, in other words when his side was at its wit's end and needed a touch of genius. That's when Miller felt inspired and when he felt inspired his performances invariably reflected his mood.

Precisely those situations stimulated him with the bat. His unpredictability both as a player and a captain for New South Wales was huge influence on Benaud who confessed a conscious effort to be unorthodox – a paradox that only Benaud could have brought off. Two Australian captains found him difficult; Ian Johnson used words such as 'impossible' and 'selfish' but both he and Bradman were hugely grateful for his presence in their sides. Johnson is probably right in his conclusion that Miller's reputation was enhanced by his role as an allrounder. Even though his natural gifts as a batsman place him close to, say, Neil Harvey or Everton Weekes. It's hard to imagine that even without bowling a ball his batting average would ever have risen to dizzying heights. He had always been careless with his wicket and always would be – just not when it really, really mattered.

As a pair Lindwall and Miller are hard to quantify. Looking at the figures alone there is not one series where their names are stamped across as the pair that won it. Lindwall's two prime series were both in England yet in 1948 Bill Johnston took twice as many wickets as Miller and in 1953 Miller only managed more than two wickets in one game. When Miller was taking wickets consistently, such as in 1950 against West Indies, then Lindwall's tally was down. But there was 1955 when both managed 20 on the batting paradises in the Caribbean. These are numbers only and retrospective numbers at that. At the time it was different – the opposition knew that Lindwall was the best fast bowler in the world and that his only peer was, on certain special occasions, Miller. The Carmody, or umbrella, field, featuring up to 10 fielders in an arc behind the batsman, could only be considered to special bowlers and Keith Carmody and, later, Hassett thought the pair special enough.

They were grand fast bowlers operating at their best against the best batsmen of their era. Whether they really qualify as a pair is debatable – Miller's batting duties and the presence of Johnston certainly muddy the waters. The figures can be massaged to lean both ways but figures are not everything. In retrospect we can see series when they were less effective than might have been expected but at the time the threat was always there that they might suddenly bounce back and turn events on their head. They were synonymous with a dominant period for Australian cricket and their legacy is undeniable. England and South Africa sought and soon found similar weapons, for other Test-playing nations the search took much longer but at the very least it was further proof that to win consistently all over the world one, two, three or even four fast bowlers was an absolute necessity.

Lindwall and Miller

Results

	Total	Won	Drawn	Lost
Lindwall	61	33	19	19
Miller	55	31	15	9
Lindwall and Miller	51	28	15	8

Test Bowling Overall

	Mat	Balls	Runs	Wkts	Ave	SR	ER	5W1/10WM
Lindwall	61	13650	5251	228	23.03	59.8	2.30	12/0
Miller	55	10461	3906	170	22.97	61.5	2.24	7/1

Test Bowling Together

	Mat	Balls	Runs	Wkts	Ave	SR	ER	5W1/10WM
Lindwall	51	11207	4383	195	22.47	57.4	2.34	11/0
Miller	51	9532	3553	150	23.68	63.5	2.23	5/0

Test Bowling Apart

	Mat	Balls	Runs	Wkts	Ave	SR	ER	5W1/10WM
Lindwall	10	2443	868	33	26.60	72.0	2.13	1/0
Miller	4	929	353	20	17.65	46.4	3.27	2/1

Best Series Together - West Indies 1951-52

	Mat	Balls	Runs	Wkts	Ave	SR	ER	5W1/10WM
Lindwall	5	1232	484	21	23.04	58.6	2.35	1/0
Miller	5	1027	398	20	19.90	51.3	2.32	2/0

Best Test Figures - Innings/Match

Lindwall (with Miller)	7-38 vs India, Adelaide – 1948
Lindwall (with Miller)	9-70 vs England, The Oval – 1948
Lindwall (without Miller)	7-43 vs India, Madras – 1956
Lindwall (without Miller)	7-58 vs India, Madras – 1956
Miller (with Lindwall)	7-60 vs England, Brisbane – 1946
Miller (with Lindwall)	9-77 vs England, Brisbane – 1946
Miller (without Lindwall)	5-72 vs England, Lord's – 1956
Miller (without Lindwall)	10-152 vs England, Lord's – 1956

YouTube Bowling Highlights

Search Phrases (sic)
Australian Bowling Greats: A Bat, A Ball and A Boy - Part 3
Third Test Cricket - Third Day (1948)
England & Australia 1948 - The Lord's Ashes Test

Trueman

and

Statham

Fred Trueman

He was a cocked trigger, left arm pointed high, head steady, eyes glaring at the batsman as that great stride widened, the arm slashed down, and as the ball was fired down the pitch, the body was thrown hungrily after it. – John Arlott

Brian Statham

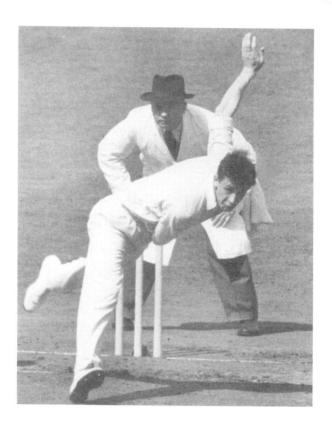

The truth about Statham's action is that it was so elastic and balanced (and double-jointed) that there was no forward shoulder-rigidity possible; his movement, from the beginning of his run to delivery, to the final accumulated propulsion, had not an awkward angle in it at all. The whole man of him was the effortless and natural dynamo and life-force of his attack. – Neville Cardus

If asked to name England's finest new-ball pair any follower of cricket with a sense of the history of the game would inevitably alight on the names of Fred Trueman and Brian Statham. Greater individual English fast bowlers may (or may not) have drawn breath but has there been a pairing of such effectiveness or redolence over such a period of time?

Fiery Fred Trueman with his mop of black hair, short fuse and unshakeable self belief. Whippet Brian Statham with a calm, self-possessed nature, almost the polar opposite of his partner. And if they were dissimilar as men they were equally unlike, if equally successful, in their cricketing methods.

Statham favoured metronomic accuracy – 'if they miss I hit' – around the top of off stump. On good wickets he was devilishly hard to score off and often succeeded through frustrating his opponents, forcing them into taking risks as the scoreboard failed to tick over. On helpful wickets his ability to move the ball off the seam made him doubly dangerous even if, as he always maintained, he didn't know whether the ball would move into or away from the batsman. He wasn't a great swing bowler but just a hint of movement in the air, with the ball well pitched up, could prove destructive as the seam then took the ball in the other direction. He revelled in this mystery, reasoning that if he didn't know what would happen then how could the chap at the other end? But he was far too good a bowler to be one dimensional – he could bowl genuinely fast when required and alter his length fractionally according to the demands of the pitch; in this the obvious modern comparison is Glenn McGrath.

Trueman was far more unpredictable. With his classic side-on action he saw himself as a genuine fast bowler who loved nothing more than to see apprehension then fear in the batsman's eyes. He employed the bouncer with a, sometimes, over-enthusiastic regularity and possessed all the aggression of his profession. Wes Hall thought that 'like all great quickies he has fire in his belly and hatred in his heart'. But as he grew older he also grew wiser; he could cut his pace where required and learnt to better control his natural ability to swing the ball, never afraid to bowl a full length when conditions favoured movement in the air.

Their bowling methods were in essence reflections of their characters. Trueman was the more complex of the two. John Arlott could find four different men in one – the man, the bowler, the public figure and the basic Fred Trueman, son of a miner. He was fiercely competitive and sometimes forgot which of the four men to be. He spent time in and out of hot water – often distrusted by authority figures, his great boots thundering equally mercilessly on green turf and MCC or YCCC carpets. Statham was far gentler although many a bruised thigh bore testimony to his whippiness and venom. 'George' was loved and admired wherever he went – Trueman could never bring himself to dislike Statham even though they were often rivals for an England place or the greater plaudits when both were selected. Uncomplainingly Statham would bowl uphill or into the wind, resignedly watching the ball beat the bat time after time. Many considered him the unluckiest bowler they ever saw. Trueman expected to bowl downhill with the wind and it was a brave captain that denied him his wish.

One a Lancastrian the other a Yorkshireman, both down to earth in their own ways and both full of admiration for one another even if one of them was quite sure who was the better bowler – the other probably didn't much care. Apparently a match made in heaven and a journalist's dream as they both represented England over the course of a decade and a half from the early fifties to the mid-sixties. Two sturdy servants who got themselves fit by bowling, were rarely injured for any length of time and gave themselves heart and soul to their counties when not on international duty. One slim, dextrous and double-jointed (removing his pullover from the hem up behind his back is an abiding image) the other built like the brick shithouse in which he was allegedly born.

Batsmen differed in their preference. Trevor Bailey could never see how to score off Statham (the barnacle meets the metronome in a battle of attrition) whereas Trueman could have his wafer-thin patience worn down by a blocker. Neil Harvey was less comfortable against Trueman as he was more likely to produce a 'wicket ball' on any surface. Harvey also felt Trueman a better bowler because of his ability outside England although the figures don't bear this out. In tours to the West Indies and Australia, Statham took 69 Test wickets at 30.6 and Trueman 59 at 29.9. Trueman's overall Test average of 21.57 compares favourably with Statham but it was considerably boosted by 75 wickets against the relatively weak batting of India and Pakistan at 16.3 while Statham took only 41 at 19.4.

The received wisdom is that the two men were a perfect fit. While Statham chipped away patiently at one end, Trueman could happily let fly at the other. Those batsmen trying to avoid the Trueman thunderbolts found themselves entangled in Statham's web while those looking for scoring opportunities ran headlong into Trueman's fury. But the reality was less symbiotic. Both men played roughly half their Tests in each other's company and both averaged considerably better in each other's absence. Their greatest performances were invariably solo efforts – Trueman took 10 wickets in a Test three times, on each occasion Statham was absent and Statham's great 7-57 at Melbourne in 1960 was with Peter Loader sharing the new ball. Statham made his England debut in 1951 and Trueman the following year and both left the international game in 1965 but they played together only 35 times – Trueman playing a total of 67 Tests and Statham 70. Furthermore they were only the natural new-ball pair for six years, from 1957 to 1963 – their respective routes to primacy had taken very different courses.

Brian Statham made his Lancashire debut in 1950 after serving his apprenticeship at clubs in an around Manchester and promptly celebrated his 20th birthday by removing Arthur Fagg (he of the two double-centuries in a match). Although his first season was unspectacular (*Wisden* reported on his 'ordinary pace' and 'awkward action'), with just 37 wickets in 15 matches, he had clearly made an impression on the future England captain, Len Hutton, for one. He had seen him rip through the Yorkshire top order in the Roses match and when the English team in Australia found themselves injury stricken Statham, much to his amazement, found himself airborne. He made his Test debut in New Zealand taking the wicket of Bert Sutcliffe, for 116, in a dreary draw. After this early elevation he remained a fringe player in an England pace attack that was basically Alec Bedser and a few others. The chance to play a full series came in 1951-52 in India – a tour any established fast bowler was happy to eschew. On the slow, low pitches Statham laboured through 120 overs for just eight wickets as the spinners dominated. But his hopes were high that on the English pitches of 1952 he would be able to show the same opposition a very different side to his bowling. He was passed over in all five games – enter Fred Trueman.

Like Statham, Trueman was born into a large family but unlike his future partner he had the good fortune to find a coach early in life. Cyril Turner imparted all the fundamental skills that Trueman was to use so expertly and the pupil never forgot the teacher. He made his first-class debut in 1949 but his first two years yielded no huge rewards. The following year, bulked up by Air Force food, his pace, attitude and 90 wickets began to capture the attention of the press and the imagination of the public. At the beginning of 1952 the selectors requested Trueman's temporary release from National Service to bowl for Yorkshire in order to secure an England place – 32 wickets at 14.2 from four matches was quite enough and he made his debut at

Headingley. John Arlott recalled the mood of the time:

> 'It is difficult for later generations to appreciate quite what Fred Trueman meant in 1952, not simply as a performer but as a symbol – heroic, epic, nostalgic, dramatic, comic and downright earthy – constituted exactly to the demands of the day.'

Yorkshire team-mate Johnny Wardle was also transfixed by the bowler and the reaction he elicited:

> 'His fiery approach, his whole-hearted attitude to the fun of fast bowling and his immensely long run-up were matters of wondering comment.'

And Trueman did not disappoint. In Hutton's first series as captain, and a professional one at that, Trueman flattened the callow Indians, suffering under unfamiliar conditions and unused to genuine pace. Victory in the first Test was achieved as Trueman reduced the tourists to 0-4 in the second innings and this was followed by eight wickets at Lord's and then 8-31 at Old Trafford as India were put out twice in a day. Even the most cautious pressmen noticed his better control and *Wisden* thought him 'the best fast-bowling prospect since the war'. The public had found the new Larwood, a tag almost as dangerous as the new Bradman. Twenty-nine wickets at 13.3 was some debut series and it seemed that finally England had an answer to Lindwall and Miller who had been crushing England for seven years. Here was a chance to fight fire with fire. It wasn't just the results, it was the drama – when Trueman took three early wickets at Leeds, one was out hooking and the other two were clean bowled. With the Ashes at stake the following summer England had found a standard bearer – Fiery Fred and Alec Bedser, the lion of Surrey, in tandem, what could possibly go wrong?

The England selectors were slightly more cautious than the general public. There was certainly no jumping the gun or being bullied by the popular press. Even his fellow Yorkshireman and captain, not a man to get carried away with rhetoric and bombast, was distinctly faint in his praise – 'a little on the colt side' who would be top class in five years. This was hardly a 'bring it on' call to arms that would accompany such a debut series today. In the event Hutton's prediction was proved correct but in the meantime a mixture of Trueman's ebullience, occasional foolishness and the English cricket establishment's mealy-mouthed bias nearly finished his career.

When slow wickets, injury and poor form caused Trueman to start 1953 slowly, the selectors were quick to forget his sensational entry to the Test arena the previous year. The country was divided – idolised and doubted in equal measure but with the doubters holding sway where it counted, in the Lord's committee room. Trueman was selected only for the deciding Oval Test which saw the Ashes return for the first time since the War. His four wickets at least guaranteed a tour to the Caribbean. Statham was even less in demand but he too had done enough domestically to book his tour ticket.

England had never won a series in the West Indies, they had been well beaten at home in 1950, Bedser was unavailable and the home spectators were expecting more of the same from their side, exorcising colonial demons. A tinder-box atmosphere was dangerous ground for a live-wire like Trueman and within two weeks he had broken the arm of the grand old man of West Indian cricket. George Headley recovered for the first Test only to be caught off a Trueman bouncer. The stage was set for acrimony that descended into violence over the course of the tour. Both on and off the field Trueman was surrounded by controversy, some of his own making and much of it fabricated. Poor umpiring led to frustration which manifested itself in cases of racial abuse and bouncers at tailenders. If any England player misbehaved either on or off the field (and many did) then it was presumed that Trueman was either that player or somehow involved. As a result his good conduct bonus, and only his, was withheld.

Senior players Hutton and Denis Compton were critical of his conduct although neither had done anything to offer guidance. Nine wickets at 46.6 was no great return, even on unhelpful pitches that often blunted his weapons. By the final Test, which England won to square the series, the attack featured three specialist spinners. Statham's progress around the islands was both quieter and more successful. Injury curtailed his tour but not before he had come to terms with West Indian pitches – both turf and matting – and West Indian batting – the three Ws – as evidenced by removing the top order at Georgetown, 'bowling with rare devil', to allow England back into the series. His 16 wickets at 28.8 was by far the best return of quick bowlers on either side.

The two men returned with very different reputations. Statham could be relied on, a real tryer with a touch of class. Trueman was too wild and his wickets might not be worth the trouble they caused. With that Trueman played just three Tests in the next three years while Statham played 22 and took 79 wickets. Not only did he pass 100 Test wickets but he was taken to the hearts of the cricketing public for his exploits in Australia and then his finest personal performance, at Lord's in 1955.

With England having finally regained the Ashes in 1953 the pressure was on to retain them in the following year. Trueman was still out of favour despite an outstanding season for Yorkshire. After the West Indies tour he was considered a liability and the fast-bowling hopes were laid at the door of Bedser, Statham, Loader, Bailey and Frank Tyson. History remembers the last named for some of the fastest bowling ever seen which flattened the hosts 3-1. Statham took the new ball in all five Tests and his record was better than that of both Miller and Lindwall. The perfect foil for Tyson maybe, but not just that. Statham produced spells of real pace and venom. He wasn't just choking an end while the main man recharged his batteries. Tyson likened the presence of Statham to having Yehudi Menuhin playing second fiddle to his lead – 'throughout the tour I owed much to desperation injected into the batsmen's methods by Statham's relentless pursuit.' His contribution was priceless and he was now a main man. Over the next few years England became increasingly reliant on him as Bedser retired, Trueman remained out of favour and Tyson battled with form and fitness.

The 1955 South Africans provided spirited opposition and five memorable Tests as England struggled to find a settled new-ball pairing. Statham was available for four games and each time his partner changed – Tyson, Trueman, Loader and finally Bailey. He was the leader of the pack and took to his new responsibility in his customary unfussy manner sending down 170 overs for 17 wickets with one performance standing out as his finest.

In the second Test at Lord's, South Africa seemed sure to win after leading by 171 on first innings. Even a fightback led by Peter May looked unlikely to be rewarded with South Africa needing 183 on a pitch that had, if anything, eased after they had scored 342 in the first innings. This time paired with Trueman, Statham proved irresistible. After removing the openers overnight he bowled unchanged (assisted by a rain break) through the entire innings removing the top seven in the order in his 7-39. His method was described as 'hostile fast bowling' – his partner, more normally associated with such descriptions, failed to take a wicket and was dropped. Without resorting to the short-pitched method of the South African's Neil Adcock and Peter Heine, he managed to be both aggressive and accurate even when bowling unchanged for two hours. Little wonder then that he nominated this his finest hour and Gubby Allen called it 'one of the greatest pieces of sustained fast bowling of the 20th century'. This was the kind of bowling that drew from AA Thomson the comment that 'Statham's near perfection in length and direction was not something to which he aspired; he achieved it naturally and without strain', hence the stamina when bowling with 'utter accuracy and savage pace'. He paid a price however; a pulled stomach muscle laid him low for the rest of the season; clearly there was strain even if it was invisible.

Spin dominated the following summer as Australia fell under the spell of English groundsmen, Laker and Lock. The one time Trueman and Statham were paired together, at Lord's, both were successful but both were apparently put in the shade by 36-year-old Keith Miller. Australian captain Ian Johnson was, however, genuinely impressed by both Englishmen despite their efforts failing to provide victory. He called Trueman's first-innings performance 'one of the most aggressive and courageous exhibitions of fast bowling I've seen' and of Statham's second-innings showing he was even more enamoured: 'the most hostile fast bowling of the match…it could be said he bowled too well to take wickets'. This was not an uncommon fate for Statham – on green wickets his seam movement was too good for all but the best batsmen. It's fortunate that his nature was essentially phlegmatic.

Trueman's 5-90 had been genuinely fast and kept England in the game – less impressive in the next match he was hastily dropped for the rest of the series. Once again the feeling appeared that the selectors needed far less reason to jettison Trueman than they did to pick him.

The summer of 1957 was a hot one and the wickets rolled out fast. West Indies were the visitors, still boasting the three Ws now aided and abetted by Rohan Kanhai and Garry Sobers. At last Trueman and Statham were first choices on largely sporting pitches.

The series proved to be less closely-fought than expected once Peter May and Colin Cowdrey had negated the threat of the West Indian spinners in the first match and England moved to a comfortable win. Statham had a largely moderate series before succumbing to injury and missing the last two matches only to see his replacement, Loader, win the Leeds match. Trueman, on the other hand, was back with a bang. His 22 wickets contained 'the finest sustained bowling performance of his career to date' at Trent Bridge; that from Jim Swanton who had hardly been one of Trueman's great advocates and later passed him (and Statham) over when writing *Cricketers of my Time*. Equally relevant was that this was the first time Trueman and Statham had prospered as a pair – Trueman 9-143 and Statham 6-196. The pitch was perfect, the weather hot, the batting strong and England had picked only four bowlers, one of whom, Bailey, tore muscles in his back. Under these circumstances both sets of figures were outstanding – Trueman delivered 65 overs and Statham 70, England narrowly failed to win. Little wonder then that the words 'sustained' and 'stamina' appeared so often when plaudits were penned about both men.

The following summer New Zealand were brushed aside as a prelude to the team of all talents heading for Australia and an anticipated comfortable victory. This was Statham's third trip but Trueman's first and the Australian public were hungry for a sight of Fiery Fred. Just to remind Trueman that past misdemeanours, either real or imagined, hadn't been forgotten he was greeted by tour manger Freddie Brown with the warning "Any trouble from you and you're on a slow boat home". Back injury was the trouble, to which Brown was distinctly unsympathetic, and by the time Trueman entered the Test arena the series was all but lost.

England had taken a battery of fast bowlers on tour hoping for wickets that had proved so helpful to Tyson and Statham four years earlier, but they were to be disappointed. The removal of the couch grass in 1954 had been reversed and the wickets were now easy-paced. Statham had valiantly attempted to rescue the second game with 7-57 but the shambolic English batting could not support him. Thereafter Statham declined (and could have lost his life in a car accident) as Trueman slowly began to prosper, buoyed by his popularity amongst the home supporters. Despite having to bowl shorter than he would have wished and finding little in the way of 'English swing' he gave it his all and was rewarded by Peter May's confidential report which called him 'the greatest success of the tour' and recommended an extra bonus. This was some contrast to what Hutton had written after the West Indies series five years earlier. Disappointing as this tour had been it heralded five years of the Statham and Trueman show.

India in 1959 were first up – a combined total of 41 wickets at 15.2 before another, far more difficult and potentially explosive, trip to the West Indies. For Trueman the tour couldn't have been a greater contrast to that of six years earlier. On easy pitches he pounded and pounded – Ted Dexter thought his overall performance as good as anything he had seen. He got on well with the management, the crowds and himself and gave everything he had, outbowling Wes Hall and making a significant contribution in Trinidad where the series was decided. For Statham the tour was less satisfactory as he was shadowed by injury and only played three Tests. However his role in the decisive Trinidad victory was recognised by John Arlott who thought it 'the finest joint operation the pair had yet carried out' and Ian Peebles praised Statham's efforts as 'an exhibition of seam bowling with a worn ball I have seldom seen equalled'. He was still, clearly, England's other new-ball bowler and as senior professional he joined the selection committee – Jim Swanton thought 'the new men could have no better model'. A remarkable example of Statham's nature came in the third Test when he warned West Indian opener Easton McMorris that he might expect a bouncer if he kept playing forward. The bouncer came two overs later and hit the batsman in the chest causing anxiety for Statham and blood spitting for McMorris.

Despite Trueman's Herculean efforts and Statham's injury problems both were back into domestic cricket at the beginning of the 1960 season. This was still the age of the County Championship and both men were the spearheads of their respective teams. Statham had bowled at least 900 overs in each of the previous three English summers while Trueman had topped 1000 in 1959 and would do so again in 1960 despite his winter exertions. And for the first time both men would play a full five-match series together. However, although they played their part in a resounding victory, 1960 was remembered for all the wrong reasons.

'Chuck' and 'drag' were terms that had become increasingly prevalent during the fifties and as the decade neared its end matters were coming to a head. England's Tony Lock was widely viewed as a thrower; in Australia Ian Meckiff's action was questioned while Gordon Rorke was a notorious exponent of drag. With no-balls decided by the position of the back foot it had become common practice over many years to plant the front foot well over the crease and drag the back foot through thus giving the ball legitimacy as long as it was released before the back foot passed the crease. Larwood had gained 32 inches by the estimation of his team-mate Bill Bowes and when at top speed Trueman was capable of 'stealing' 36 inches. Lindwall was another expert and all were, by and large, working within the laws. But umpires were increasingly applying different interpretations and making a decision on a moving foot and a simultaneously released ball was almost impossible. Rorke's extreme height meant that he was often delivering from fully four to five feet in front of the bowling crease. The situation was absurd and by 1960 a movement was afoot to introduce a front-foot rule. It may seem obvious now but at the time even Don Bradman was a steadfast opponent of altering the rule.

Throwing was proving equally obstinate but the decision of umpires Syd Buller and Frank Lee to no-ball South African Geoff Griffin at Lord's in 1960 overshadowed the entire series. Cricket was in the doldrums, due largely to negative bowling, batting and tactics and this narcoleptic mixture meant the attendances for the five-match series were dreadful even if those who did attend had the pleasure of seeing Fred and Brian capture 52 wickets – the others managed just 27. Statham's 11-100 at Lord's and Trueman's 9-104 at Trent Bridge were the work of two craftsmen in their prime. The South Africans were not at their best but this was new-ball bowling *par excellence*. Trueman was now more adaptable – he had grown into the bowler so loved by John Arlott because he had everything. Statham continued on his quiet course, his 11 wickets at Lord's a masterpiece of consistent pace, accuracy and use of the pitch that was largely overshadowed by Griffin's bent arm. It was the first 11-wicket haul by an English fast bowler since Bill Voce in 1936. South African wicket-keeper John Waite thought his team had been 'Truemanized' at Edgbaston and Trent Bridge and 'Stathamized' at Lord's.

The next summer saw the arrival of the Australians, fresh from their astonishing home series against West Indies where 'brighter cricket' seemed to have breathed new life into a stagnant game. But where Benaud and Worrell had manufactured breathless excitement and attracted huge crowds, an excellent series in England failed to have such a positive effect on attendances.

Both Trueman and Statham were at their peak of fitness. Both bowled well over 1000 overs during the summer and both were now automatic choices to open the bowling for England – both, however, found the Australian batting if not impregnable then mightily resistant. The series swayed first towards Australia and then, courtesy of Trueman, back to England. At Leeds he showed his maturity and intelligence in gaining his first 10-wicket haul. The tale is simple to tell – on a helpful wicket, but with Australia at 182-2, Trueman took the second new ball and off his long run ripped out five wickets to put them out for 237. In the second innings he cut his run and bowled off cutters into dusty patches with a tight leg trap – the result was 7.5-4-5-6. England won 'Trueman's match' at a canter and squared the series. Ironically this was the one Test Statham missed in the series. This was Fred in his pomp, leading off his team-mates in a muck sweat, jersey over shoulders in front of a Yorkshire crowd having won a Test for England and ready for a pipe, a pint and an extensive post-mortem. Never had life been sweeter and all the controversy of earlier days been further away. Within three weeks he had been dropped.

Statham was back for the fourth Test and immediately took advantage of a green wicket, taking 5-53 as England led by 177 on first innings. That Australia battled back to win and retain the Ashes was down to fine batting, dropped catches and a piece of miraculous bowling by Benaud. One ball deserves special mention as it encapsulates both Statham the man and Statham the cricketer. "Brian is the greatest. He bowled me a couple moving in. The next one was pitched in exactly the same spot but it went the other way." John Murray the wicket-keeper echoed the words of victim Norman O'Neill: "It was a beauty, moving away just enough to find the edge of the bat". And George's verdict? "It was straight!"

Trueman hadn't bowled well but his omission for the final Test was astonishing given that he was by far England's most successful bowler of the series. County stalwart Jack Flavell of Worcestershire was called up to partner Statham.

For their respective counties the two men had never been busier but the slight worry for Lancashire was that Statham's wickets cost, for the first time in a domestic season, more than 20 each. Not that it stopped him topping the county's averages, something he did every year from 1951 to 1966. Trueman took 50 more at a better average.

Both men were rested for the subcontinent tour as England looked for young talent but both were back for the home series against Pakistan and both prospered (38 wickets at 18.9 in four games) as the visitors were outclassed. One more trip to Australia lay in wait, in 1962-63.

In a moribund series England again failed to regain the Ashes, in part at least due to the shortcomings of the pace attack. Statham and Trueman had the support of just one other specialist quick bowler, Len Coldwell, and found themselves incapable of bowling Australia out or scoring runs quickly while all the time being handicapped by Ted Dexter's eccentric captaincy. Statham was clearly in decline and only avoided a dropping through the lack of alternatives, it was generally considered that he'd lost his 'zip'. But in the fourth Test he did become the highest wicket taker in Test cricket history, passing Bedser's 236. Trueman, although England's best, was outbowled by Australia's Alan Davidson. Nonetheless he was capable of producing a match-winning spell at Melbourne which David Sheppard called 'the finest sustained and accurate fast bowling I have ever seen' and by dint of staying for the New Zealand series moved past record-holder Statham. Dexter and team manager the Duke of Norfolk then wrote reports that ensured Trueman, and Ray Illingworth, lost part of their good conduct bonus.

> 'The least easy person in the team to control. Slack in his ways and not prepared to willingly lend any help in off-the-field duties.'

Trueman's response was that it was a 'filthy insult'.

And that could have been the end of Test cricket for both men. Statham played just three more times and an incandescent Trueman was minded to tell MCC where to go but neither side really wanted a permanent rift. England needed Trueman and he needed to measure himself once again against the best, and fastest, in the world – this time in the form of Wes Hall and Charlie Griffith. In the summer of 1963 Trueman, in the words of Arlott, 'blazed up like a smouldering fire fed with a handful of dry brushwood'.

Statham was tried twice in the series but in the main Trueman's ally was Derek Shackleton – if any bowler was more reliable than Statham then this was the one. But he didn't have the Lancastrian's brilliance and Trueman found himself the lone strike bowler – his response was to take 34 wickets at 17.5 despite England losing 3-1. It was a thrilling series and England responded well despite being clearly second best. Griffith matched Trueman wicket for wicket even if his performance was marred by his predilection for the occasional throw. Trueman claimed to have overheard the umpires at Lord's being given strict instructions not to no-ball Griffith for fear of political and racial repercussions.

In that very Test, Trueman took 11-152 in a thrilling and famous draw. The game, and possibly the series, was a victim of a selectorial blunder. The wicket was made for Statham rather than Shackleton's moderate pace and methodical accuracy. Griffith recalled the West Indian dressing room 'rejoicing' when they heard Statham had been omitted.

But at least the absence of Statham resulted in one of the great Test climaxes – if only the Soviet general staff had known that the UK early-warning stations were tuned to the BBC with Colin Cowdrey coming out to bat, arm in plaster, to save the game.

In the following match Trueman simply flattened West Indies with 12-119 in a 'brilliant display of controlled swing bowling' for the only English win. Thereafter West Indies asserted comfortably. It had been one final heroic deed – 236 overs of whole-hearted effort that fixed the legend of Trueman in the British mind.

Now closing in on the magical figure of 300 Test wickets Trueman was given one more crack at Australia while Statham moved quietly back to Lancashire. After two rain-affected draws, in which Trueman took nine wickets to move onto 293, the stage was set for the master showman to break the barrier at his home ground of Headingley. With Australia struggling at 187-7, still trailing by 81, and spinners Norman Gifford and Fred Titmus in full control, Dexter took the new ball with only Peter Burge and the tail to knock over. Trueman was convinced he could pin Burge to the sightscreen (as he later promised fire warden Hodges he would do to Captain Mainwaring in a magical episode of *Dad's Army*) but a series of fast-medium long hops was dispatched to the boundary. Mistaken captaincy, brilliant batting but above all Trueman's inability to recognise he could no longer summon the old pace or devil allowed Australia off the hook. The last three wickets added 211 and Australia never looked back – they won the match and eventually the series and Trueman was dropped – 297 wickets all out?

He was recalled for the final Test (magnanimous or proactive?) and when Colin Cowdrey caught Neil Hawke he had reached the magical mark. 'FS Trueman: We love him yeh yeh yeh' sang *The Cricketer*. It was a marvellous and hugely popular personal achievement but the game and the Ashes had already gone. It was no surprise when both Trueman and Statham were omitted from the party to South Africa – effectively their international careers had run their course.

Both men still had plenty more to give to their counties. In 1965 Statham's domestic form was so good that he was recalled for the final Test of the summer at the age of 35 with South Africa leading the series 1-0. Statham had said that he hoped for England's sake that his recall wouldn't be necessary – but it was. He and Lancashire partner Ken Higgs, on debut, could hardly have done more, taking 15 wickets before rain prevented a thrilling finale with England needing 91 runs in 70 minutes with six wickets standing. Eddie Barlow and Ali Bacher were his final two Test victims.

Statham continued to top the Lancashire averages and then reluctantly took on the responsibility of captaincy from 1965-67 after an advertisement in the *Times* had failed to produce a better candidate. Although he was not conspicuously successful he brought harmony back to the dressing room (even if he had to solicit help in Gillette Cup matches with counting overallocations) and it is no coincidence that that he oversaw the development of a fine team. His successor, Jackie Bond, was able to reap the benefits in the early seventies. Members of that side from Ken Shuttleworth to Farokh Engineer and David Lloyd queued up to pay tribute to Statham as a bowler, captain and man. A CBE followed in 1968.

In a less formal sense Trueman also did his stint as county captain. With Brian Close frequently absent in 1967 and 1968 senior-pro Trueman was able to show his tactical acumen. It was not a job he sought but he got huge entertainment from taunting Close with his excellent record – for years Trueman's bluster had disguised the fact, from the public if not opposing batsmen, that he had an astute cricketing brain. Of course he had – wisecracks, stares and thunderbolts would hardly account alone for 2304 first-class wickets at 18.29.

Behind the great bowling skill of both men it's often forgotten that they made other contributions. Trueman always fancied himself as a batsman and his long-handle approach did plenty of damage on the county circuit. He was also a superb close fielder, especially around the corner at short-leg or leg-gully. Statham's batting was less feared but he was an outstanding deep fielder with great pace over the ground and a fearsomely accurate throw.

After retirement from the game Brian Statham moved quietly to work for Guinness before ill-health forced his retirement and consequent financial difficulties. Trueman's career reflected his character – a born entertainer, he was frequently seen and heard on radio and television but when he heard of his old mucker's plight, testimonials were organised and the word went out. Unsurprisingly there were many genuine and generous offers from over 1000 guests at the Grosvenor House Hotel that helped ease Statham's final years.

When Jim Kilburn offered an appreciation in *Wisden* in 1962 he was inclined to deal with the two bowlers separately and recognised that they were not parts of a machine. Nonetheless, he saw the symmetry as anybody would:

> 'Statham and Trueman, playing so much together, have followed parallel careers with little more than their speed and success in common. Each has touched the topmost heights of his profession aided in considerable measure by the contemporary incidence of the other; either would have been welcomed in England teams of any age. They have been co-operative and competitive, complementary and contrasting.'

The two men saw each other and their relationship in similar terms:

> 'I have always enjoyed bowling with Fred and I reckon myself lucky to have been in harness with him for such a long time…It's a help when you know the bowler at the other end is trying as hard as you are.
>
> He describes himself as a middle-and-leg bowler, which I presume means that he starts his swing on the middle- and leg-stumps. His bowling is, in fact, a complete contrast to my own, for my target is invariably the off-stump with the ball doing little or nothing through the air but moving either way off the seam. In addition, Freddie is inclined to pitch a shorter length than I do.'

The complement was returned:

> We hunted in our own pack. That's because I moved the ball mainly away from the right-handed batsman while George moved it into them. If we had a left-hand, right-hand batting pairing against us, we'd often give them a single to enable me to bowl to the right-hander and Brian the left-hander… because his ball would then be moving away from a leftie. And the ball moving away is always considered the more dangerous delivery because there is less margin for error for the batsman.'

If the statistics of the careers of Fred and George rather dampen the case for them as the greatest pace pair ever to pull on England jerseys then the above quotes redress the balance in some measure. Both men clearly relished the presence of the other and felt it enhanced their own abilities. As bowlers of contrasting methods they were well positioned to exploit batting weaknesses and work together for their own and the team's best interests.

Trueman and Statham

Results

	Total	Won	Drawn	Lost
Trueman	67	34	22	11
Statham	70	28	26	16
Trueman and Statham	35	13	14	8

Test Bowling Overall

	Mat	Balls	Runs	Wkts	Ave	SR	ER	5W1/10WM
Trueman	67	15178	6625	307	21.57	49.4	2.61	17/3
Statham	70	16056	6261	252	24.84	63.7	2.33	9/1

Test Bowling Together

	Mat	Balls	Runs	Wkts	Ave	SR	ER	5W1/10WM
Trueman	35	8324	3684	143	25.76	58.2	2.65	5/0
Statham	35	8697	3626	141	25.71	63.5	2.42	6/1

Test Bowling Apart

	Mat	Balls	Runs	Wkts	Ave	SR	ER	5W1/10WM
Trueman	32	6854	2941	164	17.93	41.8	2.57	12/3
Statham	35	7359	2635	111	23.73	66.3	2.15	3/0

Best Series Together - South Africa 1960

	Mat	Balls	Runs	Wkts	Ave	SR	ER	5W1/10WM
Trueman	5	1083	508	25	20.32	43.3	2.81	1/0
Statham	5	1218	491	27	18.18	45.1	2.41	2/1

Best Test Figures - Innings/Match

Trueman (with Statham)	5-27 vs South Africa, Nottingham – 1960
Trueman (with Statham)	9-104 vs South Africa, Nottingham – 1960
Trueman (without Statham)	8-31 vs India, Manchester – 1952
Trueman (without Statham)	12-119 vs West Indies, Birmingham – 1963
Statham (with Trueman)	6-63 vs South Africa, Lord's – 1960
Statham (with Trueman)	11-97 vs South Africa, Lord's – 1960
Statham (without Trueman)	7-39 vs South Africa, Lord's – 1955
Statham (without Trueman)	9-88 vs South Africa, Lord's – 1955

YouTube Bowling Highlights

Search Phrases (sic)
England v West Indies, Lord's 1963 (20 June)
Australia V England (1962) Brisbane
Fred Trueman - Englands greatest ever fast bowler

Adcock

and

Heine

Neil Adcock

In short he in the main bowled just within the utmost of physical out-giving. Thus run-up and delivery were both sweetly attuned; always his arm was high above his shoulder...a plumbline from hand to ground would have brushed precisely all down Adcock's flank. Only the Australian Ted McDonald would I rate as the equal of Adcock in perfection of style among fast bowlers. – Charles Fortune

Peter Heine

He was a fearsome figure, his black hair straggling over his eyes and a great red streak across the front of his shirt, on which he viciously polished the ball. [His] attitude to his job was simple. He bowled at the batsman as often as he bowled at the wicket. – Jim Laker

As life in white South Africa settled back into something approaching its cosy and familiar routine after 1945, the population could reflect on the truth, welcome for most but uncomfortable for some, that the war years had changed the balance of power in world politics but not South African internal affairs.

Cricket had been something of a minority sport since its inception in Africa. The majority of the population was excluded from the best facilities in cricket, as in everything else, by dint of their skin colour and mixed-race games were strictly taboo. Since the glory days of Jimmy Sinclair, Aubrey Faulkner and Ernie Vogler giving Australia a few shocks and beating England before 1914 there had been precious little to cheer about. The deeds of Herby Taylor and the series victory in England in 1935 on the back of Bruce Mitchell's epic century at Lord's had been sandwiched between great doorsteps of soggy defeat.

The feeling in Johannesburg and Cape Town was that their team would be left further adrift as the breadth of international cricket grew to incorporate West Indies and India. These sides would present new tests to the established powers but they would never be allowed to play in or against South Africa. With the advent of DF Malan's nationalists in 1948 there would be a tightening of all laws that ensured whites would never share a sporting field with non-whites.

South Africa's elite were left with a slim domestic programme and the prospect of beating New Zealand and, at best, minimising the defeats against Australia and England. The game was simply too exclusive and not just through racism – the fact that it was seen as an English sport lead Afrikaners to heavily favour rugby. So the lack of competition and money meant that the pool to draw from remained tiny; an occasional pearl might be unearthed but never enough to fashion a necklace. And even these pearls soon faded, cricket was not a career and few were wealthy enough to give up 15 years of their lives to play a game for no pay.

So the team stumbled into the 1950s still guided by pre-war relics such as Bruce Mitchell and Dudley Nourse until gradually the nucleus of a new batting side appeared around Doug McGlew and Roy Maclean – but where to find the bowlers?

Not since before 1914 had South Africa possessed anything approaching a fast bowler and never had they had a finger spinner. The early battery of wrist spinners had been replaced by an inter-war mish-mash attack of bowlers largely forgotten who were fine on their day but lacking both consistency and longevity.

Then, suddenly, they all appeared at once. 'Toey' Tayfield with his dark-ringed eyes and unremitting accuracy. Certainly, and still, South Africa's only great finger spinner, he made his debut in 1949 to be closely followed by not one but two real fast bowlers. For a country that been battered and bruised for 30 years by Ray Lindwall, Keith Miller, Harold Larwood and Jack Gregory this was manna from heaven even if there was more to recommend the devil in some of the antics of Neil Adcock and Peter Heine.

The words most often associated with genuinely fast bowlers with a penchant for short bowling are 'uncompromising' and 'intimidating' with maybe an 'aggressive' thrown in. This South African pair, especially Heine, sometimes provoked a slightly deeper dig into the thesaurus and attracted adjectives of a different order; 'violent' and 'nasty' are two that have stuck. Of course they were kittens with golden hearts off the field, they always are, but given a cut strip their behaviour would have made Colin Croft or Dennis Lillee blush. There was one at each end, one blond and clean cut the other dark and straggly and their combined height was just shy of 13 feet.

Apart from their height and attitude what the pair had in common was late development. Adcock played to a moderate level at school but playing for Jeppe Old Boys under the leadership of Transvaal captain Eric Rowan he had a mad moment which was to change his life.

> "Partly from nervousness I slipped myself and bowled much faster than I had ever done before. It took everyone by surprise, including myself."

Heine's development was even more curious – as an Afrikaner he wasn't unusual in showing scant regard for cricket as a youngster but working for his local Fire Department he was asked to open the bowling and use his full height. Like Adcock he soon found enjoyment in projecting the ball at high pace and watching the fear in the batsman's eyes. Within four years he had transformed himself into a first-class bowler, initially with North-East Transvaal before moving to Orange Free State. Here he shot to prominence in 1954, already aged 26, when taking 7-29 to blast out the New Zealand tourists. This was a Test bowler in waiting.

Meanwhile Adcock had not been letting the grass grow under his feet. Rowan had been impressed by Adcock's sudden transformation and ex-international Cyril Vincent coached him hard to maintain his new-found speed. He was ushered into the Transvaal side in 1952 with immediate success. Such was his impact that with only 32 first-class wickets to his name he found himself selected for Test cricket against the same New Zealanders that Heine had already terrorised. The selectors had the delightful problem of two new pace bowlers and decided that picking both was too risky – Adcock made them think they had made the right choice.

On a flat Durban wicket he did enough to ensure that he would retain his place for Johannesburg's Ellis Park. The rugby ground was pressed into cricket service in the gap between the demolition of the old Wanderers to make room for a new railway station and the construction of the new version. The curator loved a bouncy pitch and knew just how to prepare one. Adcock was in his element and then became enraged by being run out in South Africa's long first innings. Any New Zealander who knew Adcock could guess what was coming. As if to add to the drama of what was to follow, flags flew at half-mast in recognition of the victims of the Tangiwai rail crash on Christmas Eve in New Zealand in which Bob Blair had lost his fiancée.

Adcock flew in. Eric Dempster described his bowling as 'lethal' and in the days of minimal protection it could have been. With the ball flying off just short of a length it was carnage reminiscent of Bodyline. Two batsmen were bowled off their ribs, two others collapsed after being hit, Laurie Miller was taken to hospital coughing blood after being hit on the chest and ace batsman Bert Sutcliffe was felled and suffered a burst eardrum. The fact that he later returned swathed in bandages to counter-attack (hitting seven sixes) led the crowd to boo Adcock, something he never forgot. It was a brutal display of merciless force. Five wickets followed in the second innings and 24 in the series. His best first-class figures of the season were reserved for the game against Orange Free State and Peter Heine; 13-65. When the squad was announced for the 1955 tour of England there was little doubt that the names Adcock and Heine would be included.

Despite the rate of their ascension there were still some justifiable doubts about how they would respond to the rigours of an English tour. Adcock was tall and slightly built and had relied largely on inswingers, using his chest-on action, and bouncers, using generous South African pitches and arm speed. The 'flurry of arms' was, according to Graeme Pollock, 'a fine sight to behold if you were not on the receiving end.' But there was surely the danger that his bowling might become one dimensional and ineffective in a damp English summer.

While he had shown his effectiveness in international cricket against New Zealand, bowling to Colin Cowdrey, Peter May and Denis Compton would be a different matter. Heine had yet to play a Test but looked physically stronger – whether his slingy action would suit English pitches was another matter. What soon became clear over the course of the English summer of 1955 and the next few years was that Adcock and Heine were not a pair to be taken lightly as they forged a partnership that seemed, at times, to be built on hatred of opposition batsmen, a desire to inflict injury and a line in steaming invective now known as sledging.

South Africa had waited a long time for such a pair, or even just one, of pace bowlers. Drew Forrest's book *The Pacemen* struggles manfully with this but there is no hiding place. He bridges the gap between Kotze and Heine with a selection of quick spinners and trundlers that could barely be described as fast-medium. Alf Hall, Buster Nupen, Bob Crisp and Lindsay Tuckett had much to recommend them but South Africa was not the place to nurture pace bowling. With no professionalism, little in the way of coaching or fitness training and only intermittent Test cricket it was unlikely that any bowler would last long. Turf wickets gradually began to replace the ubiquitous matting in the late 1920s and then the types laid tended to lead to orgies of run scoring that were hardly likely to inspire anyone to try and bowl quickly. Shades of India and Pakistan before Kapil Dev and Imran Khan.

The appearance of Cuan McCarthy and his success at home to England in 1948 proved that it was possible. He effectively lasted just one series and then spiralled into a decline as Neil Harvey, dreadful slip catching and a dubious action saw him fall as quickly as he had risen. But what McCarthy did achieve in that one series was to provide inspiration – Heine and Adcock were aged 20 and 17 at the time and this was bowling to emulate. It had put England on the back foot both literally and metaphorically and that was something to both relish and remember.

The 1955 tour of England would be where this pair of speedsters would start to pay back some old scores. *The Cricketer's* preview of the tour penned by Louis Duffus had little to say beyond the fact that Adcock favoured inswing and Heine outswing; certainly no mention of somewhat aggressive temperaments!

It was a memorable series, the first great contest between the two countries played on turf. Charles Fortune, who saw plenty, thought it the finest he ever saw. True, South Africa had somehow won a series in 1935 but this one ebbed and flowed throughout the summer before a memorable climax at the Oval in the final match.

The season started in typically English fashion. Cold and damp conditions meant that both the fast bowlers were kept largely under wraps and shivering inside three jumpers they were in no position to give of anything like their best in the run up the first Test. Adcock had done enough to ensure his place but Heine's much-awaited debut would have to wait. A four-day innings defeat followed at Trent Bridge giving little sign of the thrilling series that would follow. At last Heine found his rhythm as the weather improved and a 7-58 against Somerset ensured he would be joining Adcock for the Lord's Test.

To say the pitch was made to measure was an understatement – Bill Bowes reported that for the first time he was unable to tell which strip would be marked out for the match. Heine's first ball flew over the batsman's head from just short of a length, on this evidence the batsmen would be on the back foot in all senses for the duration of the game.

South Africa's new-ball pairing were in the right place at the right time and soon had a wicket apiece and appeared likely to take England apart until Jack Cheetham decided that Trevor Goddard was a better partner for Heine and this new pairing completed the rout – 133 all out. It was an odd decision both on a practical and psychological level; here was a perfect opportunity spurned for a new pair of quick bowlers to establish ascendancy over the opposition early in the series. But a first-innings lead of 161 seemed sure to take South Africa to a series-levelling victory until a century by Peter May and a superb exhibition of fast-medium bowling by Brian Statham turned the game on its head. His 7-39 showed Adcock and Heine how far they still had to go.

It had been a demoralising defeat, a winning position eradicated by the brilliance of May and Statham, and it said much for the character of the tourists that they quickly bounced back to win a thrilling Test at Old Trafford by three wickets with just five minutes to spare. Played on a fast but relatively true pitch South Africa did what they had never done before – they out-muscled England through fast bowling. Although Adcock and Heine sometimes showed their inexperience they got through 112 overs (and this with Heine needing back strapping) and took no fewer than 14 wickets. Cowdrey initially tried to replicate his front-foot tactics used in Australia but was soon forced back after receiving 'the worst going over I have ever experienced in a Test'. Tayfield and Goddard acted as wonderful support but support only and the South African pair extracted far more life from the pitch than the English triumvirate of Alec

Bedser, Frank Tyson and Trevor Bailey. It seemed that this combination might carry the fight to England in the final two Tests.

That hope seemingly lasted just eight overs into England's first innings at Headingley – Adcock limped from the field and an X-ray revealed a broken bone in his foot. In Adcock's absence Heine, Tayfield and Goddard proved to be a resilient and unflagging attack, Goddard sending down 62 overs in the second innings, as South Africa heroically levelled the series.

The deciding game was won by spin and the combination of Laker and Lock on their home ground was too much for South Africa. A number of umpiring decisions went against the visitors which would not be easily forgiven or forgotten. With Adcock injured and on a largely unhelpful pitch, Heine laboured intelligently for no great reward and the series was lost.

Heine's 21 wickets at an average of 23.52 was an indication that South Africa had another pace bowler. Adcock's injury-hit tour meant that the pair had yet to really show what they could do together. The South Africans would have to wait 16 months for the opportunity of revenge on their own pitches. It would truly be worth the wait.

The Currie Cup matches of 1955-56 further enhanced the reputation of the pair of Transvaal pacemen although Heine comfortably outshone Adcock with 34 wickets at 12.76. The following summer saw, as was the tradition, the domestic competition suspended so that full attention could be given to the MCC tourists.

These were, of course, the days of proper tours; a leisurely sea trip followed by two months and ten warm-up games which were taken very seriously by both sides. England had a viewing of Adcock and Heine, now both fit and raring to go, in the match against Transvaal and saw enough to make them realise that both men were now mature Test-class bowlers. On a largely-lifeless pitch they were every bit a match for Tyson and Statham in a narrow defeat. When, in the following game, Tayfield bowled a South Africa XI to victory at Pretoria it seemed sure that this would be a closely fought contest with little to choose between the bowling attacks but with England having superior batting, particularly as Peter May had scored nearly 1000 runs before the first Test. What England had learnt was that it would be wise to protect their premier batsmen from a new-ball battering – Peter Richardson and Trevor Bailey were deemed to be buffer and bore the brunt of some brutal attacks.

The first ever Test at the new Wanderers ground in Johannesburg in front of the largest crowd ever in South Africa was 'graced' by the then slowest century in Test cricket as Richardson ground out his three-figure score in 488 minutes. Accurate bowling, fine fielding and negative captaincy all aided and abetted the Worcestershire left hander but the mindset of the age was to occupy the crease at all costs. Adcock and Heine led the South African attack with a growling menace and were largely responsible for putting their side into a winning position of needing 204 to win with time to spare. Bailey destroyed any hopes by removing four of the top five and the collapse was completed at 72 all out.

Exactly the same score was the South African fate in their second innings of the second Test and they were 2-0 down with three to play and the fun yet to start. Perhaps 'fun' is the wrong word because this was proving to be a bruising contest. Tyson had been sidelined by illness and then injury but Adcock and Heine, particularly the latter, were bringing a new kind of attitude to fast bowling. Bailey was a particular target, having a finger broken in the third match before receiving a terrible battering in the fourth. Bailey's dour courage and phlegmatic nature was like a red rag to a bull, provoking one of Heine's famous outbursts: "I want to hit you, Bailey, I want to hit you over the heart."

The final three games of the series saw South Africa fight back in remarkable fashion but the games belonged to one man – Hugh Tayfield. In winning two and narrowly failing in the other his figures in the three English second innings were (eight-ball overs) 92.2-31-260-23. Small wonder then that the other South African bowlers were either bit-part players or the bulls that caused the cracks where 'Toey' Tayfield could creep in with his mesmerising accuracy, flight and a tiny dab of spin.

The general feeling was that England had under-performed, perhaps through tiredness towards the end of an over-long tour, and had been fortunate to avoid a series defeat. Adcock and Heine had played all five Tests together as a new, formidable opening attack – 'the rapier and the battle-axe' as they were called by Charles Fortune. Twenty-one wickets at 14.9 put Adcock amongst the best fast bowlers in the world, particularly as Statham had just 14 at 24.9. But praise wasn't overwhelming – Alan Ross's comprehensive account of the tour concluded that

'Heine and Adcock were an erratic pair, able to get more out of the wicket that promised any lift than the English fast bowlers, but more various of length and direction. Adcock was used in shorter spells, and he never gave runs away. He is a vastly better bowler than he was in England, and he always seemed to make his pace tell. Heine had a bad spell that encompassed the second, third and fourth Tests, but his vitality and steepness of trajectory made him formidable when he dropped on anything like a length.'

Lindwall and Miller they were clearly not, at least not yet, but both were young enough for the South African supporters to entertain hopes of the best part of a decade of enjoying their side being led by a real pace pair. Adcock had clearly curbed his wilder side and Heine would need to concentrate on taking wickets rather than felling batsmen, an approach which was dictating his length too often at the cost of his effectiveness as a Test bowler. Neither was he really fast enough to sustain such a method. He did not have the genuine natural pace of a Tyson or a Larwood but when roused he could, like Miller, be very quick.

The pair left behind plenty of residual bitterness amongst the English players. Laker always referred to "That bloody Dutchman" and Richardson confessed to being less than keen on one or two players – he would hardly have forgotten Heine greeting his prone body with the words "Get up, I want to hit you again". Tom Graveney termed them 'two of the nastiest customers I came across'.

After the performance against England in 1956-57 it was expected that South Africa would have the beating of Australia the following summer. Led by the surprisingly-appointed 22-year-old Ian Craig, this was a team in transition. Bradman's men had, with the exception of Neil Harvey, all gone and most of the inheritors had yet to prove themselves as worthy followers of the baggy-green tradition. Defeat in Pakistan saw the end of the pairing of Miller and Lindwall and for the first time the Kangaroos faced the Springboks as underdogs, having been termed the weakest team ever to leave Australian shores. If only those Springboks had played like top dogs they might indeed have won the series.

Heine was at his aggressive and menacing best right from the start. An Australian side featuring four debutants was reduced to 62-4 in pursuit of South Africa's 470 and yet Australia recovered to almost win. The rest of the bowling attack and the fielders failed to back up Heine who ended with 6-58 despite injuring an ankle during his opening salvo. This was genuine top-class bowling, finding bounce where no others could. Even later in the game, with a draw almost inevitable, he still found the strength to crush Jim Burke's fingers.

The second Test was on an easy track at Newlands and much to Heine's disgust he was omitted to allow his ankle to heal for better conditions later in the series. But the pitch took spin, Craig won the toss, Richie Benaud bowled like a dream and Australia were one up with three to play.

Adcock had managed little in the first two matches but now, reunited with Heine, he suddenly came back to and beyond his best. Ken Mackay had thought that Adcock ran in faster than he bowled until he was hit over the heart and needed a week to recover. Bowling with speed and life on a well-grassed Kingsmead pitch he reduced Australia to a paltry 163 in a stultifying 82.4 eight-ball overs. The match was there for the taking but South Africa failed to grasp anything in one of the worst displays of late 1950s cricket. Establishing a first-innings lead of 221 was the good part. Under normal circumstances this would be a fine position but centurions Waite and McGlew had both taken over eight hours to reach three figures – a total of 1311 balls produced just 384 runs. With still little in the wicket Australia easily held out for a draw in the dullest Test ever played. It was as if South Africa were too afraid to win, something that had dogged them for decades and would only be banished when 'Bunter' Barlow came swaggering along in the sixties.

Adcock and Heine suffered with injury and illness in the fourth Test which Benaud dominated with bat and ball (becoming the first Australian to make a century and a 'five-fer' in the same Test) although Heine again proved that he was as likely to bowl well when in pain as when not, taking 6-96 despite a recurrence of ankle trouble. Benaud recalled trying to avoid any eye contact with Heine although turning his back just opened up the invective valve; '...some of the suggestions he was making to me would, if successfully concluded, have had me a finalist in the next sexual Olympic Games.'

Australia dominated the final Test on a spicy greentop at Port Elizabeth despite a bumper barrage that Benaud thought the most dangerous he had ever seen and were left needing only 68 to win in the second innings. But this innings had some serious significance. With Burke injured, Wally Grout joined Colin McDonald to knock off the runs on a chilly evening in poor light.

'Ray Robinson described Adcock's first over to 'Mac' as the most frightening an Australian had faced since the bodyline era, 25 years before. The first four deliveries to McDonald were head high. 'Mac' chinned the third to the fence, the ball actually skidding from his bat to his chin, to the boundary. Watching from the other end I thought: "This is no place for Wallace, you can get them in boundaries or not at all."

Adcock, though told by van Ryneveld [his captain] after the third ball to cut out the bumpers sent his fourth screaming again head high down the off side. 'Mac', not interested in martyrdom, sheltered behind his bat. The ball struck it and ricocheted to second slip.

Watching from the safe end I wondered what Heine would send to me next over…though less frightening it was well studded with bouncers… van Ryneveld, however, after a conference with the umpires laid down the law and neither pace man sent down another bumper.'

Charles Fortune described this passage of play as 'the most terrifying eruption of fast bowling I have ever seen' and Graeme Pollock thought Adcock's contribution the fastest bowling he ever saw before 1970. There seems little doubt that the fast bowlers were unimpressed with their captain's collusion with the umpires. Van Ryneveld apologised to the Australians for the barrage, McDonald was furious and ashen faced when he returned to the pavilion; something not lost on one dressing room attendant, an aspiring young pace bowler named Peter Pollock – even battle hardened Test openers could be intimidated by real pace under the right conditions. Pollock would retain this information well and use it effectively over the next decade and more.

The reality for Adcock, Heine and their side was that not once had they performed well together. Heine's two match-winning spells in the games at Johannesburg had both failed to win matches because the support was insufficient – in these games Adcock took just three wickets. And when Adcock fired in Durban, Heine was ineffective. The final Test, where they should have been unplayable, was an exercise in violence.

Like the English tourists the previous year the Australians had mixed feelings about the tour. South African hospitality was legendary and men such as Compton knew how to live. There was, of course, institutional racism but privileged cricketers found this pretty easy to ignore – it suited them well not to dig too deeply. There is also plenty to support the idea that the South African attack was less than popular. Tayfield was clearly not an easy man to warm to and despite all the talk of how charming Adcock and Heine were off the field, their on-field antics were difficult to forgive or forget. The remorseless and brutal sledging was one thing but the openly expressed desire to hear ball on bone was another. Heine was by far the worst culprit and Harvey's verdict on the pair ('fire and brimstone') is illustrative. He rated Adcock highly as he could vary his stock ball and move it the other way at real pace. Heine, he thought, was considerably slower, bowled twice as many bouncers and telegraphed each one – and he was 'vindictive'. Harvey, a most generous and gentle man, was not often given to damning another player. Alan Davidson was slightly more forgiving when describing Adcock as 'the smooth wrecker' and Heine as his 'fiery support', a description that might well have suited Lindwall and Miller.

South African team-mate Goddard gave, certainly unwittingly, the most stinging criticism of the adopted style – 'They didn't have to bowl it halfway down the pitch to try and hit your head off, when you played against Adcock and Heine your bottom hand was sore because it jarred against the bat all the time.' They could have been so much better if they'd used their immense skills more wisely.

With no more Tests scheduled for two years neither bowler could harness the discipline or inclination to stay at their peak and they played just one more Test together, against New Zealand in 1962. But before that Adcock had returned to England once more, determined to atone for his miserable experience in 1955. He did. On a tour marred by Geoff Griffin's no balling, and subsequent exit from the game, Adcock showed the skill, intelligence and fitness to take 26 Test wickets at 22.57 – his best series.

In some senses the story of Adcock and Heine is one symptomatic of South African cricket prior to the 1960s. They needed coaching and professionalism to enable them to curb their wilder instincts and maintain their fitness. They needed a team ethic and strong leadership to harness their abundant skills. Neil Adcock could have been a great bowler and Peter Heine a very good one but they pale in comparison to direct contemporaries Davidson, Trueman and Statham. Their names will, however, always be linked and they paved the way for decades of South African fast-bowling pairs.

Adcock and Heine

Results

	Total	Won	Drawn	Lost
Adcock	26	9	6	11
Heine	14	5	3	6
Adcock and Heine	13	5	3	5

Test Bowling Overall

	Mat	Balls	Runs	Wkts	Ave	SR	ER	5W1/10WM
Adcock	26	15519	2195	104	21.10	61.4	2.06	5/0
Heine	14	24353	1445	58	25.08	67.0	2.24	4/0

Test Bowling Together

	Mat	Balls	Runs	Wkts	Ave	SR	ER	5W1/10WM
Adcock	13	2730	884	47	18.80	58.0	1.94	1/0
Heine	13	3614	1368	58	24.87	65.7	2.27	4/0

Test Bowling Apart

	Mat	Balls	Runs	Wkts	Ave	SR	ER	5W1/10WM
Adcock	13	3661	1311	57	23.0	63.4	2.14	4/0
Heine	1	276	87	3	29.0	92.0	1.89	0/0

Best Series Together - England 1956-57

	Mat	Balls	Runs	Wkts	Ave	SR	ER	5W1/10WM
Adcock	5	1136	313	21	14.90	54.0	1.65	0/0
Heine	5	1480	417	18	28.72	82.2	2.09	0/0

Best Test Figures - Innings/Match

Adcock (with Heine)   6-43 vs Australia, Durban – 1958
Adcock (with Heine)   7-69 vs England, Johannesburg – 1956
Adcock (without Heine)   6-65 vs England, The Oval – 1960
Adcock (without Heine)   8-87 vs New Zealand, Johannesburg – 1955
Heine (with Adcock)   6-58 vs Australia, Johannesburg – 1957
Heine (with Adcock)   8-157 vs England, Manchester – 1955
Heine (without Adcock)   2-44 vs England, The Oval – 1955
Heine (without Adcock)   3-87 vs England, The Oval – 1955

YouTube Bowling Highlights

Search Phrases
Cape Summer MCC Tour to South Africa 1956-57 Part 1
Cape Summer MCC Tour to South Africa 1956-57 Part 2
Cape Summer MCC Tour to South Africa 1956-57 Part 3
Cape Summer MCC Tour to South Africa 1956-57 Part 4

Hall
and
Griffith

Wes Hall

He's a tall man, almost ebony in colour with flashing white teeth that light his face when he smiles. He has broad shoulders, and a lithe bouncing run to the wicket, gathering himself in as the popping crease approaches, to explode in what seems a flurry of arms and legs as he hurtles the ball at the opposing batsman. He likes an occasional drink and singing calypsos…but he dislikes batsmen. – Jack Fingleton

Charlie Griffith

Griffith, coming in at the start with that noble, upright run, cradling and rocking the ball, a love-child to be sacrificed before the great leap of delivery. – Alan Ross

The 1950s had been an abundant decade for the growing cult of fast-bowling pairs. Australia had found one straight after the war and before Lindwall and Miller were finished both England and South Africa had unearthed their own versions. Lagging well behind, however, were West Indies with a reliance on spin and medium pace. From 1950 until April 1956 Sonny Ramadhin and Alf Valentine were the match-winners for their country with support coming from such as Gerry Gomez, Frank Worrell and Denis Atkinson. With the three W's churning out runs they usually had a fair total to bowl at. The great spinners bowled nigh on half of all the balls delivered for their country during this period and took almost 49 per cent of all wickets. Of the 26 five-wicket hauls, 17 fell to the famous pals.

However, by 1957 their race was all but run and the 3-0 defeat in England was an indication that the old guard was changing. Fortunately Garry Sobers, Rohan Kanhai and Collie Smith had injected some youthful genius and equally interestingly the West Indies squad for that tour included two pace bowlers – Roy Gilchrist and Wes Hall. The fates of these men were to be very different in both short and long term.

The tour of England was a disaster for Hall. The teenager could make nothing of English wickets and was unable to adapt his run-up to soft English turf. For Gilchrist the tour was more successful, but only just. Called a 'considerable discovery' and generating some real speed he played four Tests and cemented his place in the team. Hall took advice on straightening his run-up and the pair finally came together during the tour of India in 1958-59 and the results were dramatic. *Wisden* reported:

> 'In Gilchrist and Hall West Indies possessed two fearsome opening bowlers reminiscent of the days of Martindale and Constantine.'

The figures more than bear out the assessment. On largely unhelpful wickets, but against batsmen unused to real pace, they took 56 wickets at 16.9 each in a 3-0 victory. That, however, was the end of Gilchrist's brief and fiery Test career. His temper and a penchant for bowling deliberate beamers were too much for the team management and he was sent home before the Pakistan leg of the tour where Hall continued in fine form and collected a hat-trick in the only game played on turf. Even after time for reflection Gilchrist seemed bemused.

> 'A beamer is a nasty ball when it comes flying head high at a batsman from my hand. But I have searched the rule books and there is not a word in any

of them that says a fellow cannot bowl a fast full-toss at a batsman…No one makes a batsman play Test cricket, man.'

Gilchrist took his armoury into the Lancashire League and Hall was left without a pace partner. It would be a long wait. First Chester Watson was given a crack and a raw young bowler named Charlie Griffith was tried once with no great success. By the time of the great 'tied-Test' series Hall's new-ball support had reverted to Worrell and Sobers. But Hall's stock rose rapidly during a home series with England.

Paired with a new partner in Watson, Hall twice blasted out the tourists in the first innings to put his side in a winning position though twice West Indies were unable to press home their advantage as England hung on to a 1-0 lead which did little for cricket as a spectacle. Complaints about excessive short-pitched bowling were swatted away by the West Indians who had taken their fair share of the same over the previous decade without the resources to retaliate.

The next series could hardly have been a greater contrast as Worrell and Richie Benaud not only promised brighter cricket but then also delivered it. The story is famous: a tied Test, the heroic resistance of Ken Mackay and Lindsay Kline, the vast crowds and a tickertape parade for the departing West Indies. Best of all, this wasn't just patriotic fervour, the game and the way it was being played had captured the public's imagination. The fact that Australia squeezed home in the final Test to win the series 2-1 was less important than the sum of the whole which had offered an antidote to the creeping negativity that had been strangling international cricket over the previous five years. In truth neither side was studded with thrilling cricketers but they produced thrilling cricket. The batting of Norm O'Neill, Kanhai, Neil Harvey and Worrell was delightful and the bowling of Alan Davidson was the difference between the two teams. But two men captured the imagination of the public, Sobers and Hall. Sobers was well on his way to becoming the best in the world although even at this stage nobody could guess how good he would become and how long he would stay that good. With Hall it was slightly more complex.

Twenty-one wickets over five Tests is respectable rather than rampant and the one victory for West Indies was achieved by spin rather than pace. It was the manner of the attack and not the figures that captured the hearts and eyes of all who saw it. In the tied Test his second-innings opening salvo removed four top-flight batsmen and seemed to have won the game. In the final overs Hall missed a run-out, removed Benaud, dropped a catch off his own bowling and then decked a catch in front of a waiting Kanhai – it was the cricketing equivalent of Jean van de Velde pottering around in the water at Carnoustie while his Open Championship slipped away. How could you not warm to a man completely overtaken by the tension but still bowling the final, crucial over.

And as for his bowling. The magnificence of the run-up, the magnificence of the man running up, the splaying of arms, the huge leap, the sheer physicality in the entire process shouted of enthusiasm and desire to propel the ball as fast as possible. It was Keith Miller or Jack Gregory not Ray Lindwall or Ted McDonald. There was no economy, no holding back. And it was thrilling for the spectators if not for the opposing batsmen. Neil Harvey rated Hall faster than Frank Tyson in the early part of the series while O'Neill recalled being bemused, not to say scared:

> 'For the first time in my cricket career I was up against a bowler so quick that he had me wondering how I was going to cope with him in the future.'

For those watching from a safe distance the effect was magical. Australian commentator Johnnie Moyes described Hall as 'a rare box-office attraction, a man who caught and held the affections of the paying public'. When CLR James wrote that 'Hall simply exudes good nature at every pore' it was gleaned from personal knowledge, but crowds could somehow sense the truth of the assertion from his body language alone and that is a rare gift.

Hall was now the world's best out-and-out fast bowler – in fact he was just about the world's only truly fast bowler. In South Africa Neil Adcock and Peter Heine were fading, Davidson was brilliant but not genuinely quick and Fred Trueman was still capable of fast spells but at the age of 30 he had begun to be more considered in how often he unleashed his full strength. Little wonder then that Hall was in some demand. Already approaches had been made from Lancashire, and Accrington enjoyed his services from 1960-62. The Australian states were equally quick to pounce on Kanhai, Sobers and Hall for the Sheffield Shield of 1961-62. Forty-three wickets for Queensland was a further feather in the cap before a return to international cricket at home to the pace-shy Indian team who were knocked over by 5-0 with Hall taking 27 wickets at 15 each. Knocked over and knocked about. Hall was in his pomp and Tony Cozier loved it.

'He had developed into one of the most feared bowlers in international cricket and I was safely settled in the press box, relishing the thrill of that galloping approach, that explosive delivery, that menacing follow-through, that flying crucifix around the neck that I had first experienced from 22 yards, or considerably less, five years earlier.'

The selectors didn't hesitate in giving Hall plenty of support when including Watson and Charlie Stayers for the opening Test, with the big Barbadian Griffith acting understudy. The suspect technique of many leading Indian batsmen against bouncers was summarised by Dick Rutnagar as an inability to sidestep and a simple reliance on ducking and turning the face away. This approach ended the Test career of Indian captain Nari Contractor and came close to ending his life. During the game against Barbados, Contractor ducked into a high-pace bouncer from Griffith that didn't get to the expected height and hit his temple straight on. With blood coming from nose and ear Contractor was rushed to hospital and survived a fractured skull by a hair's breadth with players from both sides offering blood samples to find him a match.

Various players contest that the delivery was even a bouncer and claim the ball was barely above stump height. But when Griffith was no-balled for throwing, for the first time in his career, later in the same game by umpire Jordan Cortez he became a marked man and rightly or wrongly the stigma stuck throughout his playing days and beyond. Contractor himself absolved Griffith from any blame, placing his predicament firmly at the door of 'batting misjudgement'. Given his mental state and the furore surrounding the incident, Griffith was not selected for any of the remaining Tests but by now the cricketing world was aware of trouble brewing.

Having just emerged from a period of dubious, not to say downright illegal, bowling that saw Geoff Griffin, Gordon Rorke and Ian Meckiff removed from the game and men such as Tony Lock and Harold Rhodes forced to remodel their actions, this was the last thing anybody wanted. The situation was, as ever, made more complex by the potential accusations of racial bias, inter-island bickering and even a potential political stand-off in England. However, when the selectors met the following spring to decide on the players to travel to England the name of Charlie Griffith was included. The selection came as a surprise to many, including the bowler himself, but despite his lack of experience he looked the most likely partner for Hall. The West Indies Board were well aware of the potential for controversy and had filmed Griffith at a club game in Barbados and tour manager Berkeley Gaskin took the evidence to England should it be needed. In their own minds the selectors were clearly convinced that Griffith's action was legal but they could hardly be certain of the English response.

The West Indian islands and West Indian cricket had undergone huge changes in the five years prior to the 1963 tour of England. Federation had imploded after just four tortuous years as in-fighting between the various islands and the slow pace of the promised independence from Great Britain undermined attempts to bind the islands together through promises of strength through unity. Once Jamaica withdrew support the project was doomed. Cricket was, however, a unifying force as long as the players worked together under one banner and this was something that both manager and captain were at pains to emphasise at all times.

The ascendency of Worrell to the captaincy, having completed his studies at Manchester University, was a step as symbolically significant as it was inevitable and overdue. Only his colour and studies had stood in his way prior to 1960 and after a long campaign, headed by CLR James, his appointment was duly ratified and the immediate result was his contribution to the greatest series ever played. By now 38 years old he was fully aware that this tour of England would be his swansong and it would be played out in front of considerable numbers of ethnic West Indians.

The *Windrush* generation had grown from 15,000 to 172,000 during the 1950s and despite the dire and often racist conditions of everyday life there was an increasing confidence that a permanent life could be made and that pride in the islands of origin could be celebrated. Race riots in Notting Hill in 1958, the brutal racially-motivated and unsolved murder of Kelso Cochrane in 1959 and Oswald Mosley standing for parliament on an anti-immigration ticket were, however, clear indications that this was a transition that would not be happening quickly. Nonetheless, where black faces had been largely absent from the terraces during the 1957 series, six years later the appearance, mood and ambiance, particularly in London, had changed dramatically. Culture in the form of food and music had emerged from hidden locations in backstreets, the Notting Hill carnival was first held in 1966, the first tentative steps were being taken in professional sport and there was a slow acceptance that non-white faces were now a part of the British landscape. But integration would never be easy or quickly accepted. When Enoch Powell spoke of 'rivers of blood' in 1968 his was still not a lone voice.

But the here and now of 1963 was the opportunity to celebrate the world's best cricket team, the world's best cricketer and the world's fastest bowler and those that had been drawn to Britain by its economic advantages were determined to enjoy the performances of their heroes. They were not to be disappointed. The hallowed halls of the Test grounds had never seen the like; the sounds, sights and smells drifting down from the terraces were frightening to some but for others a welcome relief from staid crowds of men in raincoats chewing soft sandwiches. It was somehow fitting that this was also the first year of the first limited-overs competition – the Gillette Cup.

An increasingly spinning wicket at Old Trafford proved ideal for Lance Gibbs and West Indies took a 1-0 lead to Lord's where England prematurely jettisoned Brian Statham. This time conditions were very different – uneven bounce and poor light made facing Trueman or Hall and Griffith the stuff of nightmares. But the game was one of the greatest ever played as Colin Cowdrey emerged with a broken arm in plaster, courtesy of a Hall 'lifter', to accompany David Allen in playing out a draw that had almost stopped a nation and sent the BBC into a tizzy as the early-evening news was interrupted by developments at Lord's. It wasn't just the final act; the entire drama had been studded with unforgettable performances. Ted Dexter's first-innings counter-attack, Trueman's ten-wicket haul, Brian Close's battered and bruised body, Basil Butcher's solo retrieval mission and the furious pace of Hall and Griffith. The work of this pair on the final day and the resistance of the English middle order was magnetic viewing and set up the series as much as the tied Test had done in Australia. John Woodcock in the *Times* was as enraptured as anyone:

> 'For three hours 20 minutes Hall bowled from the pavilion end without relief. His energy was astonishing, his stamina inexhaustible, his speed awesome, from the first ball to the last…His partner for all but five overs was Griffith, likewise a man of the fiercest strength.'

The final few hours had everything as Hall tore in from the end with no sightscreen to find Close walking down the wicket to meet him. Bouncers abounded and Griffith's action came under the closest scrutiny, especially on the England balcony. The official word was to say nothing but in later years nearly the entire English team went on record as saying that Griffith's fast ball, usually a bouncer or a yorker, must have been thrown simply because introducing a ball of this pace without a change in action or run-up was a physical impossibility.

How close was Lord's to becoming a turning-point in the game and even causing the greatest furore for 30 years? How accurate was Trueman's account of overhearing chairman of selectors Walter Robins telling the umpires not to 'call' Griffith for the sake of a harmonious tour? Nobody still alive knows but it sounds very feasible. What is certain is that Dexter approached both selector Cyril Washbrook and MCC president Gubby Allen and was told to leave any questions of the rules to the umpires. Fortunately for the spectators in 1963 this was happening behind closed doors and they could enjoy the spectacle.

England struck back at Edgbaston as Trueman took 12 wickets, cleverly adapting himself to a pitch lacking pace in a way that was seeminly beyond Hall who was clearly still recovering from his efforts at Lord's. At Leeds, Hall was again below par but with Griffith at his best West Indies strode to victory. On a wicket offering no great assistance Griffith took 6-36, including five front-line batsmen, to virtually win the game on the second day yet he received hardly a word of praise from either *Wisden* or the *Times*. John Woodcock was more taken with his size and strength (and the English shortcomings) while Leslie Smith couldn't manage even one complimentary adjective. When Griffith took another nine wickets in the final Test the press coverage concentrated almost entirely on his length, aggression and warnings for intimidation. At the end of the series Griffith had collected 32 wickets at 16.21, Hall had half as many at double the average. In all fairness Hall had been outbowled not only by Griffith but also by Gibbs and Sobers. He had been unlucky at times but for a man in his prime and injury free it was a poor series, bar the Lord's Test, and a poor tour hidden by the excellence of his team-mates. Overall, however, the summer had been a triumph as Ron Roberts recorded in the *Daily Telegraph*:

> 'This happy breed of cricketers has achieved a popularity that has become universal. England versus Australia is no longer the sole peak of Test cricket's achievement. West Indies share the summit.'

Gordon Ross's verdict was, as ever, more poetic: 'Enriching the common idiom of the game, they restored to it not only spontaneity, but style'. That summit had been attained not only through 'calypso flair'; Worrell had realised (as Clive Lloyd later would) that hard work and fitness were requirements to continued success. Despite being selected as one of *Wisden's* five cricketers it's hard to find any affection or real admiration for Griffith in the English press, the talk was all of Sobers, Hall, Kanhai and Worrell. It was as if the chucking thing may not be proven but his bouncers are bad enough anyway – not that those of Hall were much more palatable.

It would be nearly two more years before West Indies had another international fixture and it should have been another eight years before they visited England again but MCC hastily re-jigged the programme to accommodate another popular home series in 1966. Before that, however, the Australians were due to play five Tests in the Caribbean. The tourists were well aware of what they would be getting in terms of 'hospitality' having faced up to Hall five years earlier and having heard all about Griffith while touring England in 1964. The whispers that had surrounded Griffith's action in 1963 had no doubt been passed along the players' grapevine and the first sighting of the West Indian pair was not one to forget.

On a lightning fast wicket at Sabina Park Hall and Griffith set out their stall for the series by hurling everything into the attack. Hall was at top pace and was rewarded with 5-60 after bowling better than his partner had ever seen him. Australia had no answer and were soundly beaten. For the rest of the series Hall was again somewhat below par, taking only seven more wickets with Griffith managing just five in the next three games while the series was still alive. Gibbs was the crucial bowler in winning the third Test which was sandwiched between two draws on batting wickets. Finally West Indies had beaten Australia and could fairly be called world champions under their new captain, Sobers.

But the Australians had their reservations. Benaud, now a resident of the press box, published a photo of Griffith in action during the first Test accompanied by the words 'I believe implicitly that, in this present game, Griffith has thrown a great number of deliveries.' This wasn't whispering, and within hours Dexter was penning his lines for *The Observer* to indicate that Griffith's action in 1963 had been 'doubtful', thus rendering the series 'meaningless'. Keith Miller, also a member of the press, had always been a staunch supporter of Griffith and his 'magnificent action' and he stuck with this line, pointing out that Benaud had seemingly changed his opinion since supporting Griffith in the *News of the World* back in 1963. Bill Lawry recalled that in the Australian dressing room 'the unanimous verdict was that Griffith was a chucker.' This was then compounded as Griffith struck no less than five batsmen with 'physically serious direct hits' during the second Test and was warned for intimidatory bowling in the fourth. With the cat now out of the bag O'Neill, Wally Grout, Tom Graveney and Ken Barrington amongst others joined the forces of the disbelievers while the West Indian players and officials firmly rebutted all accusations. If the controversy had previously undermined Griffith's achievements it was now slopped across the top of them. Certainly this couldn't fail to affect his partner. Hall was a thorough believer in the value of their joint endeavours:

> 'One thing I have learned in Test cricket is the value of a regular partner and the need for real pace at both ends early in an innings...The biggest disadvantage in not having a regular aide is that batsmen immediately pinpoint you as the danger man and refuse to play any strokes against you. They are content to make scoring shots, and consequently mistakes, off the other fellow. This is why, through the years, all great fast bowlers have gone in pairs.'

The world's leading coach, Alf Gover, wrote a long, explanatory article for *The Cricketer* explaining how the quest for extra speed in delivering bouncers and yorkers was compromising an otherwise legal action.

> 'In pressing for extra speed, his right foot points up the wicket. He lands on the outside of his left heel, and the whole of his left foot points towards second slip. The placing of the feet forces the hips to open so that Griffith's body faces the batsman square on. The shoulders have to do the same and just before the moment of release, he is chest-on – not towards the batsman, but even as far across as first slip. The whole of his body balance simply collapses to the left – it can do nothing else – so that there is no possibility of the normal bowler's follow-through with the body weight properly distributed. This is the point where he throws. His arm goes away from his body in a bent position with his right elbow pointing in the direction of mid-on and his hand holding the ball close to his face. From that position, he cannot bowl the ball. He must throw.'

Gover still saw fit to take Griffith on a Commonwealth tour of Pakistan which, considering his reservations, was an odd decision. The chest-on delivery, and the foot positioning it requires, has been much derided but the idea that it necessitates a bent arm is a debatable conclusion. Two umpires, Cec Pepper and Dai Davies, came down on different sides of the argument after seeing film of the contentious action.

Whichever way you turn it comes back to the issue of throwing. The career of Griffith, and by definition his partnership with Hall, is hidden under the shadows of the 'did he, didn't he?' argument. Had the 1963 England series and, to a lesser degree, the 1965 Australia series been won by illegal methods?

Not surprisingly most West Indians of the era come down firmly on the side of Griffith but sometimes the defences seem confused. Jeff Stollmeyer simply admitted that the odd ball was thrown but relies on the rarity and the lack of umpire action to exonerate Griffith. Kanhai wrote that a chucker 'skids the ball through off the pitch because of his angled action' but then claimed Griffith's 'outrageous' bouncers proved he did not belong to this company. Yet it is precisely this skidding that Grout and Farokh Engineer, amongst others, identified as proof that Griffith *did* chuck. Not that a skidding bouncer is proof-positive of a bent arm as bowlers such as Ray Lindwall and Malcolm Marshall have shown. Perhaps more pertinent is the sudden and dramatic increase in pace without any perceptible change in action that so perturbed Graveney, Barrington and many others. But then if the change in action was not detectable then how could any umpire call Griffith? In 1991, when interviewed by Stephen Thorpe, the bowler's unconvincing explanation was that his arm was bent 'during the delivery swing but straightened before release.' This beggars the question, precisely when before release?

In 1966 England won the football World Cup and Sobers dominated everything cricket. In all departments he was a masterful presence and excelled in every game as England were put to the sword. But unlike 1963 his pace attack was not the broadsword that bludgeoned England. Hall was clearly down on pace and his 18 wickets didn't come cheaply even if the wicket of Colin Milburn at Lord's took him past Ramadhin as the most prolific bowler for his country.

Once he had failed in the opening Test his psychological grip had gone – the English batsmen recognised a fast bowler trying to recapture his glory speed. Griffith was also struggling with a shoulder injury and then two bouts of influenza and his effectiveness was barely half of what it had been in 1963. The controversy was double. Called for throwing by Arthur Fagg (for the second and final time in his career) against Lancashire, hitting tailender Derek Underwood in the face with a bouncer (or was it?) in the third Test and then becoming involved in an on-field spat when Graveney inexplicably asked Charlie Elliott to call him in the fourth Test meant that Griffith was barely out of the news. Within the space of a few months the affable, cheerful Charlie had been reduced to a morose and brooding presence, afraid of where the next headline might be coming from. The fact that his 14 wickets could hardly be considered decisive to the outcome of the series probably saved the matter from escalating.

West Indies were still the best side in the world but their supremacy no longer hinged on their pace attack. They had a stellar batting line-up, the best off-spinner in Gibbs and they had Sobers. On quick wickets Hall and Griffith could still be a handful but when there was little pace they were blunted and Sobers was quick to take them off and use his own, more subtle, skills or the guile and perseverance of Gibbs.

This impression was hardly altered during a three-Test series against India in which pace was more a weapon to be used for knocking over the tail than eating into the middle order. Hall managed just eight wickets and Griffith nine, only one of which was a top-five batsman. Indian opener Engineer took his side to 125-0 at lunch on day one of the Madras Test with an unbeaten 96, something that would have been unthinkable three years earlier. One last chance for redemption lay with an English tour of the Caribbean in 1968.

The two teams were largely as they had been when they had last met – Sobers was still the fulcrum around which everything revolved and Lloyd was the only significant new blood. England had tinkered but seemed unaware that they had a secret weapon. John Snow was omitted from the first Test and then took 27 in the remaining four. The records show that England won 1-0 on the back of a disastrously misconceived declaration by Sobers in the fourth game but three of the other Tests went right down to the wire with West Indies just surviving at Port of Spain and England holding out grimly at Kingston and Georgetown. If Snow had shown the value of a genuine pace bowler then his performance could only show that Hall and Griffith were at the end of the line. Although both were still in their twenties the fire seemed to have largely disappeared and couldn't be reignited even by the heat of the fiercest battle.

Hall had been playing almost non-stop for a decade and even more importantly he had never been one to save himself, which was one of the great joys of the man. Gerry Cotter has encapsulated his appeal at the time and it is an appeal that has lasted half a century.

'There have been few cricketers who have given such pleasure as Hall. There is probably nothing spectators like more than a player who clearly *enjoys* his cricket and is ready to play his heart out, and few who saw Hall pounding in will ever forget him.'

He was a victim of his own enthusiasm and also the frequent short-sightedness of Worrell and Sobers who were too willing to use him both as shock and stock. As early as 1961 O'Neill had detected how Hall's pace dropped during the tied-Test series and his fitness and workload were never managed as they would be now. Perhaps an injury or two might have extended his span but even those he did have were ignored and he bowled on. By 1968 it had all caught up with him and even in 1966 the England players recognised he was not the fearsome proposition he had been in 1963 and before. On the cracked wicket at Kingston where Snow took 7-49, Hall removed only two top-flight batsmen. Griffith was even less impressive, 31 overs brought only the wicket of Snow.

The situation with Griffith was perhaps more mental than physical. His career had largely degenerated into a chucking sideshow from 1964 onwards and it had eaten into his enthusiasm and confidence. Whispers in 1963 had become open talk and then shouts and he naturally felt that his past achievements had been dismissed and any further performances would be tainted. His mood had darkened and words such as 'morose' were used to describe his mood. Little wonder, then, that he was a shadow of his former self. After 21 successive Tests the partnership was finally broken when Hall was dropped for the fourth match only to return for the fifth as a replacement for Griffith who had pulled a muscle.

In retrospect the denouement was inevitable when the pair were selected to lead the attack in Australia in 1968-69. In point of fact 'lead the attack' had become something of a misnomer – Hall and Griffith had been supported by Sobers and Gibbs throughout their careers as joint new-ball bowlers but over the previous three years the supporters had become the leaders as the pace and intensity began to decline. Since taking over the captaincy from Worrell after the 1963 England series, Sobers had not spared himself and was also not shy of taking the new ball when he saw fit. As each series passed so the percentage of wickets taken by the fast pair fell – less than 24 per cent of the total between 1966 and 1968 while Sobers and Gibbs took 54 per cent. With no sign of a revival it was fairly clear that if the Australian wickets didn't galvanise the pair then West Indian resources would be spread very thin with only 'Prof' Edwards as support.

Despite nagging injuries Sobers dragged West Indies into the series before the youthful vigour and talent of Ian Chappell and Doug Walters combined with the experience and skill of Graham McKenzie and Lawry to totally outpoint an ageing side. Hall and Griffith were not fully fit, the latter breaking down in the first game and missing the next two while Hall played only the third and fifth. Griffith's most noteworthy contribution was to 'Mankad' Ian Redpath in the fourth Test, something hardly designed to endear him to home supporters even if he did find a supporter in Bill O'Reilly. Their final appearance together in a Test came at Sydney in the final match. Gamely they sent down 73 eight-ball overs but were taken apart by Walters and Lawry who, throughout the series, continued to benefit from some truly dreadful catching. One of the most watchable and one of the most vilified fast bowlers in cricket history were done. Michael Manley likened the last act to watching a once great heavyweight reeling on the ropes having taken on one bout too many.

The names of Hall and Griffith seem to be conjoined for posterity but the facts don't quite fit the story. Their legacy exists almost entirely on their performances in England in 1963 and even by that stage Hall was not the bowler he had been. His record before that series was that of a truly outstanding fast bowler – 116 wickets at just 21.87 apiece. Thereafter, when sharing the new ball with Griffith, he stumbled to just 76 wickets at 33.27 in 25 Tests. It wasn't a great partnership. That requires both men to be at or near their peak for at least a series or two. It was a partnership of a once great bowler brought prematurely low by his own enthusiasm and a briefly great bowler whose legacy will always be shadowed by the words and opinions of others.

Both men relied primarily on speed and as that became harder to find they had less to fall back on than, say, Dennis Lillee. Hall's outswinger and Griffith's inspearing yorker and bouncer were fearsome weapons but without being delivered at top pace they became only moderately effective, especially on unhelpful wickets. But at their best they were amongst the greats and the legend of Hall will always be linked to his role in the dying minutes of two of the greatest Tests ever played. The legend of Griffith, if one can call it that, is far more complex.

Hall and Griffith

Results

	Total	Won	Drawn	Lost
Hall	48	21 (Tie 1)	16	10
Griffith	28	11	11	6
Hall and Griffith	23	10	9	4

Test Bowling Overall

	Mat	Balls	Runs	Wkts	Ave	SR	ER	5W1/10WM
Hall	48	10421	5066	192	26.38	54.2	2.91	9/1
Griffith	28	5631	2683	94	28.54	59.9	2.85	5/0

Test Bowling Together

	Mat	Balls	Runs	Wkts	Ave	SR	ER	5W1/10WM
Hall	23	4526	2368	72	32.88	62.8	3.13	1/0
Griffith	23	4713	2271	85	26.71	55.4	2.89	5/0

Test Bowling Apart

	Mat	Balls	Runs	Wkts	Ave	SR	ER	5W1/10WM
Hall	25	5895	2698	120	22.48	40.7	2.75	8/1
Griffith	5	918	412	9	45.77	102.0	2.69	0/0

Best Series Together - England 1963

	Mat	Balls	Runs	Wkts	Ave	SR	ER	5W1/10WM
Hall	5	1068	534	16	33.37	66.7	3.00	0/0
Griffith	5	1343	519	32	16.21	41.9	2.31	3/0

Best Test Figures - Innings/Match

Hall (with Griffith)	5-60 vs Australia, Kingston – 1965
Hall (with Griffith)	9-105 vs Australia, Kingston – 1965
Hall (without Griffith)	7-69 vs England, Kingston – 1960
Hall (without Griffith)	11-126 vs India, Kanpur – 1958
Griffith (with Hall)	6-36 vs England, Leeds – 1963
Griffith (with Hall)	9-81 vs England, Leeds – 1963
Griffith (without Hall)	3-92 vs New Zealand, Wellington – 1969
Griffith (without Hall)	4-121 vs New Zealand, Wellington – 1969

YouTube Bowling Highlights

Search Phrases (sic)
England vs West Indies - 1963 Lord's Test
Charlie Griffith big Barbadian bowling in England 1963
West Indies vs Australia 1st Test 1960 Tied Test Match

Snow To Babylon

By 1971 England were in the extraordinary position of possessing by far and away the best fast bowler playing Test cricket, though without apartheid Mike Procter would have been a worthy rival. John Snow had proved himself against West Indies and would cement his position in Australia. But for injury Bob Willis or Alan Ward might have been worthwhile partners, in their absence Snow was supported by the gentler skills of Mike Hendrick, David Brown and Geoff Arnold. Willis did come back and led England's attack into the eighties with the more than able support of Ian Botham, he of the golden arm.

India were blessed with spin bowlers as no other country has been before or since and it wasn't until the appearance of Kapil Dev that they could finally attempt to match other countries for pace. His success brought with it the belief that Indians *could* bowl fast and transformed the nature of their approach to Test cricket even if Kapil still remains the best to this day. Pakistan had found an even better practitioner in 1974 had they but known that the 18-year-old Oxford student **Imran** Khan would develop so dramatically during the following decade and form such a potent partnership with **Sarfraz** Nawaz. New Zealand also discovered her best opening bowler and over the next 15 years Richard Hadlee performed wonders while his team-mates blocked up an end and left the wicket taking to 'Paddles'.

South Africa lost the best of Procter and all of Vincent van de Bijl and Garth le Roux, both of whom showed in county cricket and rare meetings with Test batsmen what might have been. Australia, having been humbled by speed in South Africa and then at home to England, had the good fortune to uncover something even better in the form of Dennis **Lillee**. The pre-injury tearaway became the classic practitioner whereupon he was joined by another, even faster, bowler and with Jeff **Thomson** he put both England and West Indies to the sword.

West Indian cricket had gone into a decline and was only kept respectable by the ageing stars of a golden age; Garry Sobers, Rohan Kanhai and Lance Gibbs. With the exception of Clive Lloyd the new men were no match for their predecessors. Then out of the blue Caribbean sky came a new generation of aggressive batsmen, led by Viv Richards, and fast bowlers, led by Andy **Roberts**. Michael **Holding** soon emerged to support Roberts and the two decades of 'pace like fire' was born. Men like Sylvester Clarke and Wayne Daniel could barely get a game and were reduced to scaring English county batsmen witless.

In the space of just seven years pace bowling had been rejuvenated and had brought life back into Test cricket. Not just pace bowling but those who could face up to it and attack it. In their different ways Tony Greig, the Chappell brothers, Richards, Sunil Gavaskar, Gordon Greenidge and Majid Khan, amongst others, were the necessary adjunct to waves of quick stuff that came crashing down. Crowds returned to enjoy the spectacle and Kerry Packer swooped to bring them all together in coloured clothing under floodlights.

Lillee

and

Thomson

Dennis Lillee

This tall and graceful character moved meditatively back from the region of the bowler's umpire...until at about the forty-sixth pace it occurred to him that if he was ever going to get the ball actually delivered he might as well turn back; which he then frighteningly did, tearing flat out as if the hounds of hell were after him, with the wind whistling through his hair and moustache, until he rose in the last half-dozen yards of his sprint into a glorious rhythmic liberation of shoulder and elbow and free-flowing swing of release. – Ronald Mason

Jeff Thomson

Jeff Thomson...starts his run-up at a trot...casual at first, with only the light flop of his brown mane to catch the eye. There is a barely perceptible but crucial acceleration, at which point the enormous shoulders become more noticeable. Then comes the cocking of the catapult, the flinging back of the right arm, with the sliding of the right foot behind rather than in front of the left...He hurls himself almost off his feet, but the braced left leg absorbs the impact, giving way to the right as it wheels through, the body already well on its way to recovery, to balance. – David Frith

Dennis Lillee and Jeff Thomson were very fit young men when they arrived at the gates of Test cricket. This physical well-being had been arrived at in very contrasting manners and those contrasts were symptomatic of the pair. Their names will always be linked through pace, dual deeds and a somewhat anti-authoritarian stance both at and away from the crease but one was, or became, one of the subtlest protagonists of his art while the other remained at heart a bull in a china shop, albeit one with surprising grace.

Lillee drew heavily on the influence of his grandfather Len and all through his teenage years was a fitness fanatic with the discipline to match and this was a discipline he retained throughout his career.

> 'I was great at practising. I couldn't wait to get out there and I would practise as long as possible. If the session was five hours I'd be out there and involved for five hours…some thought I was a bit mad because at the end of practice I would run hard until it was dark and then do a series of other exercises.'

This work ethic and the consequent effect on his physical development would stand Lillee in good stead later in life when he was faced with long spells and injuries that would have finished lesser men. And his work ethic was all encompassing; clean living and no drinking in a spartan quest for cricketing greatness, at least until he met Doug Walters and Rod Marsh. Imagine then Lillee's surprise when, as a veteran of 11 Tests, he found Thomson in the bar the night before the first Test against England in 1974 drinking scotch with the specific intention of giving himself 'a hangover from hell'. "I bowl real well when I have a headache" Thomson explained, "It makes me just want to get in there and get them". Lillee preferred a solid meal and sleep.

Thomson's approach was clearly less organised. The fourth of five brothers he learnt to fight for his rights at a young age. These rights included intimidatory bowling in the confined area of the back yard; what was required was a bouncer off a two-step run – the Thomson method was born. Naturally strong and drawn to all sorts of sports and outdoor activities, he soon found he could bowl fast although he never took well to coaching. After a teenage, girl-sponsored hiatus he gave cricket his best shot and amidst a welter of wickets and frightened batsmen his name became familiar to State officials. Like Lillee, he took his approach into the first-class game, never wanting to over-complicate what was an essentially simple operation: 'Aww mate, I just shuffle up and go wang'. This was a man who had to ask his captain which side to hold the shiny side for the outswinger – he was playing for New South Wales and his captain was Greg Chappell! Chappell could recognise the complementary contrast of his future speed pair. One was a self-made cricketer the other was just born to do it.

What the two men did share was an ambitious temperament, huge natural ability and a great sense of theatre. They loved the thrill of bowling fast and seeing fear in the batsman's eyes and they loved the roar of appreciation as the batsman ducked or snicked or had his wicket flattened. Right from their start in first-class cricket they bowled as fast as they could with no thought of subtlety until injuries and coming to terms with unresponsive wickets required a different approach. And while remaining great friends they drove each other on. Lillee in particular was never going to be second best and watching his team-mate terrorise England in 1974-75 was the great incentive to get back to top speed after injury. But if they acted as incentives for one another they were, like all great fast-bowling combinations, truly complementary. Each had something that the other didn't and both had plenty. One, or both, always seemed to find something to work on and both could extract pace from the dullest surface given the right mood.

Growing up, both teenagers had been impressed by two bowlers in particular – Fred Trueman and Wes Hall. Hardly surprising really given the all-out effort and speed these two could generate. But in many ways the greatest and most immediate influence on the careers of Lillee and Thomson was the English bowler John Snow. In the early seventies he was, for two series at least, not just the best fast bowler in Test cricket but the only fast bowler in Test cricket. Between November 1970 and February 1971 in Australia he had a stage that energised him, wickets that encouraged him, a captain that understood and cherished him and the skill to use pace, bounce and control to decimate a team he really wanted to wallop. Australia was impressed and two weeks later Lillee was ushered into their side.

Once Snow had reminded spectators and selectors that aggressive fast bowling was not only a match-winner but also a draw card, administrators the world over were scuttling off to unearth something similar. Not only was quick bowling essential to a great team, it was box office. The physical challenge was something spectators could understand from 100 metres without the aid of a big screen, rev counters or slow-motion replays. It was theatre; Dennis Amiss recalled feeling like a gladiator (or sacrificial lamb) as Lillee buzzed one past his nose at the MCG to bring a howl of approval from 80,000 spectators.

It was this buzz and excitement that Lillee and Thomson harnessed so perfectly. There was something innately anti-authoritarian about their make up and approach that caught the mood of Australian youth. Music, culture and society in general had drifted from the swinging sixties to something more sinister – Altamont, Vietnam and anti-apartheid riots. The times were indeed changing and Lillee and Thomson, with their hair and lifestyle (imagined in the case of Lillee, real in the case of Thomson), were a perfect fit to bring a new generation to the cricket especially as they arrived together to meet a bunch of hapless Poms at the Gabba in November 1974.

In cricketing terms their paths to Adelaide could hardly have been more different. Lillee had already shown English batsmen and a select few of the world's greatest what he could do, tearing in at full pelt off a 35-yard run up. His two appearances at the back-end of the 1970-71 Ashes series were a warning but his true arrival took place the following year at Perth against a World XI gathered to replace a South African side barred from international competition. Lillee's 8-29 (Sobers, Gavaskar, Lloyd and Greig amongst the victims) announced to the world that this was a fast bowling sensation. And then for those who thought this was down to the fire in the wicket he came to England six months later and took 31 wickets in five Tests on wickets that offered little to out-and-out pace.

Then came injury, slowly and undiagnosed at first. After returning home early from a West Indies tour he was encased in body plaster to counteract three stress fractures in his back. This wonderful flowing action did, as Barry Richards had seen, have a flaw. There was a twist in the delivery action which put unsustainable pressure on the back. And that could easily have been that. But Lillee's innate and hard-won fitness, his determination and ambition, the clever and careful ministrations of various specialists and his capacity for hard work saw him back in the nets within a year. Lillee never forgot that he had to go, cap in hand, to the ACB to get his medical bills paid.

The return would never be simple, a new action would be necessary that placed less stress on the back and consistent madcap pace would become a thing of the past. Here Lillee added intelligence to his armoury and re-built his action and eased his way back into Sheffield Shield cricket at the start of the 1974-75 season.

Thomson's experience of Test cricket at this point was slightly more limited. One game, with an injured foot which he'd not disclosed thinking it might be his one chance of a baggy green, and figures of 0-110 (Lillee managed 3-149) from 19 wild overs. *Wisden* had termed him 'a comic character rather than a Test bowler' but, despite remaining wild, he was knocking over batsmen aplenty in Shield cricket and Ian Chappell did not need much reminding of the value of fast bowling in a home Ashes series. And so it came to pass in November 1974 that a crock just out of plaster, an overrated larrikin (he'd even been mixed up with Alan 'Froggy' Thomson by some English journalists) and a moustachioed Max Walker with an action like an octopus would have to walk the walk after issuing all manner of blood-curdling threats over the previous weeks.

England had arrived without Geoff Boycott, furious at being passed over as captain, and John Snow, still in the Lord's doghouse after a clash with Sunil Gavaskar but were still confident that their fast-bowling 'battery' would be quite sufficient. This confidence lasted about two days. On a horribly underprepared Brisbane wicket the English batsmen got their first sighting of that pantomime dame Lilian Thomson, and she was right in front of them. After Australia had cobbled together 309 and received a few bouncers (mainly from Greig to Lillee), Ian Chappell threw the new ball to Lillee to bowl downwind and, after a change of mind, Thomson to bowl into it. Lillee had already told the Englishmen to remember 'who started it', as if any excuse were needed. Within 42 minutes Thomson had blown enough wind of his own to remove both openers and the pattern for the series was set. Lillee easing himself back into the fray and Thomson wild, wayward and very dangerous. Greig would have none of it, meeting fire with fire and signalling his own boundaries with a swish of the hand and fighting to a glorious century having riled the pace bowlers into predictable short bowling. David Frith, writing in *The Cricketer* was not slow to spot and appreciate the showmanship:

> 'The Greig-Lillee clashes have been a kind of cricket parallel to the Ali-Foreman mini-pantomimes without the sense of spoof...Greig signalling his own boundaries was genuinely funny until one examined the cost.'

England ended the first innings only 44 runs in arrears and on day five needed 322 for victory with all wickets standing – Ian Chappell had given them a sniff with his declaration.

The sniff was soon snuffed as Thomson tore through the top order, culminating in a glorious yorker to clip Greig's leg stump. Ably supported by Lillee, who was not really the stuff of supporting casts, England were blown away for 166. The crowds had poured through the turnstiles to see this carnival of speed as Thomson in particular made the ball fly off a length. For the youth of Australia this was our boys doing it our way – there were plenty of the older generation who were dubious of the rough language and long hair but they could hardly find fault with the results.

The post-mortems were soon swinging off the presses – as EW Swanton correctly observed, 'Passions are always excited when real speed becomes a factor' and there was no doubt that Thomson and Lillee, in patches, represented real speed. Both men had come into the Test talking of blood on the wicket, hating batsmen and bowling to hurt. Thomson would amiably expand to any journalist while Lillee's publishers had rushed to stock bookshops with *Back to the Mark*. The response was predictable – 'This is the talk of the underworld, not Test cricketers' was the verdict of the *Times* man John Woodcock while in Australia Jack Fingleton, Bill O'Reilly and Ray Robinson all deplored the overuse of bouncers. The players' retort was simply that England had started it (in 1932 maybe, or 1970) and that the state of the wicket had meant some balls rearing from barely short of a length had appeared like bouncers. In some ways they were justified by the serious injuries being to the hands not heads of top-flight batsmen Amiss and Edrich.

But the controversy could not and did not hide the fact that a phenomenal cricketer had emerged. 'Thomson burst upon the scene with a suddenness that can seldom have been equalled in Test cricket' wrote Woodcock while the significance of this new pair was lost on no-one. Alex Bannister recognised that 'The Thomson-Lillee combination is for speed and danger the closest I've seen to Lindwall and Miller or Hall and Griffith' before blotting his copybook by predicting they would be less intimidating once they left the Brisbane 'mud heap'. Lillee's take on the recipe for success was simple:

> 'He just wanted to get out there in the middle and bowl as fast as he could. Thommo's mates jibed that he was not as quick as me…so initially he wanted to prove them wrong. I have no doubt he was quicker than me, quicker even than when I was bowling my fastest which was about 97 miles per hour.'

Parallel to this Brisbane game, in Bangalore Andy Roberts was managing quite well without a genuine speed partner as West Indies routed India. Gordon Greenidge scored 200 runs in his debut match, Viv Richards just seven. India had only nine fit batsmen for their second innings.

The upshot of this literally bruising encounter for England was a spate of injuries and the summoning of Colin Cowdrey to plug the gap. At 42 and a veteran of encounters with Lindwall and Miller, he bravely took the long flight to Perth and after minimal preparation went out to bat on the fastest pitch in the world. The collective memory of this game diverges markedly from the reality: Australia did win easily, English batsmen were regularly hit and Thomson and Lillee were a frightening sight. But the England top four all scored at least 20 runs in their eight attempts, none, however, managed a half-century. Lillee wasn't responsible for any of these eight dismissals, Thomson took five and Walker three. Quite simply Lillee and Thomson were still not a tyro pairing that knocked over the top four and later dipped in for a couple of sprats. Lillee was still working back to full fitness although the signs were ominous for bats-men all over the world; he could bowl consistently at a decent pace and with good control and also had it in him to slip a real fast one. Thomson was still wayward, especially with the new ball, but he could produce something almost unplayable regularly enough to keep everyone alert from batsmen to slip fielders to pressmen and spectators.

While English supporters were hiding behind sofas during the evening highlights, Australians were packing cool boxes with tinnies and making their way down to the WACA for the best show in town. The whole Australian team was energised by these new weapons. The batsmen could attack (Doug Walters hit a century in a session) and the other bowlers revelled in working on an opposition that was teetering on the brink of capitulation. Worst of all from the opposition point of view was the ability of the pair to produce shock and awe over long periods of play; at Perth they sent down 78 eight-ball overs between them, just about half the team total, and with Walker delivering 44 of the remainder there were no easy runs on offer.

For captain Ian Chappell this was nothing short of a dream, he could use his strike bowlers as he chose knowing that the game would not slip away as they rested. What he also had was close catchers of the highest order. With lifting deliveries at over 90 mph catching outside edges, the abilities of Rod Marsh behind the stumps and the Chappell brothers, Ian Redpath, Ashley Mallett, Walker and Walters in the slips and gullies were crucial for tying up loose ends and keeping the bowlers interested. Richie Benaud's TV round up concluded with the damning words "I haven't seen a more pathetic display from an England side for many years and some of those batsmen won't sleep too well tonight." Stork Hendry, who had played with Gregory and McDonald back in 1921, was less than impressed with what was so enthralling young Australians:

'Both Lillee and Thomson are bowling to intimidate batsmen with the sole objective of forcing them into errors to avoid physical injury. The methods are worse than those used in the so-called Bodyline series.'

At Perth the gully fielders were arraigned fully 25 metres from the bat – Mallett, standing at gully, had a ringside seat and loved what he saw

'They brought the crowds back in their droves. The theory that the only thing that will attract the crowds is the prospect of batsmen thrashing an attack was hit for a giant six. The two fast bowlers really captured the imagination. It's a rare sight to watch two superb express men on the same team rip into an opposition batting line-up.'

Those droves, over 250,000 during the five days, were accommodated happily at the MCG for the third Test and Lillee and Thomson delivered. Although England narrowly avoided defeat, they might also have won as the brought-back casualties from the first Test replaced those fallen at Perth. Lillee, still working his way back in, took four wickets for the third match in a row while Thomson, this time on a less helpful surface, added eight to the 16 he had from the first two matches. But the closeness of the draw meant that England, although still two down, felt that they could compete once again. A new record crowd for Sydney witnessed another Australian victory, further English injuries, the return of the Ashes and another episode in the legend of Lillee and Thomson. Lillee was finally satisfied with his form and progress:

'I was certainly thinking about my bowling more than I had ever done before. I guess that was because I could no longer simply blast batsmen out; I had to have a better worked out plan than that. It was probably something to do with me maturing as a person , the catalyst being dealing with a career-threatening injury…Maybe I bowled less quickly than before but I was a lot more accurate.'

Lillee was, of course, allowed this luxury of choice through the presence of Thomson at the other end. Without him the pressure would have been on to produce the fast stuff and leave the accuracy to Walker. A close look at the Sydney match actually shows it was an all-round team effort – Mallett and Walker both took wickets and the batsmen made runs in the necessary quantity. But the headlines were always about the two quicks, as they would be in the fifth

Test at Adelaide. And this time there was no question that they were deserved.

This was the game that England should have won. Winning the toss and inserting Australia on a rain-damaged pitch with two spinners in the side and then batting when conditions were perfect, what more could Mike Denness have wished for? Yet, even with Thomson unable to bowl in the second innings Australia won by 163 runs. *Wisden's* description of 'discouraging' was courteous in the extreme – England were now a broken team.

Thomson and Lillee had not only taken their side to a 3-0 lead but they had invigorated their own team-mates and dismembered the opposition. This time, on an easy wicket and facing an Australian first-innings of 309, Lillee took out the openers, Thomson ripped out the middle order and Mallett tied up the tail. On the rest day Jeff Thomson played tennis and ripped his shoulder. Having sent down 175 eight-ball overs in a style that would have mere mortals screaming under a surgeon's knife he managed to tear tendons serving a tennis ball and was unfit when Chappell set England 405 to win. How did Lillee react? He removed four of the top order leaving England 76-5 and then returned to recovery mode – this was just one series and he had a career to consider. England won the final Test – Thomson was still injured and Lillee left the game with a foot injury after bowling six overs. They had taken 57 wickets in the five games they had played together.

Left to reflect on a torrid four months, the England players could hardly fail to recognise a great fast-bowling pair. Denness saw that their partnership had lifted the whole Australian team to a new level of achievement, 'they all became more macho'. Keith Fletcher saw the necessary 'devil' in the pair but only an average county bowler in Walker who took six more wickets at a better average than the best of the England side. Underwood was the most illuminating:

> 'They were just too good for us. Too good because they were too fast and were still able to swing and move the ball around the wicket.'

He was also quick to emphasise the ability of Thomson to make a short-pitch ball rise like a bouncer which cut the available reaction time; unsurprisingly he also foresaw protective headgear as being inevitable. *Wisden* was less charitable: 'Never before in the 98 years of Test cricket have batsmen been so grievously bruised and battered by ferocious, hostile, short-pitched bowling.' If they had only known what the next 20 years would bring.

It wasn't just pace – it rarely is. It was the pace at which the bounce and swing had to be countered. Lillee was working largely around 85 mph although there was always the possibility of something much quicker. Thomson in the early 90s and often quicker was the more frightening prospect with the sighting of a ball being produced from behind his right buttock a challenge in itself. Even the best players could fall foul of this new menace as Barry Richards could attest after having his protective box re-arranged (*a la* David Lloyd) by Thomson on a placid Southampton pitch.

England had received a lashing but of far more permanent significance was the response of the Australian public and in particular the young spectators. Ray Robinson observed that 'it takes the extra speed of a Lillee or a Thomson to make people sit up and take notice'. The menacing predictions of this speed duo and their ability to back it up on the field suddenly made cricket cool for a generation veering away from flower power into a world of rock. Henry Blofeld called Lillee 'a prima donna who exaggerated every action and emotion on the field of play'; he might just as well have been writing about Pete Townshend or Mick Jagger playing to a stadium audience. A day in the sun with the 24-tinny allowance and the prospect of fast and furious entertainment set the turnstiles clicking.

Vast sold-out stadiums became the norm and the money came rolling in which set one man in particular, Ian Chappell, to thinking. Where was all this money going? Australian players were still technically amateurs and players were being lost to the game trying to balance work and cricket with a paltry 20 bucks provided by the Australian Board for a day's 'expenses'. Yet here were vast crowds shelling out their dollars. Something didn't add up – Ian Chappell went to Australian supremo Don Bradman to find out what could be done – "nothing" said the Don, nothing at all. Richie Benaud recalls Australian cricket being awash with money and Chappell (and an increasing number of other players) being part of "a questioning era". Sides were being formed that were on a collision course. It was as if the Australian team, and in particular their fast bowlers, had filled a box with gold and then the ACB, steered by Bradman, had snapped it shut in front of their very eyes.

Next stop was a one-day World Cup in England followed by four Tests. In that previous Australian summer, however, so much had changed in world cricket. Clive Lloyd had seen what pace could do, English batsmen felt what pace could do and Kerry Packer, Ian Chappell and Tony Greig saw what pace could generate at the turnstiles.

Lillee and Thomson made relatively little impact in the World Cup of 1975 but thanks to their all-round strength they made it to the final only to be knocked over by a stupendous Clive Lloyd century. He had history, having been playing this form of cricket for Lancashire for years against fast bowlers such as Roberts and Mike Procter. Greg Chappell was left to reflect on crowds and one-day cricket, calling it subsequently "the first day of the rest of our lives and the new era of cricket". It wasn't just at Lord's, all over Australia the midnight oil had been burnt to the bitter end as live pictures were beamed across the world. Packer was taking notice. In London it may have seemed slightly less momentous but the atmosphere (free of corporate dominance and rammed with cricket fans) was a wonder to behold and a wonder that even the older generation of Jim Laker and Benaud lapped up with real enthusiasm. Certainly most cricket lovers over 55 can remember where they were and that's a sure sign that something's going on.

After this thrilling support act it was now time to see if Lillee and Thomson could reproduce their form on English wickets in four Ashes Tests. The possibility was almost scuppered when the ACB decided to send Thomson home on the grounds of self-inflicted poor form and an incendiary newspaper article. The threat was reversed when Ian Chappell made it clear that the whole team would be keeping him company. The pair were soon up and running in a curious symmetry that saw them following Lindwall and Miller after 27 years, that pair having come 27 years after Gregory and McDonald had thrilled English crowds.

What the latest Australian pair actually got was four travesties – dead surfaces designed to kill their pace and ensure a sense of dull mundanity that might enable England to snatch back the Ashes. Fortunately the plan failed as, even on wickets designed to neuter all tom-cat antics, Lillee and Thomson again proved they were no one-trick ponies and even England managed to pull some rabbits out of the hat. Between them they took 37 wickets at 25.3 using seam, swing and all the other skills, beside pace, that a fast bowler could muster. In response England produced David Steele and the unlikely battle of the larrikin versus the bank clerk dominated the summer sport and again drew crowds where empty seats had been.

After being caught on a wet wicket in the first Test England slumped to a huge defeat and a new age was declared – Greig assumed the captaincy. But dead wickets, described as unfit for first-class cricket by Ian Chappell, in both matches in London ensured the games meandered to draws and protestors at Leeds sabotaged the wicket with the third game evenly poised.

For Lillee and Thomson it was a frustrating series in many senses but plenty had been learnt and the series won. Lillee's spell on the first morning of the Lord's Test was one of his finest, reducing England to 49-4 only for the pitch to lead the batsmen on to an orgy of run scoring. The fact that Gary Gilmour and Doug Walters were more successful than either Lillee or Thomson showed how well the English groundsmen had done their work in the final two matches – except England lost the series and the spectators missed the chance of seeing the excitement that had been so prevalent the previous winter. England's own curly tom cat, John Snow, could barely get the ball above stump height.

Despite, or because of, the pitches both Lillee and Thomson had become better bowlers with more skill at their fingertips. Tony Lewis offered astute analysis of both:

> '[Lillee] has learned the true art of fast bowling which lifts him far above the ordinary. Variation of pace, length and line are all under his control. [Thomson] looks as if he has lengthened his run. He gathers momentum on the way to the stumps now rather than jogging and straining for pace just from his action. Accuracy has come with it. Here is a bowler who has learned much in this country.'

Rod Marsh, who was in the best position to judge, agreed that Lillee had become a better bowler having mastered rolling his fingers across the ball to produce a leg cutter to complement the outswinger. Marsh also thought Thomson a better bowler with the old ball especially as he had now added an outswinger to his wide-of-the-crease inswinger.

But the job was done, the Ashes retained and now there was the little matter of the unofficial world championship in the following Australian summer. Six Tests against World-Cup winners West Indies – on quick wickets Michael Holding and Roberts against Lillee and Thomson with Lloyd, Richards and Alvin Kallicharran in one firing line and the Chappells and Walters in the other. For new captain Greg Chappell the formula was clear: 'Fast bowlers all through Test history have been the difference between a good side and a great side.'

The series was far from what anyone had expected. It turned out to be one-sided and was not dominated by raw pace although there were spells of astonishing fast bowling. Ian Redpath, Greg Chappell and Gilmour were just as instrumental in their side's crunching 5-1 victory as Lillee and Thomson. Holding had a chastening introduction to Test cricket (15 wickets at 61.4), Gordon Greenidge considered giving up the game (11 runs in four innings), Richards looked out of his depth until late in the series ('It's what I needed at the time' he later said) and only Lloyd and Roberts would have merited selection in the Australian team. With controversy about pitches, umpiring and sledging and a huge gulf in fitness, discipline and ability Lloyd and the West Indian authorities had much to ponder. Not for nothing did Frank Tyson nickname them the 'Hapless Hookers' as they attempted to meet fire with fire.

Somewhere, however, the reality of what happened has rather got lost in the mists of time. Tony Cozier's recollection that 'Thomson was the difference' is only true after Perth. He was flayed mercilessly in the first two Tests, quite simply getting carried away with bounce and pace rather as he had done with Tony Greig the previous year. During the Perth game a close friend of Thomson was killed at the wicket in a club match, an event that he said changed his thinking on the subject of bouncers and physical intimidation. At Melbourne his discipline returned without it trimming his sails. *Wisden* reported that he 'bowled just about as fast as one could imagine a human being propelling a cricket ball and the lift he found from only fractionally short of a length proved too much for the West Indies.' A return of 5-62 was the result and Australia on their way to a 2-1 lead. Without Lillee in the next game at Sydney his 6-50 in the second innings ensured a comfortable win and effectively won the series as West Indies folded poorly in the last two matches as injuries and injustice from umpires mounted; an air of defeatism settled in. This time it was a case of feeding the instrument of self-destruction as batsman after batsman took on the short ball.

If Thomson could be said to have been erratic then Lillee was quite the opposite. He too had got carried away at Perth and was mauled by Roy Fredericks but bowled throughout the series with sustained pace and accuracy as if the back injury had never happened. In the five Tests he played he never took less than two wickets in an innings and of his 27 victims a mere five were non-batsmen. He and Thomson shared 56 wickets at 27.5 but this was far from a two-man show. Gilmour had 20 at a lower average and new captain Greg Chappell amassed 702 runs at 117. But Lloyd was certain what was at the heart of his team's demise:

'In Thomson and Lillee they possessed the best combination of fast bowlers any captain could wish for, and our batsmen were constantly under

pressure. None of them had ever encountered bowling of such speed before…
it takes a lot of physical courage to withstand that threat of physical danger…,
everyone at some stage did feel the pain of a cricket ball thudding into their
bodies at ninety miles an hour.'

This was the third successive series that had featured this captivating
and thrilling new-ball pairing and if anything they were getting better. Lillee's
injury was fully behind him and if he would never again capture the consistent
explosive pace of 1972 he had gained in cunning and was certainly no lesser a
model for it. Thomson, despite his tennis injury, was back to full fury and his
occasional waywardness could easily be accommodated in a team that had such
a support staff – and when he got it right he tended to win Tests in a session.

But from such a foundation of riches little would be built – they played
just one Test together in the next three years as injury and Packer changed
everything.

The beginning of the end as far as the Lillee and Thomson combination was
concerned came at Adelaide on Christmas Eve 1976. The much anticipated
series against Pakistan, with its array of batting talents, was barely two hours
old when Thomson, having already removed Majid Khan and Mushtaq
Mohammad, charged at a caught-and-bowled chance from the prize bat of
Zaheer Abbas. Team-mate Alan Turner went for the same chance:

'He landed straight down on top of my arm while I was still in the air. I didn't
feel a lot of pain – until I tried to use the arm to get up! I thought, Shit, my
arm won't move, you know? I remember getting up and seeing Turner still
down there, dead as a maggot. I felt like laying the boot into him!'

The ligaments were torn away from the massive shoulder and despite
immediate surgery the prognosis could hardly be good given the nature and
method of Thomson's day job. This was big news and a sporting catastrophe, one
half of Australia's great duo in dire straits; Ray Lindwall predicted the end with
Thomson's 'shock value' likely to be gone forever.

Astonishingly, after missing the Centenary Test in March 1977,
Thomson was ready to tour England just five months after the premature talk
of his demise. Lillee, after prospering in the Centenary Test, wasn't, having
developed a 'hot spot' in his back. Furthermore he was closely associated with

the well-advanced negotiations for the start of World Series cricket, Tony Greig breaking the story during the tour. This meant for Thomson life without his pace partner and the uncertainties of a newly-repaired shoulder. It was a miserable English summer for Australia but a personal reaffirmation for Thomson with 23 wickets at 25, making him comfortably Australia's most successful bowler in a 3-0 defeat. Mike Brearley's erudite memory was that 'broken marriages, conflicts of loyalty, the problems of everyday life fall away as one faces up to Thomson' but the loss of Lillee and the distracted nature of some of the Australian team made them easy victims.

World Series cricket would dominate the Australian summer with all the leading players having signed up, all except Jeff Thomson. He was, of course, a natural target for Packer – a headline maker and turnstile mover. But Thomson was in the unique position of not needing and not being eligible for Packer's money – he had signed a hugely-lucrative 10-year contract with 4IP radio during the West Indies series and having first signed for Packer he then tore up the contract and pledged his future to 4IP and the national team. He was given a standing ovation at Trent Bridge for this gesture although, in truth, he had little option given his contractual obligations. With Lillee now absent for the foreseeable future along with all the other leading Australian players the five home Tests with India followed by five more in the West Indies meant a busy and challenging five months for Thomson and a hastily assembled team of raw recruits.

This Australian second XI plus Thomson captained by Bobby Simpson beat India in three tight matches and were soundly beaten in the other two. It was a great display by a moderate team and Thomson led the way with 22 wickets at 23.4. He tore a hamstring in the final Test and bowled only 27 balls, but by removing Gavaskar and Amarnath he had set Australia on her way. Just across town or state Lillee was battling with the very best in the World Series and finding it hard going. But in the very last game he bowled his side to victory and his first two victims went by the name of Richards – he definitely still had it. And he continued to give it his all – he would never do anything else. Apart from his desire to excel on the field he was a believer in the fairness of the project. He had given up the real-estate business to play full-time cricket, he was one of the best in the world and he would only be hurting himself financially by playing for his country, something players all over the world were realising. Something had to change, a fair day's pay for a fair day's work, something that cricket Boards in every country had singularly failed to appreciate. It was the end of a patriarchal system of master and servant and not before time.

Thomson was reluctant to tour the West Indies just five weeks after the India series but found himself again at the mercy of his contract with 4IP who insisted he travel. He made the very best of a bad job and showed he still had it even if his side was thoroughly outclassed by a full-strength West Indies in the first two Tests. In the second in Barbados he produced probably his finest spell of bowling, inspired by watching Roberts, Colin Croft and Joel Garner knock over his team for 250 as Graham Yallop made history by wearing fully protective headgear in a Test for the first time. The final 75 minutes of the day were unforgettable. Thomson bowling at maximum pace took the wickets of Greenidge, Kallicharran and Richards, the latter after a drop when on nought and some mighty boundaries. The effort led to further leg trouble for the bowler. Brief, but as thrilling as Test cricket has ever been. Thomson's form dipped in the last three matches as the West Indies' WSC contingent refused to play but he still took 20 wickets in the series.

With World Series cricket and injuries it wasn't until 1981 that Lillee and Thomson were re-combined for more than the odd game. In the meantime Lillee's stock had risen even further having bowled brilliantly in taking 35 wickets in six Tests in the tri-series with England and West Indies, 21 wickets in three games against India and then 39 wickets against England in 1981. Pakistan were the visitors later that year and by now Lillee was the absolute maestro with Terry Alderman his understudy and new-ball partner and, judging by the first Test, Thomson was becoming a bit-part player. Things didn't improve and his future was clearly in doubt with the West Indians arriving for a three-match series just weeks later. In the first game Thomson was left out in favour of Geoff Lawson and Australia won due to the heroics of Kim Hughes and a magnificent 7-84 by Lillee, determined to show Holding, Roberts, Croft and Garner just who was the real deal. Thomson was recalled for the second match and bowled well enough in a drawn game – not as well as Lillee but better than Alderman. In the final game, where West Indies levelled the series, Lillee hardly bowled due to injury and Thomson tried gamely to carry the attack almost alone. But for a series of dropped catches he might just have pulled it off – at least he had proved he was, despite multiple reports to the contrary, not a spent force.

Just a month later the pair were in New Zealand for what proved to be the final combined act. Despite miserable weather, the deeds of Bruce Edgar, Richard Hadlee and Greg Chappell made both completed games memorable. The great pair of speed bowlers flickered only briefly and Lillee hobbled out of the series with another knee injury. As a pair they had reached the end of the line.

Individually they continued. Thomson played nine more Tests over the following three years and collected 28 wickets, playing a significant part in the 1982-83 Ashes success with 22 scalps at under 20 each. Lillee played eight more times, taking 27 wickets and exiting with 20 wickets in a 2-0 win against Pakistan, Benaud saying that this was the best he'd seen him bowl, fully 13 years after making his debut. Little wonder that his name is indelibly etched as one of the greatest fast bowlers the game has ever produced. If he had found success in Asia there would be little argument as to his pre-eminence.

Both men had adorned Australian cricket for over a decade and terrorized batsmen in virtually every Test they played. Both entered the Test arena to a fanfare largely of their own making and both were capable of living up to the hype they had created. In all honesty they never really calmed down. Lillee remained as competitive up to his last game as he had been in his first, as driven and as determined. Thomson was just a bloke who loved life, enjoyed it and took pleasure in a god-given ability to propel a cricket ball at enormous, staggering speed.

In 1979 Channel 9 in Australia sponsored a fast-bowling shootout to measure the speeds of the world's best 12 for an A$10,000 prize. Thomson's average was higher than the next fastest and he even won the accuracy award. The highest measured was 91.86 mph/147.9 kph. This might be slightly underwhelming even given the non-match situation. More revealing was Perth 1975 when measured in play against West Indies: Lillee's top speed of 86.39/139.03 was a shadow of what he had produced before his injury but Thomson's 99.70/160.45 was just a shadow, or a blur.

Lillee and Thomson

Results

	Total	Won	Drawn	Lost
Lillee	70	31	23	16
Thomson	51	21	12	18
Lillee and Thomson	26	14	8	4

Test Bowling Overall

	Mat	Balls	Runs	Wkts	Ave	SR	ER	5W1/10WM
Lillee	70	18467	8493	355	23.92	52.0	2.75	23/7
Thomson	51	10535	5601	200	28.00	52.6	3.18	8/0

Test Bowling Together

	Mat	Balls	Runs	Wkts	Ave	SR	ER	5W1/10WM
Lillee	26	6449	3126	119	26.26	54.1	2.90	5/0
Thomson	26	5359	2778	98	28.34	54.6	3.11	4/0

Test Bowling Apart

	Mat	Balls	Runs	Wkts	Ave	SR	ER	5W1/10WM
Lillee	44	12018	5367	236	22.74	50.9	2.68	18/7
Thomson	25	5076	2823	102	26.67	50.7	3.27	4/0

Best Series Together - England 1974-75

	Mat	Balls	Runs	Wkts	Ave	SR	ER	5W1/10WM
Lillee	6	1462	596	25	23.84	58.4	2.44	0/0
Thomson	5	1401	592	33	17.93	42.4	2.53	2/0

Best Test Figures - Innings/Match

Lillee (with Thomson)	5-15 vs England, Birmingham – 1975
Lillee (with Thomson)	9-132 vs Pakistan, Brisbane – 1981
Lillee (without Thomson)	7-83 vs West Indies, Melbourne – 1981
Lillee (without Thomson)	11-123 vs New Zealand, Auckland – 1977
Thomson (with Lillee)	6-46 vs England, Brisbane – 1974
Thomson (with Lillee)	9-105 vs England, Brisbane – 1974
Thomson (without Lillee)	6-77 vs West Indies, Bridgetown – 1977
Thomson (without Lillee)	8-127 vs England, Lord's – 1977

YouTube Bowling Highlights

Search Phrases (sic)
Jeff Thomson 5-38
Lillee and Thompson 1974/75
Dennis Lillee 8/29 vs World XI 2nd test 1971/72

Roberts
and
Holding

Andy Roberts

Sir Anderson Montgomery Everton Roberts is still remembered for his wondrous days in the sun — the slouching gait, the expressionless eyes, the inscrutable menace as he walked back to his mark, before turning and starting his run, accelerating with each subsequent step, transforming into the deadpan and deadly weapon of detached destruction. – Arunabha Sengupta

Michael Holding

It began intimidatingly far away. He turned, and began the most elegant long-striding run of them all, feet kissing the turf silently, his head turning gently and ever so slightly from side to side, rhythmically, like that of a cobra hypnotising its prey. Good batsmen tended not to watch him all the way lest they became mesmerised... The cobra, I am told, hypnotises prey in a similar swaying manner. – Mike Selvey

Picking a pair when faced with the *Fire in Babylon* generation is a thankless task. There were so many and so many that were so good. The firestarter was Andy Roberts, soon to be joined by Michael Holding and they were supported minorly by Bernard Julien, Keith Boyce and Vanburn Holder. Wayne Daniel made a brief show before Colin Croft and Joel Garner appeared at the party door clutching bags of goodies. Malcolm Marshall was a slow burner but eventually graduated to life-and-soul as Roberts retired to the chill-out zone. From this point Marshall and Garner held sway supported by a re-invented Holding and Eldean Baptiste until Courtney Walsh, Ian Bishop, Patrick Patterson and Curtly Ambrose arrived. In the space of 15 years these men (and a couple of half-decent batsmen) held sway and changed cricket while bringing joy to the Caribbean and, grudgingly, the rest of the cricketing world with the obvious exception of a few hundred unfortunate batsmen.

The obvious pairs are Roberts and Holding, Marshall and Garner and Ambrose and Walsh. The last named can safely be excluded here as belonging to a later generation and thus a later chapter. What tilts the balance for the first two names is their new-ball ubiquity. In their 30 Tests together there were only five innings in which they didn't take the first two overs. Three of those were in their last series together, once when Holding was injured and once when Boyce was preferred over Holding in their second game. In those 30 games they took almost eight wickets each time between them. Marshall and Garner were even more prolific with nine a match over 36 games together at a better average but they were often not *the* pair. Holding played in 26 of those 36 matches with Marshall and Garner and Walsh played in the same side as Marshall 42 times and that pair managed eight wickets per match. It wasn't until their 13th match together that Marshall and Garner were called on to open the bowling and for the rest of their time together they had the support of two top-line speedsters in almost every game. Croft himself wrote that 'Somehow the fast-bowling pairs seem to have more of a place in history than the four-pronged fast bowling attack, which seems to be more associated with clinical carnage.' So Roberts and Holding it has to be.

Two young Antiguans arrived in England in November 1972 to be greeted by typically dank and gloomy London weather. Money had been raised by crowdfunding back home even in the days before social media. The aim was to put Antigua on the map. It worked. Both men developed their trade at Alf Gover's cricket school and played for their country with such panache that both are now prefixed with a 'Sir'.

Andy Roberts was already fast but some expert tinkering eradicated his tendency to fall away in the delivery stride. Viv Richards could already bat like a dream – Gover tightened his technique without inhibiting his flair. Within five years the pair would be the backbone of the best cricket team in the world. Backbone would be needed, and not just backbone. As Roberts and Richards were honing their skills and hording 10p coins for the gas meter, West Indies were in the middle of a horrid trot of 20 Tests and four years without a victory. New men were needed to replace the giants of yesteryear; Garry Sobers, Rohan Kanhai and Lance Gibbs. The first signs of green shoots appeared in 1973-74 as England were beaten 3-1 over two series with Lawrence Rowe and Alvin Kallicharran adding youthful vigour to the batting. But Keith Boyce, Vanburn Holder and Bernard Julien were no pace cavalcade and the debut of Roberts, the first Antiguan to wear the maroon cap, at Bridgetown didn't bring any immediate fanfares – three wickets and then dropped for the returning Boyce.

The next series would be in India. The last time the teams had met in the Caribbean, in 1970-71, India had won the series 1-0 through a spin trio and over 1400 runs by Sunil Gavaskar and Dilip Sardesai. To say that new captain Clive Lloyd was facing a difficult first series would be an understatement. But Lloyd had at his disposal a group of exciting young players who, though novices in Test cricket, had put in the hours playing English county cricket. They'd learnt their trade in the middle on a variety of pitches and this would hold them in good stead, none more so than Roberts.

After the months in the Gover school Roberts suffered a severe knee injury back in Antigua that seemed likely to end his career. Not only did he recover, within two years and after dominating the English bowling averages in 1974 (Lloyd topped the batting), he was being hailed as the fastest bowler in the world. But on English pitches it was, according to team-mate Barry Richards, 'the one he gets to nip back off the wicket' that was proving his most fruitful weapon. Already there were clear indications that here was a bowler with all the natural attributes required and a brain to match. The series in India would emphatically support this contention.

West Indies won 3-2 and Roberts prospered although he took only 12 wickets in the games West Indies won and 20 in the two they lost. Twelve more wickets followed in Pakistan so while Jeff Thomson and Dennis Lillee were dismembering England a few thousand miles further south, another new Test bowling star was rising in Asia. And there were batsmen too. Gordon Greenidge hit 200 runs in his debut match and Richards played maybe his finest ever Test innings at New Delhi on a turning pitch against three of the best spinners in the world. This was certainly a side on the rise and it could only be helped by a prodigious new fast bowler when they landed in Australia in late 1975 for a six-Test series. Enter Michael Holding.

Already this was being billed as a clash of extreme pace to decide which was the best Test team in the world. Even without Holding, West Indies had claimed the one-day crown during the English summer and the scene was now set for what in retrospect was perhaps the most significant Test series ever played.

In the space of just two years Roberts had proved himself under all conditions. Thomson had done much the same against England and Lillee had returned untamed from a major back injury. The case for Holding was still not proven. After success for the under-19 and then full Jamaica side he had been considered for the World Cup squad of 1975 and then rejected on the grounds of his lack of experience. There was no doubting the quality of his action or his pace but he had yet to learn about subtlety or the value of strength and fitness for fast bowling in long spells on often unhelpful pitches. But with a promise of fast pitches from helpful Australian curators there was an unarguable case for including the young man to partner Roberts.

To say that this series was much anticipated would hardly do it justice. The home crowd had loved what they'd seen the previous summer as Mike Denness's tourists were sent home with their heavily-bandaged tails between their legs. The World Cup final at Lord's had kept half the country up all night as satellite technology brought live pictures into the Australian winter. Now there was a chance for revenge over a period of three months and all cricket lovers wanted to catch some action in the flesh.

Bowling out New South Wales to win the fourth match of the tour secured Holding's place. The scene was set and Clem Jones, Brisbane's curator, proceeded to ruin the first Test. He might even have ruined the tour if Lloyd had objected to his illegal watering of the pitch after a first day on which it became increasingly apparent that the crumbling surface would barely last two days, let alone five. Lloyd was either very sporting or very naïve and he let the indiscretion pass, much to the surprise of Australia's new captain Greg Chappell. Where Lance Gibbs would probably have spun West Indies to victory they sank to an eight-wicket defeat as Chappell scored two centuries. The much vaunted opening pairs managed just 11 wickets between them, none for Holding and one for Thomson. Both teams had included two spinners and both jettisoned one for the next match at Perth. This time Gibbs and Ashley Mallett managed one wicket between them on a wicket built for speed.

If anything it was a wicket out of control – too hard and too bouncy – and the bowlers lost control as well. Persistent short bowling and brilliant batting from Ian Chappell allowed Australia a decent score. With Roberts too ill to bowl after taking out the openers, Holding christened his account to the tune of four (the first of which was on the explicit advice of Roberts) and then the real fun started. The Australians got carried away with the pacey pitch and Roy Fredericks carted them around the ground for 169 off 145 balls in a truly breathtaking display. Sadly all film record was lost in a fire many years ago – maybe not sadly for Lillee and Thomson who, much to the disgust of the Chappell brothers, bowled like over-excited teenagers.

Then a now-recovered Roberts showed everyone what to do by taking out Australia's top seven for just 54 runs. Sparing with the bouncer despite the bounce and bowling at a pace that forced wicket-keeper Deryck Murray to stand deeper than his counterpart Rod Marsh, he was utterly irresistible in one of the great exhibitions of fast bowling. Ian Redpath quickly resorted to wearing rib protection. In typical Roberts fashion he reported he had bowled better in India. What he had done, however, is learnt to get his arms higher at the point of gather to facilitate away swing. This was done on the basis of a *Sunday People* article by Fred Trueman that he chanced upon. By great good fortune a team of West Australian scientists chose this game to measure ball speeds. Thomson was the fastest, just shy of 100 mph, followed by Roberts, Holding and slow-boy Lillee at 86 mph. Lillee had been much faster before his back injury, Holding would be faster and Roberts was measured during the first innings when below par but still the speeds were scary and this had absolutely nothing to do with the surface beyond its inducement to the bowlers to seek an effort/reward delivery.

Perth was a stunning win but the reality was that West Indies were a fragile team. Inter-island rivalry and disagreements over tactics still bedevilled the side and Lloyd was some way from assuming the control and loyalty he commanded in later years. Greenidge, Richards and Holding were, astonishingly, all in need of an arm round the shoulder to bolster their wafer-thin confidence. While they were winning these issues could be papered over but when things went wrong they went really wrong. This is what Tony Greig had in mind when he misguidedly spoke about grovelling a few months later.

The vast crowds that flocked to Melbourne for the Boxing Day Test could hardly know what was to come. No less than 85,000 were in the ground on day one while a quarter of the population were watching ABC's live coverage. The newspapers were loving their sub-racist metaphors of wild animals and calypso cavaliers, some of the crowd were less subtle but on the field Ian Chappell ensured this ugliness was absent. The unravelling started with some poor umpiring, including allegedly allowing over-stepping to go unpunished, public tears of frustration from Holding, monumental batting from Greg Chappell and bad luck/poor preparation leading to injuries. The wheels came off and the series went west by 5-1.

Roberts struggled with an ankle injury after the third Test but finished the series with 22 wickets at a respectable average. Holding had 10 wickets at 61.4. Little wonder that he wrote of 'bewilderment and anger' being his companions on the way back to the Caribbean. Nor was he alone; Greenidge's self-belief was shot and Richards only managed to resurrect some pride late in the series. For the captain the challenge was an enormous one – to establish what exactly had gone wrong and then make sure it never happened again. It was more than chastening, it was humiliating. There was the carping from journalists who 'knew' that Caribbean flair was all very well in the one-day game but would never cut the mustard when it came to the real thing. At this point Roberts and Holding looked far from the new Hall and Griffith.

Roberts was by far the more mature of the two. The in-cutter that had been so successful for Hampshire was far from his only weapon. There was extreme pace where required, at this stage only Thomson could bowl faster, an outswinger that was as reliable as it was difficult to defend and the double-speed bouncer. With barely any indication of a change in action the first, quickish bouncer would lull the batsman into some sense of safety before a brother, two yards faster, quickly unlulled him. For the batsman that survived there was the inevitable incredulity. Some onlookers even suspected an illegal action, not because the arm was bent but because the increase in pace was so dramatic and so lacking in a warning sign from the bowler's body. Holding's prime asset was simpler – pace. The smooth approach to the crease and the easy but whippy delivery with seemingly minimal effort allowed control as well. If there was no great movement in the air or off the pitch there were also few half-trackers, full tosses or leg-stump gimmees.

Fitness, team spirit and fast bowlers – that was the requirement after the lessons learnt in Australia. There was precious little time to re-group, just six weeks after the last rites had been said in Melbourne the side reconvened at Bridgetown to meet India. Roberts was still struggling with an ankle injury and played only two of the four Tests but Holding took on the mantle of chief destroyer with relish and his 19 wickets cost less than 20 runs each. West Indies won 2-1 but the most significant game was the one they lost in Trinidad. Given the conditions, West Indies fielded three spinners and then failed to bowl India out as they broke the Test record for the highest winning fourth-innings total. Never again would Lloyd make this mistake. If he didn't have good enough spinners then he would rely on pace whatever the pitch. For the final match of the series four fast bowlers were picked and Wayne Daniel joined Holding in the absence of Roberts. The resultant carnage on a fast pitch left India shattered. Captain Bishan Bedi virtually conceded the match amid a welter of injuries and fear of injury. Holding was praised and castigated for his skill and his methods. A round-the-wicket short-pitch attack was both effective and brutal – the relative importance given to the two adjectives varied from supporter to supporter and writer to writer.

Holding had proved himself capable of leading an attack but with England the next opponents only a few months later there still remained the question of Roberts and Holding as a pair. Both men had proved themselves individually but not as part of a combination. There was no obvious reason for this – as room-mates and friends there was a healthy rivalry but no underlying issues. Both men were part of a team that now wanted to win more than ever, especially after England's captain uttered the word "grovel".

The early part of the 1976 tour was difficult for Holding. Lacking the requisite footwear for soft English turf it was Roberts who pointed him to the right supplier, a specialist company in Northampton. No sooner was this rectified than Holding came down with mumps and missed the first Test before returning, undercooked, for the second. Both games were drawn as neither Richards' double-century in the first nor Roberts' 10 wickets in the second could force a result. But for the second year in a row the Lord's crowd were treated to a masterclass of fast bowling – where Lillee had trodden Roberts was likely to go.

And so on to Old Trafford. Both men fit and well and a hard fast pitch with a nasty crack at one end and an England top three mixing baldness, grey hair and guts in equal measure. Guts alone was never going to be enough as the two men took 16 wickets (the others went to Daniel) in a crushing victory which also announced Greenidge as one of the most exciting batsmen in the world. After medium-fast Mike Selvey had terrorised West Indies it was a fair assumption that Roberts and Holding would be a terrifying proposition on the same pitch. They were; England 71 all out with Roberts happy to ease off slightly and leave the tail to Holding.

This was every bit as difficult and frightening as anything Lillee and Thomson had produced over the previous 18 months. More was to follow in the second innings as Holding and Daniel reverted to the folly of Perth and hurled down short-pitched deliveries at Brian Close and John Edrich when their wickets were ripe for the picking using more appropriate methods. Order was soon restored and England were blown away again and the gulf in class between the two teams was laid bare. Only five months earlier David Frith had recorded a far from controversial view when describing the West Indian players as 'fickle' – 'England awaits them eagerly.'

The fourth Test was far closer. The English press, having lambasted the West Indies pace battery, now had to watch as the selectors brought in Bob Willis, John Snow and Alan Ward to match fire with fire. The fact that England came close to winning was largely due to an injury to Holding with England in trouble at 80-4 in the first innings. By the time he was back with a ball in his hand England required a gettable 259 to win. Now it was time for these fast bowlers to perform under pressure. Roberts removed the top three and then both men, aided and abetted by Daniel, chipped away at the rest until the series was won with one to play. It was a performance of real discipline, of professional cricketers doing their job. And it was a triumph of team-work, keeping the danger men tied down while attacking the weaker links. The value of Roberts' fine diving catch to remove Peter Willey, when well set, off Holding was inestimable and it's somehow indicative of Roberts that he nominated this his most satisfying performance in Tests.

Although the series was now dead there was the greatest theatre still to come in a summer of high drama. Thanks to the writing of David Tossell and Simon Lister and the wonders of YouTube the parched outfield and the seemingly unending run up of Holding at the Oval in August 1976 can never be erased. On a lifeless wicket on which Dennis Amiss and Richards scored double-centuries, Holding prospered. A combination of England's opening bowlers and Roberts managed two wickets in 86 overs of toil, sweat and heartbreak, Holding took 14 in 53 overs of gliding majesty. This wasn't a West Indian partnership of equals, it was a one-man hit squad complete with the bull's-eye wrecking ball that shattered Tony Greig's stumps. Maybe the pitch was taking pace off the ball and offering little bounce or movement but the speed through the air after it left Holding's hand was too much for all bar Amiss. Roberts was as impressed as everyone else ('I've never seen anyone bowl like that on a flat pitch'). And he took some impressing. Lloyd was a succinct summariser: 'For sustained speed and accuracy it would be impossible to improve on Holding's performance.' The carping about Holding's methods at Old Trafford and Sabina Park could be forgotten. Fast bowling had never been so beautiful and rarely so effective.

Roberts and Holding had equally split 56 wickets during the series at a combined average of just under 16, with Holding's 12.71 the clear superior. On the face of it they had arrived as a great opening pair. Yet when Roberts excelled at Lord's Holding was only partially fit, ditto Headingley. At the Oval Holding ploughed a lone furrow. Only at Old Trafford did they truly combine.

So what? Did Lloyd care which of them took the wickets and whether they had an equal share? Hardly. They were formidable in more than wickets or even results, the threat was enough to send shivers down the spines of the world's best batsmen. If one had an off day then the other could step up with Daniel also lurking in the shadows. And if three were fearsome then what about four, which would provide the magical sweet spot of non-stop speed?

West Indies next opponents were Pakistan and certain to provide a much harder test for the bowlers. Where England's batting was mediocre, Pakistan could boast the skills of Zaheer Abbas, Majid Khan, Asif Iqbal and others. Holding missed the entire series through injury but with great good fortune West Indies could pull Croft and Garner off the bench (26 wickets in their first two Tests). Roberts led the attack and a bruising series was won. There was to be no immediate re-uniting of Roberts and Holding, at least not in Test cricket. A great searing hole was cut into both Test careers – two years and three full series passed while the world's best players spent two Australian summers knocking seven bells out of each other and finally earning sums of money at least approaching their real worth based on the crowds they could attract. Cricket boards the world over bleated their protests at the blunderbuss tactics of Kerry Packer without ever really considering their own culpability in the process. Did they really feel that players would pack grounds and ask for a pitiful remuneration forever? Or perhaps they had forgotten the players weren't amateurs.

World Series cricket changed the game for good. There was positive encouragement for a blood-and-thunder approach as Packer estimated that crowds would want coloured clothing, floodlit games and, above all, lots of very fast bowling. With this fast bowling came self-defence in the form of helmets. There was also the chance to watch other players at close quarters, something Lillee took full advantage of as he remodelled his run to the wicket based entirely on the easy and rhythmical approach of his West Indian rivals. By the time the various Test cricket boards reintegrated their leading players the game had moved to a higher level of organisation and fitness. For West Indies Dennis Waight, an Australian with a rugby background, was the great new asset. His fitness regimes and strength-building exercises allied to the latent natural talent of his charges would make West Indies well-nigh unbeatable for the next 15 years.

The beginning of the new era was 1 December 1979 and the venue the Woolloongabba stadium in Brisbane. It was West Indies first official Test since February of that year when India had completed a 1-0 series win at Kanpur. Only one player, Alvin Kallicharran, played in both matches. The other ten were returning from the Packer adventure and even Marshall couldn't keep his place in face of this influx. If anything the Packer years had accelerated the West Indian certainty that they were the number-one side in the world. Richards was the best in his field, Lloyd and Greenidge amongst the best in theirs and Roberts, Holding, Croft and Garner were so far ahead of any other pace attack that it was hard to see how they could be beaten. Not that Australia were slouches. Lillee and Thomson back together with Rodney Hogg and Lenny Pascoe supporting. The masterful Greg Chappell now backed by Allan Border, David Hookes and Kim Hughes. If anybody could beat West Indies then surely Australia were the ones. But they couldn't and they didn't, receiving two hidings in a three-Test series. After so many near misses West Indies had finally won in Australia and exorcised the ghosts of 1975-76. Little wonder that both Roberts and Holding nominate it as their career highlight.

The new ball was with Roberts and Holding and they did what they should with 25 wickets. The back-ups were Croft and Garner who did more than expected with 30. In some senses this is where the idea of a pace pair falls down. True enough no batsman could possibly relish the prospect of 'Fruity' and 'Whispering Death' at the best of times but with 'Big Bird' and 'Crofty' waiting in the wings these could only be the worst of times. This wasn't 'hunting in pairs', it was 'hunting in packs' and the like had never been seen before. At this stage it was hard to imagine anyone challenging West Indies over a series.

The first to try would be New Zealand – and against all odds and expectations they succeeded. True West Indies were tired after the Australian series and an exhausting tri-nation one-day series. Richards was absent, the umpiring was lamentable not to say biased and Richard Hadlee, Bruce Edgar and others were inspired. But it was the umpiring and the West Indian response that decided the series. The wheels came off, Holding kicked stumps out of the ground and Croft barged an umpire. The team were close to forfeiting a Test and going home. Lloyd may have thought that he had driven discipline through the side but this was a sign that it was still a work in progress. Imran Khan's insistence on neutral umpires for Tests seemed even more sensible and the fact that West Indies remained unbeaten in every series over the next 15 years was an indication that through hardship comes redemption.

Ian Botham had seen plenty of the West Indian players during the one-day series in Australia and with England preparing to receive them for a full series in 1980 penned an article for *The Cricketer* entitled 'I've a gut feeling we can defy the odds'. Over two pages he offered no grounds for this prediction, in fact it was more a paean to their brilliance. Holding was, in his opinion, the fastest in the world, Roberts the only bowler who could challenge Lillee and Garner likely to be better than both in England. Not to mention 'a tremendous array of batting stars'. But Beefy had a 'gut feeling' and he was the new captain of England.

England came within a whisker of winning the opener but lost after a late flurry of hitting by Roberts. After that the home side never looked like winning again in a wet summer that clouded over the remaining four Tests. Botham was right in one thing, Garner was the outstanding bowler of the series but Roberts and Holding were clearly no back numbers.

They had been sharing fields and dressing rooms for the best part of a decade and while they were welcoming and helpful to new arrivals they had a bond which had been forged in adversity back in Australia in 1976. Their first contact had been as respective twelfth men in a Shell Shield game at Sabina Park. Roberts was slightly older and Holding immediately recognised he was slightly wiser and had the good sense to listen. This continued throughout their career; Roberts wasn't a great talker and some mistook this for a frosty personality but he was simply the antithesis of the clichéd Caribbean stereotype. A deep and quiet thinker he was also hugely generous to his pace partner as the pair exchanged tips on how best to dismiss opposition batsmen. Here is an aspect of pace pairing that is probably as important as any, the willingness to share knowledge.

With 26 wickets at a skinny average in England Garner was now the new number one for West Indies with Marshall completing the latest quartet. Roberts and Holding were still the new-ball pair but they had only shone briefly, Roberts at Trent Bridge and Holding at Lord's, before their partnership was curtailed by injury. Holding was sidelined from the next series, against

Pakistan. Roberts also withdrew, mindful of a workload that needed increasing management after years of service to Hampshire in county cricket on top of his domestic and international commitments in both formats of the game. Pakistan were beaten and it was some testimony to the enduring belief in Roberts and Holding that they were ushered straight back into the team for the visit of England only six weeks later. Marshall and Croft were the unlucky bowlers forced to make way.

This was the attack that Holding thought the best. He himself was bowling as fast as ever he had but with more control than before World Series cricket. Roberts was in his pomp and it tends to be forgotten today how good he actually was, his brilliance somehow clouded by those who followed. Lillee, amongst others, was in no doubt that he was the best of his time.

> 'He had almost perfect line and length with an economy of run-up and action, and he was really whippy at the end. It was X factor stuff. He was uncompromising, unsmiling and just got on with the job…Andy was unusual because there weren't many around in those days who had such a good change of pace. It wasn't just that, it was the control. He was always on the right spot. He almost crept in rather than indulge in the big arm-pumping run most of us used. His secret was stealth.'

Deryck Murray had a unique view and his verdict was simple on the bowlers of his era. Holding was the fastest and Roberts the best and being the best was achieved by allying natural ability with deep thought. Perhaps more than any other fast bowler he applied his brain to his art. Typical of the man was hours spent practising a deft flick of the ball in his delivery stride so that the shiny side was reversed and the eagle-eyed batsman confounded.

One match of England's 1981 tour was cancelled due to the 'Jackman affair', two were easy home wins and two were draws that West Indies dominated. Holding had rarely bowled faster and in Barbados he produced the famous over to Boycott that still drives any red-blooded West Indian into paroxysms of joy. The England team was pretty average and West Indies won in a hack canter with Holding and Croft as star bowlers. Roberts took just eight wickets in the first three games and was dropped for the last. Any other side in the world would have delayed such treatment but West Indies had Marshall cooling his heels. Roberts might have gone a game earlier but for the fact that the fourth Test was the first ever to be played in Antigua, pretty much a direct result of the exploits of the two boys that had wandered the grey London streets nine years earlier. Richards took full advantage with a century but Roberts failed to take a wicket and it looked as if his Test career could be over at the age of 30.

Michael Manley later wrote that the series 'confirmed the emergence of Holding as the leading bowler in the West Indies' in spite of the fact that Croft had proved more intimidating and more successful. What Manley actually meant was that Holding had now, without any doubt, moved past his long-time partner. Roberts had been the first of this new generation and for six years his position had been unquestioned even when Holding performed miracles at the Oval. Now the press was turning against Roberts and with Marshall's sustained excellence he was increasingly seen as a man on the way out. The selectors now seemed to agree, but they weren't sure.

Although Roberts was down on pace he was up on variation and this made him an increasingly clever one-day bowler and with the next tour to Australia featuring just three Tests and a three-nation 'World Series Cup' the full battery was required. The number was soon reduced by one as Marshall succumbed to a back injury. This put Roberts and Holding back together.

The shock of losing the opening Test was profound. On a nasty wicket Kim Hughes made an astonishing century and both Holding and Lillee took 10 wickets. Roberts took but one and was promptly replaced by Sylvester Clarke who managed little in the drawn second Test. With one to play West Indies' record was on the line and Roberts was recalled. Lloyd won the toss, put Australia in and watched his old faithfuls take two each and reduce Australia to 17-4. This is what real opening bowlers did.

Despite the efforts of Border the game was won and the series levelled. West Indies pace supply was suddenly cut by two as Croft and Clarke elected to try their luck for South African money, knowing full well they would never play for their country again. Even if Marshall were to return to full fitness Roberts was back on board as a key player. His pace had dropped but his final outings against India were something of a triumph as Holding recalled.

'He was 32, not as quick as he used to be, and the pundits wanted him out of the team. Andy didn't listen. He took 24 wickets by outthinking the batsmen instead of blasting them away. He varied his pace, got the ball to move off the seam or flummoxed them with his slow-one-quick-one bouncer routine.'

This was 1983, the year that West Indies and India grew heartily sick of the sight of each other. Eleven Tests in a calendar year and a World Cup final thrown in.

Seven years earlier India had been knocked about badly in the Caribbean and the top four in their 1983 batting order had played in that series. With Marshall recovered to aid Roberts, Holding and Garner the Indians would have had a fair idea about the nature of the next 10 months when they took the field at Sabina Park in late February. They were a fine team – experienced batsmen such as Gavaskar and Dilip Vengsarkar were now led by the all-action Kapil Dev but they were simply no match for a West Indian side now entering the most golden of years. To lose 2-0 was no disgrace but Roberts did indeed outthink them with his 24 wickets costing just 22.7 each. Marshall was not far behind, Holding had an unaccountably poor time. Roberts' interventions were crucial in both games that West Indies won and suddenly he was back at the top with a World Cup to collect in England.

After a slow start West Indies moved smoothly to the Lord's final and prepared to be crowned as Roberts removed Gavaskar for two and India crumbled to 183. As everybody knows, West Indies lost. If ever revenge would not be served cold then this was it. Just four months later the two teams were back in Test-match opposition at Kanpur.

Roberts had, on the face of it, a minimal influence on the series, playing in just the last two games and taking five wickets in what proved to be his final series. The two bowlers who dominated, however, both owed a huge debt of gratitude. Marshall took 33 wickets and from here on was West Indies number one, having benefitted from the generous advice he received from his predecessor at Hampshire and a man who had found a way to take wickets in India back in 1975. Holding took 30 and his debt to Roberts was even greater.

Following a cartilage operation on his left knee in 1982 he was down on confidence and favouring the left leg which was throwing his action out of kilter. Roberts' reputation as a deep thinker and close observer of the game was not limited to his own performances. Watching from the dressing-room at Kanpur he suggested Holding should cut down his run in order to gain greater control over his body and regain confidence in his repaired knee. It worked and Holding stuck to this approach. Up to this point in his career Holding had taken 151 wickets at 24.47, he went on to take another 98 at 22.46. Of course he may well have reverted to this approach anyway but who better to offer advice than the man who knew his bowling best. Certainly he lost little if anything in effectiveness as the averages show and Lillee, for one, thought that 'when he learned to swing the ball both ways, even though he lost some pace, he was a better all-round bowler.' And Lillee knew better than anyone having made the same transformation himself after injury.

For Roberts the series was a sad and bitter departure from Test cricket despite the success of his protégés. Passed fit for the first match he stepped down for the good of the team as he was unsure of his ability to last five days. An easy win in the first Test might have excused his omission from the second except for the fact that Daniel was brought back to replace Baptiste. Somehow the unconvincing Daniel and Winston Davis were retained for the next three matches as Roberts' mood sunk lower and lower. Holding remains convinced that he was treated badly – nobody spoke to him and he was never given the option of announcing his retirement rather than being slowly shuffled out to pasture. Ironically when he was recalled it was his batting, in a partnership of 161 with Lloyd, which proved to be a match winner. For Holding it was a sad time:

> 'His exit marked the end of an era. He was the cornerstone of the pace policy and was the one who initially carried the other fast bowlers in his slipstream. In the early days he did the bulk of the work and never flinched from it. We just supported him before the four-pronged attack was developed with everyone pitching in and performing as a team.'

From the team point of view the India series had great significance. Lloyd described the umpiring as the worst that he'd ever seen (for the third time) but the response this time was far from the tantrums and sulks of Australia and New Zealand. The fifth Test also gave an inkling of the now supreme confidence, bordering on arrogance, of the team. Leading 2-0 with two to play it seemed the wicket might take spin so the rare sighting of Roger Harper was noted; just to be sure, four quick bowlers were also selected. It looked like backfiring before Roberts joined Lloyd and the bad blood was put behind them for the sake of the team. This was the Roberts that Greg Chappell knew and sort of loved:

> 'He hated losing. He could bat and won a couple of games with really pugnacious innings. I think behind the scenes he would be standing a few up in the corner and asking them to have a look in the mirror.'

Fortunately for West Indies, Antigua had bestowed two great competitors on the national side. Mystery surrounds the final act – Roberts said only 'There are many reasons that come to me as to why I was sent home from that tour to India. And it had absolutely nothing to do with cricket or my performances…' One of those reasons was certainly his insistence on helping a young out-of-form batsman in the nets. Richie Richardson.

Over the following years Marshall established himself as one of the greatest fast bowlers in history – given his achievements in India and later Pakistan it seems quite reasonable to place him ahead of Lillee – and Garner became his new-ball partner with Holding enjoying a fruitful time as first change. As one left another appeared, Patterson, Walsh and then Ambrose and Ian Bishop.

In 2014 the pair gave a combined interview to *All Out Cricket* which revealed much about their work together:

> MH: 'We were different. Initially, Andy was the quickest of the two. I was just learning my trade. So, early in my career I didn't know a lot to work out many opposition batsmen and that sort of thing. But by the time I'd got to learn more about fast bowling and learned more about the game, Andy and myself would work out the opposition and we would target different batsmen in different ways. Because of his skills and my skills. I developed a great deal of pace; I was quicker than Andy at a lot of stages. So, he would use his guile, I would use more pace than anything else. But in the evenings, we would always discuss opposition batsmen and who would be better at bowling to which batsmen.'
>
> AR: 'We complemented each other by looking at what we thought were the weak points of the batsmen and pinpointing them to one another. Michael had pace and I was using variety, I'd bowl at different paces. Plus, Michael bowled at different lengths to me so you could not play both of us the same. You had to play Michael more in-between. You couldn't go forward, you couldn't go back because it was not short enough to go back. Whereas with me, you would have to play me more off your front foot because I would pitch it up a little more than Mikey did.'

These words offer an insight that statistics alone can't, about teamwork, advice and friendship. Like many other pairs, Roberts and Holding produced many of their greatest performances when the other was either below form or absent and in their case the water was often muddied by the presence of one or two other fast bowlers. The tendency was often to share the wickets around and this leads to sometimes unspectacular figures. There are, after all, only 10 available wickets in an innings and if Daniel, Garner or Marshall are waiting in the wings you have to be quick out of the blocks to grab a lion's share. This was slightly less of a problem for Richard Hadlee or Kapil Dev.

The abiding images of this magical pair are many and varied. The beauty and speed of Holding and the force and stealth of Roberts. It was the fact both men could mix these qualities with so little apparent effort that made them so exciting to watch. Cricket has rarely offered such a sight, as long as you weren't standing 22 yards away.

Roberts and Holding

Results

	Total	Won	Drawn	Lost
Roberts	47	21	18	8
Holding	60	31	21	8
Roberts and Holding	30	14	12	4

Test Bowling Overall

	Mat	Balls	Runs	Wkts	Ave	SR	ER	5W1/10WM
Roberts	47	11135	5174	202	25.61	55.1	2.78	11/2
Holding	60	12680	5898	249	23.68	50.9	2.79	13/2

Test Bowling Together

	Mat	Balls	Runs	Wkts	Ave	SR	ER	5W1/10WM
Roberts	30	6521	2951	117	25.21	55.7	2.71	6/1
Holding	30	6498	3027	116	26.09	56.0	2.79	7/2

Test Bowling Apart

	Mat	Balls	Runs	Wkts	Ave	SR	ER	5W1/10WM
Roberts	17	4614	2223	85	26.15	54.3	2.89	5/1
Holding	30	6182	2871	133	21.59	46.5	2.79	6/0

Best Series Together - England 1976

	Mat	Balls	Runs	Wkts	Ave	SR	ER	5W1/10WM
Roberts	5	1330	537	28	19.17	47.5	2.42	3/1
Holding	4	957	356	28	12.71	34.1	2.32	3/1

Best Test Figures - Innings/Match

Roberts (with Holding)	7-54 vs Australia, Perth – 1975
Roberts (with Holding)	10-123 vs England, Lord's – 1976
Roberts (without Holding)	7-64 vs India, Madras – 1975
Roberts (without Holding)	12-121 vs India, Madras – 1975
Holding (with Roberts)	8-92 vs England, The Oval – 1976
Holding (with Roberts)	14-149 vs England, The Oval – 1976
Holding (without Roberts)	6-21 vs Australia, Perth – 1984
Holding (without Roberts)	11-107 vs Australia, Melbourne – 1981

YouTube Bowling Highlights

Search Phrases (sic)
Andy Roberts 10 wickets vs England 2nd test 1976
Michael Holding, 8 for 92, and 6 for 57, Pace Like Fire, 5th Test 1976
West Indies Fantastic Four Roberts Holding Garner Croft 1980

Imran

and

Sarfraz

Imran Khan

He ran in off increasingly long strides, a run up meticulously calculated over the years. It helped him gather momentum and then, as he approached the umpire, that leap, so high, and from side on, such an exquisite and elegant portrait of taut human musculature…of the innate but often accidental aestheticism of athletics, there can have been few better manifestations than Imran's bowling action.
– Osman Samiuddin

Sarfraz Nawaz

He would hold the ball in both hands until three strides in front of the crease and then his right hand would flop down, like a faulty trafficator, before he would gather and deliver. He didn't drive through the crease but relied on the remarkable strength of his shoulder as his arm whirred through. Sarfraz made every delivery look like an effort ball. It was as if the brain was more refined than the body but it had worked out a utilitarian method that gave his mind a vehicle to express itself. He was not so much a bowling machine as a bowling Dalek.
– Rob Bagchi

It's irresistible really, the sorcerer and his apprentice. But like so many of these neat phrases or preconceptions it is largely untrue. From a distance of 30 years or more and without an intimate knowledge of the careers of both Sarfraz Nawaz and Imran Khan it is easy to imagine the older and more experienced man imparting the mysteries of shine, seam and reverse swing to the young pup who would eventually outgun the old dog and pass those secrets, and his own additions, down to his own brood. It sort of happened like that but only sort of, so the details are worth recalling.

For starters, the age difference is not so immense, just under four years. Sarfraz beat Imran to international recognition by just over two years and both men had the misfortune to make pretty awful debuts and then find themselves jettisoned from the national team for over three years.

Sarfraz had to deliver 34 overs without reward over three days on a Karachi pitch on the other side of stultifying. Even Colin Milburn was becalmed and then rioting brought the game to a premature conclusion. The raw, over-confident teenaged Imran was drafed into the Pakistan team at Birmingham in 1971, Sarfraz was injured, where the rioting was confined to the run variety flowing principally from the bat of Zaheer Abbas. Imran began with a spray of full tosses to a bemused Colin Cowdrey and if he improved from this he still couldn't be trusted with any real spells and finished with no wickets where fellow opening bowler Asif Masood had nine. Given that England fought out a draw it was hardly surprising that Imran was singled out as the primary reason for the failure to force a victory. Like Sarfraz, he would be back.

The backdrop to the early development of these two nascent stars was political turmoil, bloodshed and eventually a split as East Pakistan seceded under the name of Bangladesh. Both men came from privileged backgrounds, both from Lahore but not sharing a common language – Punjabi was spoken by the older man and eventually shared with the younger who spoke Urdu.

Sarfraz was quick to seize an opportunity in England after his name was passed forward by Roger Prideaux, who had faced him in Pakistan, to his county, Northamponshire. With the sporting and political situation at home unappealing to a young man with an appetite for life and experience outside his own country it was hardly surprising he took up county cricket before switching to the Lancashire League and then back again once he truly mastered English conditions. With Imran at Oxford and Worcestershire both men were learning skills that would hold them in good stead all over the world and not just on dead subcontinental wickets.

Not that there wasn't plenty more to do. Imran later complained that often it was too easy in England just to pitch the ball up and let the conditions do the work. He was the kind of man that wanted to control his bowling himself and being a stock swing bowler was never going to be a satisfactory day job. When eventually confronted with Faisalabad and later Perth he realised that he would have to add genuine speed to his armoury. Perhaps Sarfraz was more set in his ways or maybe he was less driven to explore new disciplines, or perhaps just physically incapable of sustained spells of fast bowling. His amble to the wicket and action remained that of a club bowler but his deliveries were certainly not. A strong upper body and plenty of height allowed for the occasional genuinely fast delivery but mostly he relied on variation, control and movement off the seam or in the air when conditions allowed. His particular pride remained his ability to find the chink in the armour of even the best batsmen and then have the control to exploit his discovery. When conditions didn't suit he had to improvise, something he did well as his record attests even if his best bowling was invariably when the going was good.

Imran frequently reserved his best for the most unforgiving conditions for bowlers, extracting life where there was seemingly none. Such an attitude, and the ability to achieve success with it, is given to few. Equally important was a determination to equip himself in any possible way for any fights that lay ahead. A rigorous training schedule, endless practice and a large ear for advice from wise mouths were the groundwork for the triumphs that would follow. John Snow helped modify his action to more side-on when he moved to Sussex, with this came the ability to swing the ball both ways. Later still, Mike Procter rebuilt a 'mincing' run up so that he could generate more speed into the crease. He learnt wherever he went, a keen brain fired by the ambition of being the best at what he did.

The return to Test cricket came first for Sarfraz and within two games he had announced himself as a fine exponent of medium-fast bowling on a helpful surface with eight wickets in defeat at Sydney including both Chappells, Ian Redpath (a player whose name had always fascinated Sarfraz) and Keith Stackpole. Despite following this with a lean run he had learnt prodigiously and was an obvious selection for the party to tour England in 1974. Imran, still waiting for his second cap, was named as well after a spell in county and university cricket where his reputation both as cricketer and devastatingly handsome man about town blossomed in equal measure.

The three-match series ended 0-0 and for Sarfraz and Imran it was proof that one was a real Test player and the other had much still to learn. However, ending the tour unbeaten in all matches was a further mark of Pakistan as an improving team. For the first time Imran had been encouraged by his captain, Intikhab Alam, to concentrate on speed rather than control. While he appreciated the freedom, his confidence and technique were not really up to the task but on returning to Pakistan after graduating at Oxford, Imran set out to make changes. Having seen enough of Snow, Denis Lillee and Andy Roberts, Imran sensed that speed might well be the future and this impression was strengthened as he found that all his 'English tricks' came to nothing on Pakistan pitches. 'Fast and straight' was the way to go. If he was going to bowl in this fashion then the opposition's response when he donned the pads was predictable. He decided it was time to learn to hook and began intense practice to master another skill even though Pakistan's batting strength was such that he was now a lower middle-order regular.

Pakistan might be a coming team but they would now be tested by the best in the world. At home there was the belief that Majid Khan, Zaheer, Asif Iqbal and the rest were a match for anyone – the question was could the bowlers complete the work of the batsmen. A short home series against New Zealand was a useful step up the ladder. Mushtaq Mohammed as captain had brought a new confidence to the team, a batting genius named Javed Miandad averaged 126, Pakistan won easily and Imran and Sarfraz became a new-ball pair and both prospered. Richard Hadlee could do nothing with the pitches but Imran and Sarfraz found things he couldn't, albeit against lesser batsmen.

This progress was all very nice but the organisation and funding of the game was lagging horribly behind the performances on the field. Ongoing arguments over payment weren't just confined to Pakistan as Ian Chappell, Tony Greig and Kerry Packer were preparing to throw a bomb underneath cricket's financial structures. With major overseas tours to Australia and West Indies in 1976-77, six leading players refused to sign contracts thus jeopardising the progress made over the previous years and potentially confining Pakistan to another decade as a second-rate team. Prime Minister Zia Bhutto was well aware of the potential of this generation and was equally aware of its relevance to national identity, profile abroad and even his own political future. King of Pakistan cricket AH Kardar was sidelined and a new age was ushered in; Pakistan and world cricket was entering an age that would be the most significant for 110 years in redefining the way cricket would be watched, paid for and played for the next 40.

With these issues largely settled there was now the matter of four months on tour and eight Tests against the strongest two teams in the world. On paper, at home or against lesser opponents, Pakistan had been impressive but Greg Chappell, Viv Richards, Lillee, Jeff Thomson, Roberts and Michael Holding would be a considerably more challenging experience. Imran and Sarfraz would be bowling to the best in their own backyards and that would require them to harness all the skills that they had learnt over the previous seven years. For Imran in particular it was time to lead his country's attack – he had craved the responsibility but could he actually handle it? Lillee referred to him as a 'trundler' in the run-up to the first Test. Lillee's later words indicate how perceptions of Pakistan were changing: 'Now they offered a much tougher attitude than we had seen from them before.'

It was a rapidly developing side, more aggressive in every area. Mushtaq had insisted, 'whatever they say to us in the field, we stand up and give it back to them'; this clearly extended beyond mere verbals. Australia should have won the first match but chickened out of a run chase. They romped the second on the back of 10 wickets from Lillee and were then thrashed in the final match at Sydney. In the second game Imran had given an indication that he was a force to be reckoned with, sporting a classical side-on action and big leap into the crease, in sending down 381 balls and claiming five second-innings wickets and bowling flat out – it was time to match Australian aggression with an Asian version instead of with obdurate blocking, wristy flicks and military medium mixed with leg breaks. Sarfraz had missed the second match but was back at Sydney for the finale and his partnership with Imran reached its first high-water mark.

Greg Chappell arrogantly chose to bat on a bowlers' wicket and his side was bundled out for 211 – nine wickets for the opening pair. As if inspired by this performance, Asif led his side to a big lead before Imran and Sarfraz ripped Australia up again with nine more wickets to draw the series. Mushtaq had piqued Sarfraz by offering Imran first over and the result could hardly have been better. Imran bowled for four hours unchanged while Sarfraz used all his skills with new ball and old. The wily captain had played his new-ball pair off against one another and got the best from both.

Bouncers aplenty, animated gestures and umpires' warnings flecked the game but it had been a thrilling contest, the kind of game that Packer wanted to buy and package. The pitch had been helpful but Imran and Sarfraz had outbowled Lillee, Max Walker and Gary Gilmour. Imran called it a turning point both for himself and Pakistan cricket. Osman Samiuddin agreed with the profound relevance:

> 'They emerged from it, hardened men, in their modern incarnation; racy, colourful and mostly successful and a bit messy but one peopled by reckless batsmen and equally reckless fast bowlers'.

It was an image that was increasingly capturing the public imagination. Now they had to prove themselves in the West Indies where reports that Imran was bowling as fast as Lillee were greeted with plenty of scepticism from Garry Sobers.

It wasn't just that Pakistan could now mix it with the best on the cricket field; they had ceased to be an oddity from the third world with clever tricks that would get found out in the heat of battle. Hanif Mohammad had done much to dissipate this image but the speed and skill of Imran and Sarfraz completed the process. They could match Lillee and Thomson for aggression and weren't far behind in other departments. They could also match them for flared shirts, gold chains and a *Miami Vice* aura. Experience in county cricket had played a huge part in the hardening and honing of skills. Most of the side had spent years excelling against battle-tried county pro's and the likes of Barry Richards and Keith Boyce while dealing with an alien culture and persistent low-level racism and sniping. They were now, however, part of the first-world cricket community, a position that needed cementing in the Caribbean. The first tour there for 20 years.

The good news greeting Pakistan was that Holding would miss the series; the bad news was that Colin Croft and Joel Garner would make their Test debuts in the opener at Bridgetown. Two months later Pakistan had been beaten after an epic series by two to one. The sad fact is that these two countries will never play such a series again, nor, probably, will any others bar, maybe, England and Australia. The wonder of the five-Test series has been sacrificed at the altar of money, public apathy, ODIs and T20.

West Indies eventually outmuscled the visitors as they would have any other touring side but it was only in the final games that the cracks really showed; up to that point Pakistan had matched West Indies in almost all departments. The differences were the batting of openers Gordon Greenidge and Roy Fredericks and the bowling of Croft – 33 wickets at 20.5. Majid and Wasim Raja weren't far behind the Windies pair but even Imran's efforts of 25 wickets at 31.6 couldn't match Croft. Sarfraz was disappointing – in the deciding Test on a fast and bouncy wicket he managed just four tailenders after Imran's opening burst had put West Indies on the back foot.

Certainly there was disappointment that the series had been lost but there were 'plenty of positives' to be taken from the tour. Perhaps the most significant was the advent of satellite coverage of both tours back in Pakistan. It would be easy to over-emphasise the reach of such coverage but in the major urban centres huddles of men around flickering pictures in the small hours became a feature of a country undergoing a cultural awakening and associated national pride. At the front end of this was Imran Khan, with Majid and Asif not far behind. Unsurprisingly these were the three who had received the whispered overtures of Tony Greig during the West Indies series.

The advent of World Series cricket took the cream of all the major cricketing nations. The pace of their reintegration varied from country to country. In Pakistan it was relatively quick despite some ugly and acrimonious interludes. The reason was simple – a Test series against India, the first for 18 years, which *had* to be undertaken with the best available players. During the Packer hiatus Sarfraz played a bit part in two forgettable series against England while Imran pitted his wits against the world's best in front of Channel 9's mass of cameras in Australia. This was his finishing school. Already compared to Ray Lindwall and Keith Miller by Len Hutton, who was impressed by the 'fanatical self discipline' of the 'smooth Asian lad', and grudgingly accepted as 'a bit brisk' by Sobers, while peppering Greenidge with bouncers, he now strove to outbowl Roberts, Lillee and the rest. And he could bat too, even if that seemed less important at this stage.

So when India arrived for the much heralded series in October 1978 it was to face a team chomping at the bit. With India still relying on spin and a talented batting line-up led by Sunil Gavaskar (they couldn't know what Kapil Dev would become based on his debut) it was only a matter of time before a home-friendly pitch was prepared. Twice it appeared and twice India were overwhelmed by Sarfraz and Imran with 28 wickets in two games. This was now an opening pair capable of leading their side all over the world and displaying skills that were the envy of most other nations – the fact that the old ball was often proving as useful as the new was raising eyebrows and is the single fact that remains in most memories when this pairing is considered.

In the Bridgetown Test of the 1977 tour an incident had occurred that can be considered crucial to the legacy of Imran and Sarfraz. With West Indies at 183-5, facing Pakistan's 435, the new ball was due. Despite the protestations of both opening bowlers, Mushtaq insisted that a breakthrough could better be achieved by accepting the offer and dispensing with an old ball that wasn't coming onto the bat but *was* swinging. All movement ceased and Clive Lloyd smashed 157 which eventually enabled West Indies to save the game. The obvious question posed was, why the tatty ball swung and the new one didn't against all conventional wisdom of fast bowling? Graham Roope recalled Imran hooping an old ball around at the Oval later that year in a Championship fixture – the response was 'disbelieving stares' and 'subsequent muttering'. What is now a stock delivery requiring great skill and dedication was, over the next two decades, to cause more controversy and recrimination than any other legal ball in cricket history bar the bouncer.

If Sarfraz is usually acknowledged as either one of or *the* founding father then behind him stood an older relative, one Farrukh Ahmed Khan who chanced upon an 18-year-old Sarfraz one afternoon at Lahore Gymkhana.

> 'I was in the nets one day and he told me how, if the ball gets old enough on one side while remaining fairly new on the other, bowlers can generate extravagant late swing with it. He didn't know why and he only gave me the idea about it. He didn't show me how to do it.'

That at least is Sarfraz's first version. Like many of his tales there was more than one. In the revised edition told to Peter Oborne, Khan became merely an instructor in basic inswing as learnt from Alf Gover. The real secret Sarfraz later discovered when tinkering around with a set of old balls and experimenting in the nets although in a further interview he claimed it was 'on a friend's suggestion'. It appears that Sarfraz did have a genuine fascination with the cricket ball in the way that other young men worship at the temple of Fender or Apple. By 1976 he was skilled enough to know exactly what he was doing and was duplicitous enough to hide it from Imran by roughing the smooth side at the end of each over so his team-mate would appear inferior. At this stage he was not confident enough to share his knowledge even if the team might suffer as a consequence. His largesse came later.

But the question is how to make sure one side shines more than the other when the law of averages dictates that both sides will receive an equal battering from the batsman? Firstly the fielding team can ensure that all returns to the wicket-keeper are not on the full and bounce on the same side; secondly the fielding side can actively polish just one side of the ball; thirdly the fielding side can weight the rougher side using spit and sweat and fourthly the fielding side can ensure premature ageing of one side of the ball illegally. The fourth method is much the quickest. Once the ball is in prime condition a skilled practitioner can make it swing late and at speed and watching that skilled practitioner, even in slow motion, the inswinging yorker seems to be the most impossible ball in cricket to either attack or defend.

Sarfraz worked on this method of swing over many years but unveiled it only when conditions were ripe. Imran had come across the same phenomenon once in Australia but it was the decision of Mushtaq at Bridgetown that pricked Imran's enquiring mind and he then picked Sarfraz's 'great cricketing brain'. It wasn't as if this became a new wonder weapon overnight but it was a potential addition to the ever-expanding arsenal being amassed by the two men that would be fully exploited for the first time five years later. It then passed down to a younger generation of Pakistan fast bowlers before crossing the oceans and becoming the property of all skilled exponents. But accusations of malpractice in altering the condition of the ball abounded, sometimes muttered and sometimes, such as in the case of Allan Lamb, splashed across the media. Court cases were threatened and brought as a history of raising seams with bottle tops and smearing wrist bands or hair with polishing agents became rife. Usually the Pakistan team were the prime suspects, as they tend to be in most corruption cases.

Sarfraz went to war over such allegations as was inevitable for a man who could pick a fight with David Attenborough if he was at a loose end. To say he was a cussed cove would only tell half of the story. Having not joined the big six in the pay dispute with the BCCP before the Australian tour he then launched his own claim against the same organisation barely a year later. That is not to say he was not dedicated, in his own fashion, both to personal and team success. It was no coincidence that Imran was to benefit from his knowledge once Sarfraz felt secure in his position:

> 'He taught me more about swing bowling than anybody else did, disclosing little tidbits to me as he got to know me a little better during our tours – that that was something he refused to discuss with other bowlers.'

State secrets were sacrosanct. Like Richard Hadlee, Sarfraz was obsessive about choosing the match ball. Not that Imran hadn't been making his own discoveries. Reverse swing was common practice on Pakistan's arid pitches but, like any delivery, it requires great skill to bowl it well. The theory of the googly or flipper is one thing, to send it down with the disguise, pace and forethought of Shane Warne is another. Imran had first utilised the technique against top batsmen at Melbourne in 1977 – five wickets was an indication that this was a skill to nurture and expand.

Although India had been comfortably beaten there were bigger tests awaiting – Australia and West Indies, neither of whom would make the mistake of underestimating their opponents this time and India again, this time away from home. Equally grounding was the certain knowledge that the golden generation of batting built around Mushtaq, Majid, Zaheer and Asif was coming to the end of the road and of the new boys only Miandad could be considered in the same class. For Imran this would inevitably result in taking on the responsibility of playing long innings and shepherding the tail from five or six rather than being shepherded or applying the long handle at eight or nine. Inevitably this would have a negative effect on his bowling as allrounders such as Miller had discovered.

A two-Test trip to Australia was one to forget for all concerned, mired as it was in questionable behaviour followed by a Mankading, a handled ball 'incident' and an all-round display that just wasn't cricket. Of equal concern for Pakistan was the failure to beat a team still shorn of its Packer players despite Sarfraz's famously miraculous spell at Melbourne, one of the greatest in Test history. The tale has been perfectly told by Rob Bagchi in *Supreme Bowling*. With Australia closing in on victory Sarfraz took seven wickets in 30 balls and won the match. The fact that it was done by swing with a worn ball created a legend of reverse swing despite Sarfraz's denials. Overhead conditions suited conventional movement and why would Sarfraz deny it anyway? Well he was Sarfraz, always mischievous and sometimes downright maddening. In the second match Imran and Sarfraz managed 5-382 where Alan Hurst took 9-155 against better batsmen. Imran blamed Mushtaq's defensive mindset and injuries amongst the thin bowling attack. Already tired, both opening bowlers sent down 50 eight-ball overs. Still, this was inconsistent Pakistan *in excelsis*.

After successful English summers for their respective counties both Imran and Sarfraz were, with a two-month rest, ready to get back onto the Test treadmill in India. The older partner found, however, that his services were not required. On form he was an obvious choice to partner Imran but new captain Asif 'felt he could not handle him'. Perhaps he had been taken in by Gavaskar's kidology when the Indian said 'Imran and their other bowlers are a different class to our guys.' Shorn of his opening partner and plagued by a rib muscle injury Imran's form fell back over the 2-0 defeat. When a recall for Sarfraz was suggested mid-series Asif, now seeking calm through tranquilisers, was unimpressed:

> 'Never, never, never. It was made clear to me that our government expected there to be no incidents of any kind while we were in India. These were two countries that had been at war, remember, and our even going there was a huge event. Under the circumstances Sarfraz was literally the last man I would have sent for.'

Another leading player commented, 'The guy was a time bomb'. Whether it was on- or off-the-field behaviour that was most feared is unclear. Whether or not Asif's intransigence, justified or not, cost Pakistan the series is also unclear but if Sarfraz had bowled to his best form the result would have been much closer.

Although still his side's most potent threat, Imran was comfortably displaced by Kapil Dev as the pride of Asia. Joyous celebrations had greeted Pakistan's victory in 1978 but vicious recriminations were now the order of the day. The most significant failing had been the inability of experienced men such as Zaheer and Majid to cope with the pressure but the injury to Imran, loss of form of Abdul Qadir and absence of Sarfraz were a toxic triad. A press that had revelled in the image of thoroughly modern men performing on and off the field the previous year now turned on the wining and womanising that had allegedly weakened Imran's muscles.

With Asif now replaced by Miandad and Sarfraz back in favour Australia, now with the Packer heavyweights, were beaten by deep batting and Iqbal Qasim. A change of heart in pitch preparation had overtaken Pakistan and it did little for the quick bowlers. The reasoning was that Australia and then West Indies could probably overpower Pakistan on fast or bouncy wickets but if spin were in the ascendant then Iqbal, and maybe Abdul Qadir, would hold the key as both sets of pace bowlers were left toiling in the heat. It worked against Lillee (who vowed never to return) but not against West Indies whose combination of Croft, Garner, Malcolm Marshall and Sylvester Clarke made light of the unsuitable pitches as the ball dominated the bat (except for that of Viv Richards) in all four Tests. Sarfraz barely featured and Imran struggled, but at least they could relish the prospect of Australian pitches in the reverse series. Unfortunately so could Lillee, having developed a rare old antipathy to Pakistan's cricketers who were now in some disarray. Imran recalled that 'it was clear that disaster lay ahead.' The spirit and togetherness of a team on the rise had been replaced by the in-fighting and anger of a team in decline.

For Sarfraz, now aged 33 and with just six wickets in his last six Tests, this was the last-chance saloon only 20 months on from his greatest day. As an opening attack Imran and Sarfraz were now broken, as the older man's form and fitness led to a variety of alternatives being tried. Despite the team's travails and his injury problems Imran's star continued to rise. Increasingly he was seen as captain in waiting; with tactical skill, experience and a proven ability to lead from the front with both ball and bat (he had scored his maiden Test century against West Indies) his time had to come especially when Richards referred to him as 'the Great Khan'.

Before the Australia series began the reverse swingers had been dealt an unwitting trump card by the TCCB's edict standardising the ball for all first-class cricket. The thicker seam enhanced the distance between the rough and smooth side and thus the amount of late swing that could be generated. Christopher Sandford described the new seam as acting like a rudder.

When Pakistan took the field at Perth for the first Test of the 1981-82 series it soon became apparent that swing, reverse or otherwise, would not play a part. In fact the only memorable swing was that of Miandad's bat as Lillee offered to punch his lights out. Imran's predictions of disaster seemed imminent but for the first time in almost two years Imran and Sarfraz shared the new ball and looked like an opening pair worthy of serious respect on a predictably fast and bouncy wicket. However when Lillee and Terry Alderman got to work the Pakistan effort was made to look pedestrian – the pair took 9-54. Australia won the second Test equally easily on a slower pitch and again the Australian opening bowlers outbowled their counterparts, albeit against spineless batting. Greg Chappell had few problems against anyone.

The third Test was a complete reversal as Imran and Sarfraz shared 10 wickets on a spin-friendly surface with Iqbal Qasim in the ascendant. By contrast Lillee's figures were 0-104. On the face of it the 2-1 scoreline wasn't disastrous but behind the scenes discipline had completely collapsed and Imran's verdict was that 'we had been shown up as a team of limited resources under conditions that did not favour us.' For Imran there was the kudos of being voted man of the series; his overall figures were better than those of Lillee but the Australian's 15-228 in the two games Australia won effectively sealed the series. Sarfraz was moderately successful, at least enough to have saved a Test career that was close to ending.

After a final showdown between Miandad and Zaheer it became clear that neither would play under the other's captaincy. Into the breach came captain Khan to pour oil on troubled waters and lead by example. That was certainly the plan of the PCCB. Imran had understandable reservations, he had been around long enough to realise the pressure of captaining any leading Test side and the hatred, as well as adulation, it could bring. On the other hand, he could hardly be more divisive than his predecessor and he could insist on having an active role in team selection. The immediate beneficiaries of this stipulation were his long-standing new-ball partner and the out-of-form and favour Abdul Qadir.

The next series should have been perfect for Sarfraz with his years of experience gained at Northampton but injury wrecked his final tour of England. In his only Test, the second, he removed both openers but his lack of fitness betrayed him. However Pakistan levelled the series, the first match having been lost despite Imran's 7-52 in the first innings and 87 runs. Even eight more wickets and 113 runs couldn't steer his side over the winning line in the final Test, two contentious umpiring decisions being the difference between the two teams. Personal triumph was mixed with disappointment over the team effort. For Sarfraz the sands of time were running out.

Those sands fell quickly as he missed the next series in which Pakistan whitewashed Australia. Imran and Qadir, posing as forerunners of Glenn McGrath and Warne, did the most damage with Zaheer finding his best form. It was a perfect preparation for a six-Test series at home to India. Imran knew that his future would rest on this series. There was also the little matter of Kapil Dev who had eclipsed an injured Imran three years earlier. Sarfraz, now fully fit, was aware that his place was far from secure and that he was probably playing in his last major series.

The second Test of the 1982-83 series at Karachi was the crowning of Imran, grown to a world beater. 'He changed ends [at my suggestion] and started bowling into the wind, at which point he generated some staggering movement' recalls Sarfraz who thought it the most memorable spell of fast bowling and extravagant exhibition of reverse swing he had ever seen. His 8-60 was a masterpiece; Arun Lal was one of the unfortunate batsmen.

> "The wicket was a placid one, good for making runs. But Imran bowled this phenomenal spell and erased our top order. There was a bit of cross-breeze, and once the shine was off the ball, Imran got into business. We were completely caught unawares by the huge amount of swing that he managed to get – both ways. We asked ourselves how he could do that when our own bowlers, including Kapil Dev, who was known for swinging it, couldn't.

Imran himself was more popular for bowling fast, digging it in short and hitting the ribcage – more of a tearaway than a swinger. But in this game he got it to swing both ways with the new ball, and then got reverse swing too, which we didn't even know existed.

The one wicket that summarises his efforts was that of Viswanath, who shouldered arms to an off-side delivery; the ball suddenly swung back in, a couple of feet almost, and disturbed his off stump. He didn't know what was happening; no one did. It was like a secret weapon that was unleashed, and we couldn't defend ourselves."

Pakistan won the next two Tests as a hitherto quiet Sarfraz rose to his captain's challenge. At Faisalabad Imran collected another 11-wicket haul and Sarfraz chipped in with five of his own and then at Hyderabad the pair shared 15-221 after Pakistan had declared on 581-3. The series was won with two to play and the two men bottomed out, Imran with a shin problem that was later diagnosed as a fracture – he didn't bowl again in Test cricket for 32 months. By the time Imran returned, Sarfraz had left the Test scene after taking 14 wickets in three matches in a series win over England, also recording a Test-best 90 in his final game. Contrarian to the end.

Imran's performances over the India series had almost defied belief and must rank amongst the greatest ever for a full series. Although the pitches were dripping with runs to the degree that Zaheer, Miandad and Mudassar Nazar scored over 2000 of them at an average of 125 (Imran's paltry 247 was played at 62 apiece), Imran took 40 wickets at under 14 each. The fact that Gavaskar was supported by, amongst others, Vengsarkar, Gundappa Viswanath, Mohinder Armanarth and Kapil Dev only adds further lustre to a wondrous record, the fact that the shin injury had made itself known on the second day of the second Test make the figures barely credible and they represent the absolute pinnacle of Imran's Test career, as they would in any career of any bowler ever to play the game.

The miracle was that the shin bone didn't shatter under the strain of 56 overs in the third Test or his 'fastest ever spell' of 5-3 in a handful of overs in the fourth. True enough Imran had the hex over India by the middle of the series if not before but he stuck to his belief that 'if you have your enemy down then you never let him up.' It was somehow typical of Sarfraz that while Imran was sending great rockets of achievement into the sky he was busy supporting at ground level with little sparklers of his own. His 19 wickets represented nearly half of those not taken by Imran. This was to be their last series together as an opening pair and they went out in style. Pace, guile, intimidation and, above all, swing of both the old ball and the new had completely undermined one of the strongest batting teams in the world. As in 1978 they had reserved their best for their most significant opponent on their own grounds. Somehow this was also typical of both men. Equally typical was that their other best displays were in Australia where antipathy and suspicion towards Pakistan cricket was rife throughout their careers.

As a pair of bowlers Imran and Sarfraz could hardly have been more contrasting although that is something that many of the great opening pairs seem to have in common from Gregory and McDonald through Trueman and Statham to Ambrose and Walsh. Imran worked incessantly, even obsessively, on every aspect of his game. Sarfraz got fit by bowling and his obsession was the cricket ball. Imran became a genuine fast bowler, Sarfraz had 'the demeanor of a genuine quick bowler'. Geoff Boycott admired Imran as 'a thinking man who was very clear about what he was doing' while Sarfraz often seemed unclear about what he was doing, thinking or saying. Imran called him 'outspoken and unconventional' and then, later, after some public spats 'selfish'. Osman Samiuddin thought his various theories on corruption left him 'sounding like a paranoid parody of himself.' Calling Ian Botham 'a drug-crazed opium pusher' hardly adds credence to Sarfraz's reliability even if it is an arresting and rather disturbing image. But with a ball in his hands he was no fool.

> 'I did not boast of any lethal weapon in my armoury. I tried to bowl according to the particular batsman's strengths and weaknesses. For instance, Sunil Gavaskar was very good at playing inswing but not that comfortable with outswing.'

These are not the words of someone who hasn't applied himself to the game and used his abilities, both mental and physical.

On often unresponsive wickets he collected 177 victims in 55 Tests. When one considers the records of his supposed predecessors Asif Masood (38 wickets in 16 Tests) and Saleem Altaf (46 in 21) it is clear that he was a major figure of his time for his country.

His reputation has certainly suffered by his proximity to Imran (362 in 88) as would most bowlers'. Perhaps this is the reason that the pair are not often mentioned when great partnerships are discussed; there was too great a gulf in ability. In their first couple of years together there was no huge disparity but after that Sarfraz was strictly the foil, except for that memorable spell at Sydney. Not that Imran didn't appreciate the importance of his support and what he had learnt from him, but it could never be considered a partnership of equals. But a partnership it was, over more than a decade, despite frequent interruptions for injury and absence. It was also a partnership that, allied with great batting, drove Pakistan into a position of prominence in world cricket that they had never occupied before. It also destroyed the idea that Asia cannot produce fast bowlers but thankfully didn't insist that Asia must produce only fast bowlers.

It's a shame that the court cases, accusations and bitter words of the last 30 years have somewhat masked the achievements of Sarfraz and his partnership with Imran. Also there is the fact that Imran's most famous hour of many was to come as late as 1992 when he stepped out of retirement to steer his country to World Cup victory. It's also a shame that Sarfraz is remembered more for what he invented than what he did – Troy Cooley once claimed that reverse swing is more complicated than rocket science – but the simple fact remains that it requires a very good bowler to use it effectively. Almost despite himself Sarfraz was a very good bowler and his partnership with Imran was central to the emergence of Pakistan in world cricket.

Imran and Sarfraz

Results

	Total	Won	Drawn	Lost
Imran	88	26	45	17
Sarfraz	55	16	31	8
Imran and Sarfraz	35	13	17	5

Test Bowling Overall

	Mat	Balls	Runs	Wkts	Ave	SR	ER	5W1/10WM
Imran	88	15519	8258	362	22.81	53.7	2.54	23/6
Sarfraz	55	24353	5978	177	32.75	78.8	2.49	4/1

Test Bowling Together

	Mat	Balls	Runs	Wkts	Ave	SR	ER	5W1/10WM
Imran	35	8953	3904	155	25.18	57.7	2.61	9/3
Sarfraz	35	8976	3771	120	31.42	74.8	2.52	2/1

Test Bowling Apart

	Mat	Balls	Runs	Wkts	Ave	SR	ER	5W1/10WM
Imran	53	10505	4354	207	21.03	50.7	2.48	14/3
Sarfraz	20	4975	2207	57	38.72	87.3	2.15	2/0

Best Series Together - India 1982

	Mat	Balls	Runs	Wkts	Ave	SR	ER	5W1/10WM
Imran	6	1339	558	40	13.95	33.4	2.50	4/2
Sarfraz	6	1447	633	19	33.31	76.1	2.62	0/0

Best Test Figures - Innings/Match

Imran (with Sarfraz)	8-60 vs India, Karachi – 1982
Imran (with Sarfraz)	12-165 vs Australia, Sydney – 1977
Imran (without Sarfraz)	8-58 vs Sri Lanka, Lahore – 1982
Imran (without Sarfraz)	14-116 vs Sri Lanka, Lahore – 1982
Sarfraz (with Imran)	9-86 vs Australia, Melbourne – 1979
Sarfraz (with Imran)	11-125 vs Australia, Melbourne – 1979
Sarfraz (without Imran)	6-89 vs West Indies, Lahore – 1975
Sarfraz (without Imran)	8-109 vs Australia, Sydney – 1973

YouTube Bowling Highlights

Search Phrases (sic)
Sarfraz Nawaz 9/86 against Australia in 1978 Post Interview Also Included
Rare Imran Khan Gold 8/60 vs. India
England 1st Inning vs Pakistan 2nd Test, Lords 1982

End of Century

As Test cricket recovered its equanimity after the Packer hiatus it seemed inevitable that speed would be both the draw card and the recipe for success. West Indies and Australia were reunited with the men who had served Packer so well and seemed likely to resume their position at the top of the tree. For West Indies it came to pass but Australia found the return much more complex and it took master builder Allan Border almost a decade to return his country to the position to which she believed herself entitled.

The international game was becoming more complex. The growth of the one-day formula was now becoming viral and this, together with the growing number and competitiveness of Test-playing countries, made lengthy series more of a rarity. Three-match meetings replaced five with the necessity of an accompanying one-day contest and in England two sides became a regular fixture in a shared summer.

Sri Lanka had earned the right to compete as equals and took to the challenge with remarkable speed, South Africa emerged from isolation and India and Pakistan became complete sides with a full complement of batting and bowling skills. For the traditional 'big boys' there was no longer an easy series to blood new players; even the traditional minnows, New Zealand, had proved themselves capable of beating all three of the heavyweights.

The final 15 years of the 20th century may have been dominated by fast or fast-medium bowling but it was also significant for the emergence of some of the greatest spinners the game has ever seen; Pakistan being a case in point. The period is best remembered for Imran Khan and his two successors, Wasim Akram and Waqar Younis, but the spin options were outstanding. First Abdul Qadir, then Mushtaq Ahmed and finally Saqlain Mushtaq. While Wasim and Waqar remained the big wicket takers there was little respite when they rested or found a pitch they couldn't exploit.

Australia had a one-man insurance policy for any fast-bowling shortcomings from 1992 onwards. A succession of excellent quick bowlers had filled the gap between Dennis Lillee and Glenn McGrath but remain largely overlooked precisely because history says they filled a gap in an often beatable side. Craig McDermott, Merv Hughes, Terry Alderman, Bruce Reid and Geoff Lawson deserve more. Once McGrath arrived to join Shane Warne and, crucially a generation of top-class batsmen and close fielders, Australia were in a position to dominate. McGrath and Warne formed the most potent combination Test cricket has ever seen.

West Indies cheerfully continued to rely on speed. As the 'Babylon generation' moved into retirement it was left to Curtly **Ambrose** and Courtney **Walsh** to continue the tradition. How much more effective would they have been with a Mushtaq Ahmed or Anil Kumble in support? Certainly without their phenomenal fitness records as well as their talent, West Indies' cricket would have sunk much sooner than it did. Kumble himself was more than just a support for his country; he was the main attacking weapon with Javagal Srinath, Venkatash Prasad and Kapil Dev backing him up. India had moved into the modern age with quick bowling but her ability to produce great spin bowlers could hardly be ignored.

South Africa and England were more old school. Allan **Donald** led a pace-based attack and with the advent of Shaun **Pollock** found a partner that could match any in the world. England were less fortunate, only Devon Malcolm was genuinely fast but he lacked the consistency of a Walsh or Wasim. For the rest there were great days for Angus Fraser or Darren Gough but never the feeling that they were from the top draw of Fred Trueman or John Snow. The distrust of spin didn't help the balance of the side.

New boys Sri Lanka were hardly likely to produce a fast-bowling dynasty in their early years but Chaminda Vaas was a fine practitioner. The real reliance was on Muttiah Muralitharan who was, well, just Murali.

Wasim

and

Waqar

Wasim Akram

The technique itself was actually one of cricket's great wonders, defying all the usual injunctions of coaches to perfect a balanced run of gathering speed and a smooth action of seamless grace. After a breakneck sprint, Akram barrelled through the crease, front foot pointing down the pitch, back foot toward the sightscreen, arm a blur. That he was able to repeat this almost 41,000 times in international cricket beggars belief. – Gideon Haigh

Waqar Younis

On a roll, Waqar, sprinting in, was a thrilling sight, often an inevitability about the outcome, as another batsman, knowing full well what was coming but powerless to respond, found his toes crushed or his leg stump plucked from the ground by a yorker that had sped in a straight line all but the last few yards, when it dipped sharply in. Waqar, at such times, was brutal. – Mike Selvey

Pakistan cricket has been well served over the last few years by two outstanding histories – Peter Oborne's *Wounded Tiger* and Osman Samiuddin's *The Unquiet Ones*. The years between 1989 and 2002, which encompass the often glorious and sometimes ignominious years of the joint enterprise of Wasim Akram and Waqar Younis, make for particularly fascinating reading.

It is hardly surprising that three themes act as a backdrop to the Pakistan drama played out on cricket fields all over the world. Firstly there is the dressing-room discord and the 'hardest-job-in-the-world' narrative of the life of the Pakistan captain and his warring troops. Then there is ball tampering and the 'cheating' of Wasim and Waqar, especially during the 1992 tour of England. Finally the match-fixing allegations which came to their ugly told-you-so climax with that ludicrous no-ball from Mohammad Amir at Lord's in 2010. Shadowing all this there is the sometimes sub-racist commentary from the media outside Pakistan, led by the British tabloid press.

Oborne has given an excellent flavour of the tone of 1992 when the uppity tourists were adding injury to insult by being really very good at cricket. The British public had already been prepared by the vitriol aimed at Pakistan and her players by Ian Botham and Mike Gatting amongst many others. 'Hordes' of Pakistan supporters bent on violent confrontation had been noted at Edgbaston in 1987 most of whom, presumably, would have flunked Norman Tebbit's 1990 'cricket test'.

The 1992 team was a 'brat pack' led by 'cricket's Colonel Gaddafi', a wild man drawn from an ambush on the Khyber Pass. Mike Langley of the *Daily Mirror* was joined by Simon Heffer's questioning of Javed Miandad's 'ethical deficiencies' making him 'the last man to captain his country, even if it is only Pakistan.' Many England players bought into this shabby bigotry behind closed doors and when the room was aired once they had been swung to defeat England coach, Micky Stewart, was happy to pour innuendo into the mix without ever being precise enough to have to defend himself in court. His views at that time were conspicuously absent when his biography appeared in 2012. Later still Allan Lamb sought to top up his pension pot with some repetition of the ball-tampering tales but by this time reverse swing was accepted and coaches and fast bowlers around the world were finding out that the skill was possible but very, very difficult to acquire.

Yes, Pakistan were clearly cheats from the third world. In their own country they could rely on biased umpiring even though Imran Khan had led a campaign for neutral umpires for 15 years. Away from home their alleged dark arts and frenetic manipulation took cricket to a new low from Melbourne to

Manchester and all points between. Fortunately the dust has largely settled on this period, if not Pakistan cricket in general which is still perceived as something vaguely suspicious. The two brilliant and innovative fast bowlers of the period stand tall as two of the finest exponents of their art ever seen. Truckloads of bowlers have been trying to imitate but none have ever been better.

The second indictment of the period is that the Pakistan sides were often an ill-disciplined rabble prone to in-fighting and back-stabbing. It's a bit harder to find a defence against this charge although only one team suffered and that was the culprits themselves. It was all somehow as predictable as the implosion of post-Tito Yugoslavia. Once the charismatic strong man who had done so much for his country was gone then there was an inevitability that post-Imran Pakistan would be ungovernable. And so it proved. Captains came and went, being undermined by vice-captains, fellow players, politicians, members of the cricketing elite and poor performances on the field. The year of 1994 had ended with a historic series win over Australia but in 1995 no less than five captains were tried and it was a calendar year of thumping defeats in virtually all the important games. There was improvement thereafter; inevitably with a team that boasted the talents of Wasim, Waqar, Mushtaq Ahmed, Saeed Anwar, Saqlain Mushtaq and Inzamam-ul-Haq; but there was always the danger of a further descent into anarchy.

The final charge, and by some degree the most serious, was that of match fixing. There was no great surprise amongst journalists or players when rumours began to surface about a pair of one-day internationals against South Africa early in 1995. Even Pakistan's most avid supporter will know that the players are under greater pressure, and therefore greater temptation, than any others in the world. The prevalence of illegal bookmakers and the relatively poor pay received by national team members made them obvious targets for insidious approaches. Everybody knew these facts so it only needed an inexplicably bad performance, a few dropped catches or an unexplained injury to set tongues wagging. Salim Malik achieved that in bucketloads when he twice elected to field at Cape Town and Johannesburg in conditions where batting first was a given. Soon afterwards three Australian players accused Malik of offering them bribes. This was just the beginning.

In fact it was another beginning. Rumours had never been very far away including fixing the toss in 1980 and throwing the World Cup semi-final in 1987. When Pakistan beat Australia by one wicket at Karachi in 1994 the final act was a missed stumping and four byes. Nobody suggested for one minute that

Ian Healy deliberately fluffed it – but if it had been Moin Khan or Nayan Mongia tongues would certainly have wagged.

Salim Malik was eventually cleared for lack of evidence (not the same as proclaiming his innocence) but rumours were constantly circulating, one of which had Wasim feigning injury in the 1996 World Cup, until the Pakistan Cricket Board (PCB) under Majid Khan decided that the only way to clear the air and wipe the slate was to have a full judicial inquiry after an administrative hearing found that Wasim, Malik and Ijaz Ahmed had been involved in match-fixing. A commission under Justice Malik Qayyum was to be the answer. The report was finally published in May 2000 by which time the PCB was under new management appointed by the new government of Pervez Musharraf – nobody could say that cricket wasn't of national importance in Pakistan. Also Hansie Cronje had confessed to match-fixing, in India Kapil Dev and Mohammad Azharrudin were under investigation and Shane Warne and Mark Waugh had admitted to selling information to a bookmaker. Qayyam's report found only Malik and Ata-ur Rehman guilty of match-fixing but pointed accusing fingers at all the leading Pakistan players of the decade for turning blind eyes, being economical with the truth, not being above suspicion, developing 'partial amnesia' and bringing the game into disrepute. In Oborne's summary it was 'too heartbreaking for words.'

Sadly the above is the backdrop to the Test careers of two of the greatest fast bowlers to grace the game and certainly one of its most potent combinations. They didn't owe their reputations and achievements to either match fixing or ball tampering, rather they had to operate despite constant accusations from both outside and within and clearly there was infrequent team unity and very often little or no unity between the two bowlers themselves. If anything this makes their individual and combined achievements all the more impressive.

Wasim Akram came to cricket through those three old mediums, a fanatical parent (in his case grandparent), an inspired coach (Khalid Mahmood) and hero worship of players in the national side (in his case Zaheer Abbas and Imran Khan). India's 1983 World Cup win was another incentive – the one-day game was as quick and glamorous as Imran and if India could win it then so might Pakistan. A cricket obsessive by 16, Wasim made his international debut at 18, a beneficiary of good fortune in being spotted by the right people, especially Javed Miandad. Pakistan has never been slow in promoting a promising player quickly, a policy that has been the making of some and the breaking of others. Wasim had the backing of Miandad so with one one-day international under his belt he was selected for a tour of New Zealand in December 1984. Ten wickets in the final game at Dunedin was almost enough to win the game and level the series, but not quite. If Test cricket seemed relatively easy at this point the next few years were to show that there was still plenty to learn. But Wasim was a learner and enjoyed the delights of beating India away over five Tests in early 1987 and then repeating the trick in England a few months later. With his mentor Imran at his shoulder he was growing from a fine prospect into a fully-fledged and much-respected international cricketer.

Behind the improvement in this gauche and star-struck teenager was experience, hard work and the guidance of Imran. He and Mudassar Nazar spent hours in the nets helping Wasim develop and perfect the art of reverse swing, then during matches Imran would field at mid-off to offer further guidance. Next up was the yorker, followed by the reverse-swinging yorker and finally a re-working of the run-up completed the process.

England were beaten again at home in the same year and then it was time to face West Indies, unbeaten in their previous 14 series. But for an injury to Imran, Pakistan would have won the series 2-0 but in his absence West Indies scrambled to victory in the final game to square things and would then remain unbeaten for another 14 series. With this being their first Test defeat in nearly two years nobody could argue that Pakistan were not at, or very near, the top of the tree and their reputation as flaky and unpredictable needed redrafting. They would soon be augmented by a new and very fast bowler for the home series against India.

All four games were drawn on dreary wickets and new-boy Waqar missed two games with a back injury but his potential was as obvious as that of another debutant on the other side, Sachin Tendulkar. Waqar's elevation into the national side had been as rapid as that of Wasim and was again largely the doing of Imran. At 17 Waqar was already bowling very fast (although it is possible he was, in fact, older than his 'official' age) but was too wayward to make any great progress. However, within a year both his pace and control were up and Imran insisted he should join the national one-day side in Sharjah. It became apparent that his pace was real enough to have Desmond Haynes dodging on a dead wicket and his reputation as one-to-watch grew when Qamar Ahmed's reports appeared in the *Times* and on the BBC:

> 'I was amazed by Waqar's fluency and pace. I'd never heard of him before, and yet here he was, a mere teenager, frightening the life out of the West Indian

batting. I wrote in my report that Waqar was the fastest bowler on either side.'

By 1990, with Imran's pace dropping and Wasim showing against Australia that he was ready to lead the attack, there were was a nice big Waqar-sized hole in the Pakistan team as an opening bowler. For the first time in Test history batsmen would consistently face a left-right combination at high pace. The West Indian pace battery had offered variety in the skiddiness of Marshall, the height of Garner and Ambrose, the width of Croft and the pace of Holding, but not one left-armer. With the angles of attack mixed up, genuine speed and the ability to swing the ball both ways it was clear that once Waqar had added more control to his pace this would be a formidable pairing for many years to come.

'He had such a positive attitude towards bowling, and was greedy for wickets. I've never seen anyone improve as quickly; in a short space of time he had grasped what it had taken me three years to learn.'

Wasim was the number one but was impressed by his rival's progress. For both men a spell on the county circuit would add to their rapidly expanding repertoire, Lancashire and Surrey being the beneficiaries. Wasim had been a regular match-winner since 1988 even though injuries and international commitments dogged his red-rose career. In 1991 Waqar was the leading bowler in England by a country mile, and this after two three-match Test series in which he had collected no less than 45 wickets to Wasim's 31.

Although Pakistan's batting hadn't looked too strong, in 1990 New Zealand were brushed aside and once again a series with West Indies was drawn. Both series were accompanied by the inevitable ball-tampering mutterings without any concrete or actual proof of any kind beyond the swing that Wasim and Waqar were finding. What was perhaps most interesting about the new pair was the change of tack from speed underpinned by short-pitch bowling, as championed by Australia and then West Indies, to the Pakistan preference of full lengths and swing.

Imran had always been prepared to trade bouncer for bouncer and his inheritors would do the same if the pitch merited it but the reality was that few did, especially in Asia. Great fast bowlers adapt to the 22 yards of turf in front of them and that turf was likely to be very different in Faisalabad, Johannesburg or Headingley. Full, fast bowling is fraught with danger as the margin for error is so small – a few inches either way and it is a half-volley or a full toss and a likely boundary ball to a top-class batsman. With one-day cricket increasingly gaining ground on the five-day match, economy was becoming ever more essential. At the end of 1991 Waqar was rated number two in the world and Wasim number four and 1992 promised to be one to remember with the World Cup in Australia and New Zealand followed by a tour of England.

The great Imran-led triumph of 1992 has been well documented as has how his heir apparent castled England in the final at Melbourne. Pakistan had looked anything but winners earlier in the tournament and had lost Waqar to a back injury before a ball was bowled in anger but under inspired leadership fought their way back into the tournament and matched India's achievement of 1983.

As World Cup winners the reputation of Pakistan had risen but an away series against England was a different discipline altogether. Wasim had already twice experienced England and disliked what he found. The Rana/Gatting dust-up and the petulance of Chris Broad were hardly likely to endear and the spiteful and childish mother-in-law comments by Botham and the general cold-shouldering by many English players added a frisson. Waqar had recovered from injury and a full five-match series would certainly allow a settling of scores and a chance to see if Wasim and Waqar could reproduce their county form under Test conditions.

There was something for everyone. Contentious umpiring and a response described as 'monstrous' in the third Test. A narrow victory for Pakistan at Lord's courtesy of valiant batting by Wasim and Waqar, a comfortable win for England at Headingley engineered by a Graham Gooch masterpiece and then, with the series tied, the denouement at the Oval.

All summer it had seemed that Pakistan's twin strike bowlers backed by the irrepressible Mushtaq might run through England and in the final Test they did. Wasim with 6-67 in the first innings matched by Waqar's even more impressive 5-52 in the second was more than enough. England were brushed aside by 10 wickets. The two shared 43 wickets and the player-of-the-series award. Ball tampering had, inevitably, been raised but the most significant facts went largely unnoticed by a tabloid press that was hardly known for investigative journalism. Three of the Tests were played on dry wickets and Pakistan were lucky with the toss for choice of balls. The Reader suited reverse swing, the Duke conventional swing. Geoffrey Boycott was one who saw the reality behind the summer: 'Wasim and Waqar could bowl our lot out with an orange, because they are great bowlers.' This was the version later adopted by those closest to the action. Alec Stewart was England's most successful batsman of the summer and loved the challenge:

> 'It takes huge talent to master reverse swing and they were whizzbang bowlers…They always attacked with fielders close to the bat, so the gaps were there. We folded like a pack of cards against them regularly, but that was due to wonderful bowling, not bad batting. [At Old Trafford] They bowled at the speed of light, with short-pitched bowling that really tested your reflexes and physical mettle. This was proper Test cricket.'

Bit by bit they were conquering the world in Test cricket having already ascended to the peak in the limited-over game. West Indies and Australia stood between Pakistan and their ambition to top the rankings in both forms of the game.

Of the three charges thrown at Pakistan it was now in-fighting that took over from alleged ball-tampering as the prime destructive element with Miandad having taken over the captaincy from Imran. To say this was a hard act to follow would hardly do it justice and Miandad was scarcely a graduate of the Brearley/Border University of man-management and team-building. As long as the team were winning and Miandad was scoring runs things should have chugged along nicely as they had done in England but within six months the poisoned chalice had passed to Wasim.

A series of poor performances, blamed by Wasim on complacency, led to the sacking of Miandad. Wasim's appointment to the number-one job brought no great turnaround in results, and resentment at his methods added to an unsubstantiated marijuana sting in the West Indies led to further changes. Waqar had been mixing masses of wickets (97 wickets in 14 Tests since the end of the England series) with plotting for the captaincy. Wasim (75 in 13) was almost as prolific while being isolated by the pressures on his position. Despite the efforts of the two premier fast bowlers Pakistan had sunk from challenging for the position of world's best team to disorganised also-rans.

There were the occasional bright spots and these tended to coincide with the form of the opening bowlers. The first Test against Australia at Karachi in 1994 was a case in point. On a flat wicket Waqar and Wasim took 15 wickets against the best batting side in the world, including a trademark obliteration with an old ball which reduced Australia from 171-2, and a winning position, to 232 all out. The Pakistan batsman, inspired by this performance, showed great discipline to chase down 315 and win by one wicket in one of the greatest finishes in all Tests. By the third game both Wasim and Waqar were out injured and only some obdurate batting enabled Pakistan to hold their hard-won advantage. New captain Salim Malik was at the forefront of this resistance but amid match-fixing allegations his tenure was short and did nothing to halt the slide, neither did the efforts of Moin Khan or Ramiz Raja so the call went out to Wasim, once again.

Equally worrying was the form and fitness of Waqar. After five years of almost uninterrupted success Waqar had accumulated 150 Test wickets quicker than anyone barring SF Barnes, but 1995 was more than just a reality check. Back problems curtailed appearances and his speed was down and when he finally rejoined the team Wasim had started to show the first signs of a shoulder problem that would dog him for two years. With the pressure of a 12-month cricket calendar and the importance of the pair to the team there was little opportunity for rest or recuperation for either man.

In retrospect it is almost inevitable that injury would strike. Both men were on a treadmill of quick bowling and neither was inclined to save himself either in international or county cricket. Paul Allott, on seeing Waqar's run-up in an early appearance for Surrey, joked that county cricket would soon curb his enthusiasm. It never did. Waqar's action, combined with a naturally powerful physique, was always going to put pressure on his back, something he recognised and worked to prevent early in his career. Wasim was described by Imran as 'not a naturally fit person' and like Waqar he took steps to improve his all-round strength. However his action put great stress on his groin and lower abdomen while his reliance on arm speed to generate pace and swing was a huge strain on his shoulder. The fact that both men were equally effective with new and old balls meant that their workload was always likely to be heavy. There was no stage in the opposition innings where they could hide and recuperate, except for the occasional spinning pitch they were always the go-to men.

Injury and fast bowling inevitably go hand in hand. The perfect approach and action are never guarantees against physical damage which can take so may forms. Ankle, shin, knee, groin, hip, shoulder and most other body parts take a fearful battering in an attempt to project a ball at upwards of 90 mph. Some bowlers such as Fred Truemen and Courtney Walsh seem to have been born with a physique that kept injury to a minimum. Others such as Dennis Lillee and Malcolm Marshall might have disappeared into the Shane Bond category of 'what might have been' without good fortune, expert help and remarkable self-discipline.

Wasim chose, like Imran before him, to try and bowl through his injury. These were dark days for Pakistan cricket. The occasional bright performances were masked by an overall malaise. Ijaz Ahmed or Aamer Sohail could play brilliantly one day and then poorly for a month. Wasim and Waqar were struggling with both form and fitness and the addition of an inadequate slip cordon made their task all the harder. Then came the 1996 World Cup and crashing out in the quarter final to, of all teams, India. Effigies were burnt and bricks were thrown, upheaval followed at the PCB but somehow Wasim survived as captain, quite possibly because nobody else wanted the job. Fortunately a tour of England beckoned and that was likely to bring out the best in a team that could only be helped by courtroom action involving Imran, Botham and Lamb. Continuous scrutiny of the ball by the umpires and racist abuse at Headingley spurred on a new-found will to win.

It wasn't the Wasim and Waqar *tour de force* of 1992, Mushtaq's bowling was the key element in the 2-0 win, but Waqar proved again that he was almost impossible to play when he got things right and even with an injured shoulder Wasim was more than a match for England's brittle batting. He had the pleasure of completing victory at the Oval with his 300th Test wicket. The most memorable passage of play was on the fourth evening when Pakistan's finest 'bombed' the English openers (and county team-mates) Atherton and Stewart for over an hour without success. The four men concerned were the last to leave the England dressing-room, honours shared and respect mutual.

Within months Pakistan had returned to a game of swapping captains willy-nilly and alternating fine performances with dreadful ones. Promising young players such as Saqlain Mushtaq and Azhar Mahmood bolstered the side, and Saeed Anwar and Inzamam could bat as well as anyone but bubbling in the background was the Qayyum inquiry and the realisation that it would not be a whitewash.

For Wasim and Waqar the lustre had gone. Only rarely did they both appear in the team both fully fit. Typical was a stifling series against Australia in 1999, surrendered meekly without Waqar and with Wasim seemingly neutered by the wickets of his youth that had first driven his search for reverse swing. If any game was typical of the period it was that against South Africa at Port Elizabeth in 1998. With the series level at 1-1 and South Africa sporting an attack of Allan Donald, Shaun Pollock and Fanie de Villiers, the PCB decided that Waqar and Shoaib Akhtar now needed the help of Wasim even though he was only half-fit. The chairman of selectors resigned, Waqar was inspired to a brilliant opening spell before Donald and de Villiers trumped his efforts and sealed the series. The presence of Wasim could still inspire Waqar – it was in his nature to prove who was top dog and Pakistan were a better team for it.

> 'We both have had long talks about how good we feel when we are bowling together. I feel more confident when Wasim is bowling at the other end, because I think we are the people that are going to take the wickets. If Wasim takes a wicket, then I think that I'm going to take one as well; if he takes two, then I think I'll take two.'

There is something not quite right here. This is the dull, diplomatic Waqar. What he *really* enjoyed was outbowling his partner. 'They compete against each other – there's always been a bit of rivalry, so they try to outdo each other.' Mark Waugh's version sounds more plausible. For Wasim, writing in 1998,

> 'It's a terrific boost to have another fast bowler firing away at the other end, especially when he is so different in style…Early on he just blasted out batsmen by sheer speed and reverse swing…When Waqar is in rhythm he can be unplayable, but if not he can get hammered. He relies on getting it just right after that surging, long run and if the timing is astray he can lose his accuracy.'

Mike Selvey has summed up their combined threat as well as anyone:

> 'They were chalk and cheese. One was tall, angular, whippy, left-arm, with a high action and a short silent pitter-patter run. The other was shorter in stature, right-arm, low, slingy, muscular action and a long, straight, pounding gallop of a run. Both were rapid, frighteningly so at times, and masters of reverse swing. They didn't even like each other very much. Yet their names were synonymous, forever linked together in the pantheon of fast-bowling giants.'

This compare-and-contrast approach is best expressed by Osman Samiuddin:

> 'Waqar Younis, opening partner, best friend, vice-captain, foe and rival, was a bomb waiting to go off; Akram, a sword slicing his way through with care and poise.'

Against his instincts Waqar was now heeding advice and relying more on subtlety than naked aggression as his bowling at Port Elizabeth had shown. With two stress fractures of the back behind him he was well aware that another could see the end of his career. The figures show that he had become a less effective bowler. The beginning of 1997 marks the halfway point in his career and up to that time he had taken 227 wickets in 44 Tests at an average of 21.3. Thereafter in 43 more games his numbers were down to 143 at 27. In the first of theses periods Wasim also took 227 wickets in the 40 games they played together while in the second it was just 21 matches together and Wasim managed just 72 wickets. When both fit they were still a menacing proposition for any batsman but such occasions were rare.

The glory days had not entirely disappeared. Winning the 1999 Asian Test championship and beating India was one, Wasim's 11-wicket match haul at Antigua in 2000 another, even if defeat ensued. A double-century against Zimbabwe was a reminder of the all-rounder that Wasim could have been without all the other pressures. But with the evident decline of Wasim and Waqar came a falling off of results and reputation. Beaten at home by England in 2000 when Moin Khan's delaying tactics in the dark were satisfyingly stymied, Pakistan were offered just two Tests in England the following year as a warm-up for an Ashes series. The old stagers gave it one more go and shared eight wickets, seven of them batsmen, in a series-levelling victory at Manchester where they 'bowled like men possessed.' For Wasim there couldn't have been a more fitting venue.

There were just two more games together, both against Bangladesh. In the second, at Dhaka, a hamstring injury saw Wasim leave the field for good in the fifth over of the match after which Waqar 'sliced through the card to take the last six wickets for seven runs in 29 balls.' It had been almost four years since he had last claimed five wickets in an innings. The position of Pakistan in world politics was, however, already in the process of being reinvented by the terrorist attacks in New York. Over the next decade this would transform how and where the national team would play cricket.

The legacy of Wasim and Waqar is not simple to estimate. Did the allegations of ball tampering that reached a crescendo in 1992 ever really go away? There seems little doubt that the ball was 'worked on' by every team. The definition of illegal was, and is, vague. Certainly Aqib Javed got caught by the cameras crossing the line. The real problem was that Wasim and Waqar could do tricks with the ball that were beyond mere mortals. Imran added fuel to the fire with a make spectacularly mistimed interview in which he admitted having used a bottle top while playing for Sussex. No grey areas there as Lamb and Botham were quick to point out before a war of words ensued and finished in court.

On the dry pitches of 1992 little help from outside was required. The ball roughed up naturally and it was maintaining the shine on one side that required the work and there was nothing new or shady in this. Furthermore Pakistan had plenty of practice in their own country. By and large the allegations came from one country and one team although New Zealand and West Indies were later to make their unhappiness quite clear.

As to the match fixing, it seems pretty clear that both men were surrounded by a culture of gambling that was bringing huge pressure into the dressing-rooms of a number of Test playing countries. Some big names fell for the bait and most, if not all, others have been reticent in talking about what they saw or heard. This was the indictment aimed at Wasim and Waqar by the Qayyum report. Yet even Wasim's greatest admirers were inclined to think that maybe he got off lightly. A journalist associate wrote:

> 'He is a decent guy at heart. He's not the kind of guy smart enough to initiate this by himself. After Imran left, he lost that figure of authority. He lost his moorings and he was fuelled by people around him into doing more and more.'

Somewhere in this is a presumption that Wasim was a lucky boy.

What really remains is in the statistics and the reverence and fondness with which their contemporaries speak about them. It is not just that they were great fast bowlers, they were artists. Wasim can comfortably lay claim to being the best left-arm quick bowler in the history of the game while Waqar, on his day and under the right conditions, might fairly be called the most unplayable bowler of them all. Mike Atherton mulled over how to deal with the fast, reverse-swinging yorker. His conclusion didn't get much further than keeping a low back-lift. Robin Smith's advice was 'reinforce your toe-caps'. The 1992 conclusion was 'we had to admit that Wasim and Waqar had proved too good. It was no disgrace to lose and we hadn't lost badly.'

This led almost inevitably from flattery to imitation. All over the world the genie was out of the bottle. Imran and Sarfraz Nawaz had been a formidable pair incorporating reverse swing into their methods in the 1980s but Wasim and Waqar had taken the art onto a higher plane. Sarfraz had never been quick enough to be as effective with this method and Imran probably lacked the pin-point accuracy of his pupils even if he could make up for it in other ways.

Coaches and fast bowlers had watched the 1992 World Cup final and then seen that the same could be produced to devastating effect in Tests. The principle was simple; rough side, smooth side, bowl full and the ball will swing towards the rough side. Adding to this was the correct seam position and preferably a somewhat slingy, front-on action. None of this was over-complex and with advanced technology it was simple enough to watch the masters at work. Great bowlers such as Allan Donald were soon studying the template and lesser men such as Darren Gough and Craig White found they were able to offer partial impersonations. But it wasn't a magical panacea. Just like short-pitch bowling it requires immense skill, even if the rules are apparently simple. A bouncer from Jeff Thomson or Frank Tyson was a challenge for any batsman but the same ball from a medium-fast trundler is a half-tracker destined for the boundary. Reverse swing requires high levels of skill that are possessed by very few, the fact that the two finest ever exponents spent much of their careers playing for the same side was quite some coincidence. In fact it was such a coincidence that it's barely credible. The influence of Imran and the willingness of the two men to combine and work together were crucial ingredients.

Maybe the legacy of this pair goes even deeper. They didn't make the bouncer redundant but it became *a* weapon rather than *the* weapon. Mark Taylor believed that Wasim could hit the same spot on the pitch and produce four different results, rather as Brian Lara could hit the same ball to four different boundary areas. Waqar was slightly more inclined to brute force but the precision of his length was key to his strike-rate. Both men could offer aggression and pace to match any West Indian but were less reliant on the short-pitch attack and as such have remained a solid influence on the Steyns and Johnsons of the 21st century.

Wasim and Waqar

Results

	Total	Won	Drawn	Lost
Wasim	104	41	36	27
Waqar	89	39	22	26
Wasim and Waqar	61	28	17	16

Test Bowling Overall

	Mat	Balls	Runs	Wkts	Ave	SR	ER	5W1/10WM
Wasim	104	22627	9779	414	23.62	54.6	2.59	25/5
Waqar	87	16224	8788	373	23.56	43.5	3.25	22/5

Test Bowling Together

	Mat	Balls	Runs	Wkts	Ave	SR	ER	5W1/10WM
Wasim	61	13877	6016	282	21.33	49.2	2.60	20/4
Waqar	61	11643	6351	277	22.92	42.0	3.27	17/3

Test Bowling Apart

	Mat	Balls	Runs	Wkts	Ave	SR	ER	5W1/10WM
Wasim	43	8750	3763	132	28.51	66.3	2.58	5/1
Waqar	26	4581	2437	96	25.39	47.7	3.19	5/2

Best Series Together - England 1992

	Mat	Balls	Runs	Wkts	Ave	SR	ER	5W1/10WM
Wasim	4	1013	462	21	22.00	48.2	2.73	2/0
Waqar	5	996	557	22	25.31	45.2	3.35	3/0

Best Test Figures - Innings/Match

Wasim (with Waqar)	7-119 vs New Zealand, Wellington – 1994
Wasim (with Waqar)	11-110 vs West Indies, St John's – 2000
Wasim (without Waqar)	6-91 vs West Indies, Faisalabad – 1986
Wasim (without Waqar)	10-128 vs New Zealand, Dundedin – 1985
Waqar (with Wasim)	7-86 vs New Zealand, Lahore – 1990
Waqar (with Wasim)	11-119 vs Sri Lanka, Kandy – 1994
Waqar (without Wasim)	7-76 vs New Zealand, Faisalabad – 1990
Waqar (without Wasim)	13-135 vs Zimbabwe, Karachi – 1993

YouTube Bowling Highlights

Search Phrases (sic)
Waqar Younis 5/91 & 2/40 Vs England 1992 Lords
Wasim Akram Superb 6/67 Vs England, Oval Test 1992
Wasim & Waqar Destroy Australia at Karachi (1st Test) 1994

Ambrose
and
Walsh

Curtly Ambrose

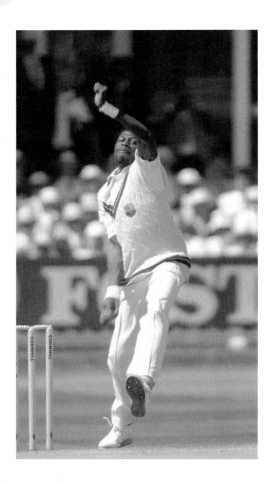

Quality bowlers essentially need two of three things: pace, movement and accuracy. Ambrose had all three. – Mike Atherton

Courtney Walsh

Courtney Walsh was not born great nor did he have greatness thrust upon him. He has achieved greatness and, coupled with his accomplishments and humility, that is why he is so popular, so loved by the people. To them, to his multitude of fans, he is one of them. His has been the triumph of the common man, the triumph of the underdog. – Tony Becca

Watching these two giants of West Indian cricket leaving the field for the last time together at the Oval in 2000 was, for most spectators, heart-breakingly sad. For a decade and more they strode across all fields in all formats, almost ever-present for their side and for one another. Walsh, who Peter Willey said could bowl a team out on one leg, was the model of consistency; always there, always on the button and the epitomy of reliability. Ambrose, perhaps more prone to moods but also perhaps the most destructive fast bowler the game has ever seen when the stars aligned.

But the sorrow in seeing them leave wasn't just for two great pace bowlers, it was the fact that for the majority of their careers they, with Brian Lara, had carried a team in a decline. They weren't ever part of some strident squad of bully boys winging from one victory to the next, safe in the knowledge that their batsmen would score stacks of runs and that the other bowlers would fill in if they had an off day. For eight years West Indies had relied on their skill and stamina. From 1992 onwards there were occasional days when Kenny Benjamin or Ian Bishop might strike but in the 25 games West Indies won Ambrose and Walsh took 60 per cent of the wickets. It wasn't a great period for Caribbean cricket, although better than what followed, but when they were at their best they could still beat anyone and that meant getting the best out of the three star players.

Courtney Walsh came of age under the wings of a still dominant West Indian side. When he made is Test debut at Perth in 1984 he didn't even get a bowl in the first innings as Malcolm Marshall, Joel Garner and especially Michael Holding rolled the hosts out for just 76. He did have a crack second time round and his two wickets were a late contribution to an innings victory. West Indies went on to win the series 3-1. Walsh played all five Tests and took 13 wickets at 33. He was very much the second-change bowler.

At the same time as Walsh was establishing a Test career Curtly Ambrose had finally discovered ability in, if not love of, the game of cricket in the village of Swetes in Antigua. Despite a fanatical follower of the game in his mother Hillie, who bestowed the third name Lynwall on her fourth child, Ambrose had shown little interest during his teenage years. His height and natural pace saw him rise quickly to debut for his island in 1985 and share a field with Andy Roberts in his last competitive game. Less than a year later came his Leeward Islands first-class debut under the captaincy of Viv Richards.

Walsh's first series had been greeted with plenty of enthusiasm. *Wisden* noted that 'Holding's protégé did a good job as a support bowler, always into the wind.' For the next year Walsh fought a losing battle to find a regular place. Such was the abundance of riches at West Indies' disposal he played only bit parts in home-series victories over New Zealand and England with Winston Davis preferred in the first and Patrick Patterson in the second. Even as his performances for Gloucestershire and Jamaica grew in confidence and skill his international career continued to stall behind the current incumbent fast bowlers. His next step up came with a full series in Pakistan when Holding and Garner were absent. He did well enough but Tony Gray returned better figures. A trip to New Zealand brought similar results but this time with a full-strength attack available. The new ball was offered to Walsh in the second Test and a first five-wicket haul was the result. Finally, he was emerging as a frontline bowler.

He had been a team man, chipping in with wickets here and there but without explosive pace or an aggressive attitude or action he wasn't looking like the new Holding or Marshall, just a good fast bowler. For the next series, in India, he was back down the pecking order. Second change in the first Test he took six wickets, first change in the second he took nine and then with the new ball again in the final two matches he added 11 more and the series was drawn. Having been christened 'the best old-ball bowler in the world' by David Graveney at Gloucester he was now moving into the position occupied by the ageing Marshall as rivals for his position either retired or fell away. Twenty-six wickets at 16.8 was evidence enough that West Indies had found a new star, not just a very good bowler. It was the recognition of this fact by his fellow players, especially his captain Richards, that kept him in the team through two fallow series in which he took just 16 wickets in eight games. Even if his performances in India had kept him in the side they couldn't prevent his slide back down the bowling order. Marshall was still top dog and Walsh was now leapfrogged by Winston Benjamin and Ambrose. At times he must have thought that this was to be his lot in life.

Clearly, while Walsh had been uncomplainingly bowling into the wind with a tatty old ball Ambrose had been making the kind of giant strides expected of a man standing 6 feet 7 inches. Thirty-five wickets in the 1988 Red Stripe Cup were enough to get Ambrose noticed throughout the Caribbean and the fact that it had been done under the captaincy of Richards was a huge advantage. He was being earmarked for the national team when Pakistan arrived for a three-Test series and duly made a low-key debut where West Indies were rescued from the fire by Marshall and a stand between Winston Benjamin and Jeff Dujon when it seemed that their long unbeaten record had gone. Richards shed tears of pride;

his old stagers and young bucks had fought back and denied the irrepressible Imran Khan a famous win.

With Holding and Garner now finished it was Marshall leading the new brigade with the batting still reliant on the experience of Richards, Gordon Greenidge and Desmond Haynes. The English side of 1988 were full of optimism that, despite their woeful recent record, they could turn over a West Indies team in transition. They couldn't and they didn't. In a bowler's series Marshall took 35 wickets at 12.6 and England were swept aside 4-0. Ambrose and Walsh played all five games and most spectators saw quickly that Ambrose was a star in the making as he collected 22 wickets at 20 each. Walsh continued to play a minor role, strictly into the wind with the old ball. This was a state of affairs he would soon rectify.

West Indies were still top of the tree, but only a nose in front of Pakistan. The overall quality of England, India and Australia was moderate with New Zealand a bit further behind and South Africa still excluded. Beyond the top two it was far from a vintage period. Even Pakistan and West Indies could look with concern at the future; with Marshall now over 30 and Imran reaching the veteran stage both countries would need replacements.

Ambrose already seemed to have that extra something needed to lead his country into a new era. Immediately recognisable by all, he had, under the advice of Andy Roberts, begun to explore the area between full and short which had been largely ignored in his early days. Two seasons playing league cricket and the tour of Pakistan were valuable introductions to new wickets and conditions that required new skills and approaches. The 1988 tour of England showed a work progressed but still in progress and Ambrose was determined to improve. He closely observed a master at work in the form of Marshall and increasingly became aware of what would be required in due course when he became the latest link in a chain dating back 13 years to Roberts.

For Walsh the series against England was a grievous disappointment. Having collected 262 wickets at 20 in the previous three seasons for Gloucestershire he was in pole position to stake his claim to a permanent and unchallenged position at the front of the new wave of West Indian quicks. His unerring accuracy and ability to move the ball both ways with no obvious change of action or grip made him an almost impossible prospect for the average county batsman but when bowling to Graham Gooch or Allan Lamb with an old ball he found wickets much harder to come by. He was quick but never showy, always bowling to the conditions which meant rarely opening himself up fully, surely one reason why he lasted so long and was so rarely affected by injuries. He could bowl very fast but only if the match or pitch conditions required it. His unruffled and uncomplaining nature made him a valuable member of the team but not, as yet, one of the leading lights.

Having safely put England back in their box the next objective was to show Australia that they, like England, should underestimate West Indies at their peril. Like England, Australia lost at home having been taken apart by West Indian quick bowlers once again. Ambrose began his love affair with the bounce of Perth by taking eight wickets and finishing the series as by far the most successful bowler – Marshall and Walsh were now his main supporting players. Mark Taylor recalled his debut at Sydney, twice being bowled by a perfect yorker from Ambrose in one innings, the first being a no-ball. It was a delivery he would see a few more times:

> 'The Ambrose yorker was a lethal delivery because it came from such a height. Your first reaction was that it was a full toss. Next thing…bang!…it was through.'

Like Garner before him, he presented batsmen with the conundrum, when paired with Marshall, of totally different trajectories at each end. Marshall's flatter, skiddy style was diametrically opposed to the Ambrose just-short-of-a-length delivery that suddenly kicked to shoulder height. It was a brave man that looked to play forwards to Ambrose and those that favoured discretion were prey to his yorker. Walsh was less obviously threatening yet his regularity in taking wickets was testimony to his skill with an old ball. The final Test against India the following year at Sabina Park showed that he could be a leader; 10-101 ushering his side to victory.

West Indies were still shuffling their pack. Ian Bishop was the latest kid on the block and shared the new ball as Marshall began to take a back seat. Ambrose kept his position and achieved almost nothing against India, leading some commentators, Holding amongst them, to question his ability in his own back yard. Once again at the end of a series it was unclear how the attack would look the next time West Indies took the field in a Test. Ambrose was riled, with a point to prove against England in 1990. Walsh was fresh and with his first ever ten-wicket Test haul could reasonably expect to have sealed his position as first-change bowler if not opener. Once again Walsh found his career stalled, this time not by any lack of form but by an unaccountable whim of the selectors.

Both Ambrose and Walsh were dropped during the series before both came bouncing straight back as West Indies won a series that they had been losing over the first two matches.

Ambrose was left out of the first game, not a decision that went down well, and one he blamed on island politics. With the second game washed out, after England had won the first, West Indies were on the back foot. The third game ended in a draw that England might and should have won but for rain. Marshall and Richards had both missed the drawn game and their return at Bridgetown meant that someone had to make way. In an intervening one-day match Ambrose and Walsh shared the new ball in what was essentially a bowl-off to stay in the Test side. It was at this point their relationship grew from team-mates to close friends, as Ambrose recalled.

> 'We had a little talk and I said to him straight up, "One of us is going to be dropped for the Test match but let's not worry about that. This is the West Indies and we must do our best for the team. If you get the nod ahead of me I wish you all the very best." And he said the same to me. There was no rivalry from that point and our strong friendship was cemented at that moment.'

In fact neither did especially well but it was Ambrose who joined Marshall, Bishop and Ezra Moseley in a traditional attack. Moseley's most significant contribution on his debut had been to break Gooch's hand. West Indies were on top throughout and after reducing England to 10-3 in the second innings looked on course to win until Alec Stewart, Robin Smith and, especially, Jack Russell dug in. At 166-5 the game seemed safe and the new ball was the final throw of the dice. Ambrose threw a five and tumbled England over for 25 more runs, finishing with 8-45. This was the arrival of Ambrose the destroyer as described by Christopher Martin-Jenkins:

> 'If ever there was a natural fast bowler it is this giant yet lissom Antiguan with his straight approach and high flowing action, the delivery stride marked by a little wave of the right hand like a tennis player signifying new balls to his opponent.'

The series was wide open and Ambrose was an instant hero, all catcalls and doubts hastily retracted. If Ambrose had been venting his spleen on the selectors then at St John's Antigua in the deciding match it was the turn of Walsh whose excellent bowling on the first day was ill-rewarded. West Indies romped to victory amid a welter of wickets and broken bones and the natural order was restored before a championship play off in Pakistan.

Rarely, if ever, can a single Test match have boasted such bowling brilliance as that at Karachi in November 1990. West Indies fielded four bowlers in the world's top 10 and Pakistan had four of top 13, only Abdul Qadir and Mushtaq Ahmed were not high speed. The series was shared with the last game in the balance. The oddity was that pitches were prepared to nullify pace when Pakistan had three men of their own chomping at the bit to prove their worth against the accepted best.

The guard was changing. Marshall was now an excellent first change, Richards was missing injured and Greenidge and Dujon were nearing the end. On the plus side Bishop was proving to be a natural partner for Ambrose with the willing workhorse Walsh in reserve. Two new batsmen, Carl Hooper and Brian Lara, also showed a bit of promise.

After a couple of months to draw breath there were back-to-back five-Test series at home to Australia and in England. For West Indies this was another test of their mettle and it would also strain the stamina of the older generation while exploring the staying power of the younger.

Australia were beaten but handsomely won the last Test and the green shoots of their revival under Allan Border were plain to see. England came back to share the series in the final Test at the Oval to ruin the departure of two of the greats as both Marshall and Richards quit the Test arena. Marshall left as still, marginally, the team's best bowler; Richards failed to score a century in any of the 10 Tests, which says quite enough. When the dust settled on the West Indian bowling attack Bishop was back from injury to join Ambrose, and Walsh was still toiling in the ranks despite a rating of number eight in the world. Ambrose was number one.

Ian Bishop might have been one of the great fast bowlers of the last 30 years given a stronger back. Having adjusted his delivery from side-on to chest-on to prevent a further recurrence he returned to something like his best in 1993 only to miss another two years. He played another 25 Tests afterwards but was never the same threat. Where Ambrose and Bishop might have gone was now the path followed by Ambrose and Walsh. But the real Walsh, the mature Walsh, had yet to appear. He played his part but the pack leader was clearly Ambrose especially when re-united with Australian pitches where 10-120 and 9-79 in consecutive Tests saw his side cling onto an unbeaten record dating back 13 years.

The second of these games featured the famous spell of 7-1 in 32 balls. It left a lasting impression on three of his opponents:

> 'Only once in my career did I face up and say to myself, "I don't know how I'm going try score any runs. This is too hard."…I was cooked mentally, like a pulverised boxer awaiting the death knell. No escape seemed possible.' – Steve Waugh

> 'He exploited pretty much every bit of help in that pitch. His greatest strengths were his control, his ability to obtain bounce out of an pitch…I firmly believe he bowled within himself the majority of time and he had the ability to step it up when he really needed to.' – David Boon

> 'You feel suffocated because you can't move, you can't score…That's what Ambrose did. You just could not score runs against him. I got off the mark in Test cricket with three runs down the ground at the Adelaide Oval, and I honestly reckon that's the last time I ever drove him.' – Justin Langer

No wonder he was now the most feared bowler in Test cricket. Just over a year later he was at it again. Chasing 194 to haul themselves back into the series at Port-of Spain, England were dismissed for 46. Once again the testimonies of three opponents are enough:

> 'I played a beautiful forward-defensive, the only problem was that I was about two minutes too late.' – Robin Smith

> 'I think there was a bit of shock. I was probably just thinking, "Crikey, Test cricket is a pretty brutal game. You play well for three days and you're in the game all the time and then – bang! – game over.' – Graham Thorpe

> 'Ambrose, sensing a match to win and a wearing pitch to exploit was only interested in wickets. Of course there was the occasional bouncer…but Ambrose's general length was full and the effect was dramatic.' – Mike Atherton

Hillie Ambrose kept ringing the bell ouside her house and her son could have later told her, "Made it ma, top of the world." With a rating of 912; only ever bettered by SF Barnes, George Lohmann and Imran Khan; he was.

Walsh was now, at long last, established as Ambrose's partner. West Indies were still unbeaten in a series since 1980 but, with Pakistan seen off, Australia were emerging as a new threat in a new world where Brian Lara and Sachin Tendulkar would face Shane Warne and Glenn McGrath. At this stage in their careers Walsh was averaging 3.42 wickets per game at an average of 25.6, Ambrose 4.65 per game at 20.5. But with the new ball in his hand Walsh was embarking on the second half of his long journey to 500 wickets with his best pal by his side. The real battle, however, would be how to maintain West Indies' position at the top of the table..

New Zealand were never likely to reprise their achievement of being the last team to beat West Indies back in 1980. With Richie Richardson unavailable the captaincy had become vacant and Walsh was the obvious choice to keep the seat warm for Richardson and, eventually, Lara. Of course it wasn't put quite like that but everybody, including Walsh, knew the way the land lay. A short series was never likely to attract much notice but it did give Walsh the chance to lead his side in all ways. His 13-55 on a flat wicket where West Indies had scored 660-5d was his single most impressive performance. Perhaps the batting was not as strong as that knocked over by Michael Holding at the Oval in 1976 but the ability to remove batsmen on a dead wicket was rather reminiscent. It is easily arguable that these are the most impressive match figures since 1918 bar Jim Laker's 1956 masterpiece. It was quite a way to celebrate becoming the first specialist bowler to captain West Indies.

Six weeks later the much-anticipated contest for the Frank Worrell Trophy began at Bridgetown with Richardson back at the helm. Since the two sides had previously met much had changed. On one side Haynes, Bishop and Marshall had gone and the replacements were not of the same class. On the other Michael Slater and McGrath had arrived and the Waughs, new captain Taylor and Warne had grown in stature and skill. West Indies were reliant on their two quicks and the batting of Lara, Richardson and Hooper.

Steve Waugh was the outstanding player of the series and Australia deservedly won 2-1. It was a sobering time after so many years of domination even if there was an inevitability about it. Walsh had done his best to bowl his side to victory in the drawn second Test and he and Ambrose had shared 15 wickets in the victory at Port-of-Spain but ultimately the series was decided by the Waugh twins' partnership at Kingston. Unfortunately the best remembered incident of the series is the confrontation between Steve Waugh and Ambrose, endlessly and boringly recounted by all who saw it and many who didn't.

The English summer of 1995 offered the chance of immediate

redemption. An unwieldy schedule and internal bickering meant that West Indies were unable to do themselves justice. Ambrose in particular was out of sorts and the series, which could have gone either way, finished 2-2. Despite being below par, Ambrose and Walsh still collected 47 wickets but the main talking point was Lara, 765 runs and the first signs of outgrowing his team.

With the retirement of Richardson and a disastrous one-day World Cup in 1996 the captaincy reverted back to Walsh and with it the unenviable task of touring Australia, who had now added Mathew Hayden and Ricky Ponting to a bulging roster. With Ian Bishop back West Indies at least had some support for their two premier bowlers but over the course of five games they were simply outgunned by a better team. Lara failed to fire amid increasing dressing-room tension and the fielding was a constant source of frustration. Ambrose and Walsh even had injury problems. After falling behind 2-0 Ambrose's nine wickets at the MCG opened the series up again. Then he was injured in a one-day match and the deflation was obvious in his team-mates as they crumpled to defeat in the next match. The final, dead-rubber Test was West Indies' cricket of the late nineties in a nutshell. Lara scored a century, Ambrose took five wickets and then in the second innings Walsh took five, bowling 20 overs in a row with a torn hamstring after which he could barely walk for two weeks. It was a heroic victory but a series defeat.

Walsh had bowled through injury before: a pulled hamstring at Adelaide, a neck injury at Nagpur and back spasms to win his side a Test at Mohali in 1994. Only physio Dennis Waight and Walsh himself can know just how he managed. Indeed part of the reputation of Ambrose and Walsh lies in their fitness record. Ambrose was never a man for the gym; football, basketball and a lot of bowling was his recipe. Walsh just had to keep on the move, sluggishness and weight his enemy and bowling his friend. Both had actions that were relatively stress free and both, crucially, were good enough to be effective even when bowling within themselves. Only on rare occasions did they really let rip but when they did they could be very fast.

Compared to, say, Allan Donald, Waqar Younis or Wes Hall, they were models of restraint and this was crucial factor in their remarkable fitness records. Walsh in particular was also capable of throwing in the unexpected and almost undetectable fast ball in the manner of Charlie Griffith, but without the debate over its legality. Once in a while an entire spell could be devoted to pace as, for example, when he targeted England's young captain Mike Atherton with two hours of unremitting vigour at Sabina Park which he recalled as 'among the fastest spells that I ever faced.' Jack Russell had plenty of time to observe Walsh from behind the wicket at Gloucestershire:

> 'He always troubled me the most. I still have trouble working him out. Ambling in off that smooth run you just don't know when he will produce that "effort" ball, the one that appears to be bowled with the same action but picks up pace angling into the batsman, sending the keeper off balance as he tries to get near the ball jagging back.'

For Ambrose the secret was more about inspiration than technique. He was blessed with an easy rhythm and something of a languid personality until something, or someone, fired him up. Sometimes it might be a triviality like Dean Jones complaining about his wrist bands but usually it was the requirements of the team.

> 'When things are going your way, everything comes natural and easy. But when your backs are against the wall and you are down for the count, can you beat the count, get up and win? That is what separates great cricketers from the average. Myself and Courtney Walsh have worked together in tandem through several of those moments and that has been where our true greatness shines...Implementing and executing your skills when all seems lost – that is what makes the difference. I thrive on challenges, negative comments or anything where people doubt my ability.'

While Ambrose was the more obvious epitomy of thriving under pressure it was Walsh's ability to maintain his equilibrium and poise in the tensest situations that saw his side to some of their greatest wins. Who else would be bowling at the death in Adelaide in 1993? Tim May and Craig McDermott had added 40 and brought Australia to within three runs of a win and a series victory after Ambrose had demolished the top order. Australia Day, the whole country clustered around televisions, a crowd swollen by late arrivals – but Walsh remained unflustered behind those sleepy eyes and proceeded to bowl six balls, concede one run and have McDermott caught behind. This was combination bowling; Walsh, the cool assassin, taking over as Ambrose's fire began to die.

Only a year earlier the pair had produced one of the finest combined efforts in history when dismissing South Africa in their first visit to the

Caribbean. Set 201 to win on a decent pitch Ambrose tore into the task while Walsh 'chugged along on two cylinders' at the other end before bursting into life to take four wickets for eight runs from 11 overs. The pair's combined figures were 10-65, the rest 0-66. Richardson was captaining for the first time and recalled Walsh begging for the ball and sensing that something would happen by the 'sweat and determination on his face.'

The contrasting methods of the two men were part of their danger and appeal. Left-hander Graham Thorpe was hexed above all by Shaun Pollock but he didn't have much fun against West Indies.

> 'Ambrose was a handful because he projected the ball from such a great height but he didn't swing the ball and his deliveries generally went across me. Walsh was very different. He varied things a lot, bowled a fuller length and could swing the ball.'

Nasser Hussain offers a similar appraisal.

> 'For a young batsman Ambrose was a frightening prospect. For some reason I never feared him as someone who would consistently get me out because I saw him as a 'straight line' bowler and I could line him up a lot better than Walsh...[who] was the most difficult bowler I ever faced. He was all arms and legs and would bowl from the side of the crease so you thought it would be coming in at you, and then at the last moment it might hold up... Walsh would turn me into an S shape which was embarrassing. I never felt 'in' against Courtney Walsh.'

If Hussain sounds a little lukewarm in his assessment of Ambrose he was a little more fulsome in his praise of his bowling at Queen's Park Oval in 1994: 'Awesome. Just incredible. His accuracy from such a height was a wonder to behold.'

The defeat in Australia in 1996-97 had been predictable but still showed West Indies to be a force in world cricket. They had certainly pushed the hosts a lot harder than most. A home win over India despite the poor form of the opening bowlers offered some hope that new boys Franklyn Rose and Shiv Chanderpaul might be a way forward but that hope was short-lived. An astonishing set of three series followed – embarrassing whitewashes in Pakistan and South Africa sandwiched a comprehensive home victory over England, with dressing-room dissent bubbling under the surface.

Pakistan was a disaster, the dam had seemingly broken in the face of a phenomenal bowling attack. Mushtaq Ahmed and Saqlain Mushtaq won a game apiece – in front of them were Wasim, Waqar and Shoaib Akhtar. Walsh resigned, Lara took over and Ambrose had to be talked out of retirement. The argument that persuaded him was that he should go out on his own terms and at the top, not on the back of a miserable shambles. The sight of England in the Caribbean again had a galvanising effect. The series was won 3-1 and Ambrose named top player with 30 wickets at 14.26. Walsh would never sulk in the ranks and he chipped away at England 22 times. But the rest of the team managed just 37 wickets and of those 25 were taken by spin. Even in the moment of victory it was clear that even though England had been a relatively soft target only two men could knock them around.

South Africa were always likely to be tougher and the West Indies' players prepared by having a protracted stand-off with their Board over pay and conditions. With various squad members littered around the world the main action centred on the Excelsior hotel at Heathrow airport for a foregathering of the current heavyweights and those of the previous generation. A deal was eventually thrashed out to temporarily mollify the players and Ali Bacher arrived with a message from Nelson Mandela. Finally a bitter and despondent team made their way in dribs and drabs to the Cape to lose 5-0 in the Tests and 6-0 in the one dayers. There were no positives to be taken although that didn't stop Walsh from matching Pollock and Donald wicket for wicket.

If Ambrose had felt like retiring after the Pakistan series it was inevitable that those thoughts resurfaced after this trouncing but the lure of Australia at home, one more time, was too much. One of the great series of all time was about to be played and Lara was to astonish even those who thought they'd seen it all.

It didn't start well. Ambrose and Walsh had just about kept their side in the first Test with 12 wickets only to see their batsmen capitulate for 51 in pursuit of a target of 364. Surely no team could pick themselves up after this and no captain could perform under such pressure knowing his job would be gone after one more defeat?

History records that Lara played two of the greatest innings back-to-back and West Indies won both games after being in the mire. Amid the plaudits heaped upon Lara it was almost inevitable that the contributions of Walsh would get forgotten – it just always seemed to happen that way. He had opened up the first of the two games by removing the Australian top order and in the Sabina Park epic it was his 5-39 in the second innings that gave West Indies just a sniff after surrendering a lead of 161 first time around. Lara's unbeaten 153 did the rest with Walsh at his side at the death offering the most ostentatious 'leave' in history as McGrath tried to tempt him to drive for glory with no fielders on the off side in front of square. Courtney was never going to take that bait.

The effort couldn't be sustained despite another Lara century and 13 wickets for Ambrose and Walsh. The support was just too weak and a spellbinding series was drawn. Ambrose considered retirement yet again after West Indies dramatically, again, beat Pakistan at home with a one-wicket win in the final Test. Two glaring umpiring errors and two absurd missed run-outs added to the sense of unreality as Walsh batted out for an hour with Jimmy Adams. In the absence of Lara this was some achievement and Ambrose was happy to go out on that note at his home ground of St John's. Then Walsh got in his ear. There he was with 388 wickets, so close to joining Walsh, Kapil Dev, Wasim Akram and Richard Hadlee.

> 'There was never any rivalry between us – ever. If it was his day to take wickets then my job was to just keep the pressure on at the other end. If it was my day he would do the same thing. So I told him that game was going to be my last and he immediately protested and said that I should carry on…On this occasion I thought, "Cuddy's got a point, 400 would be quite nice."'

Walsh's memory of their partnership offers a perfect mirror image:

> 'On my good days he would support me and on his good days I would support him - and when we both had good days batsmen were in trouble! We worked well in tandem, we had a good understanding and we were more than cricketing friends, we were like brothers. We had that understanding, we worked for each other, he would die for me and I would die for him. The days that he struggled were the days that I tried to make sure I didn't struggle.'

Five Tests in England, 12 wickets to take? Piece of cake. England to beat again? Slightly more difficult, but Ambrose and Walsh had done it a few times before. Ambrose did get the wickets but was down on pace and nothing in the five games convinced either him or his supporters that he should delay retirement. After winning the first Test West Indies began to look increasingly bedraggled as they lost three of the remainder. With Lara failing to fire, the batting was weak and even a below-par Ambrose was way better than the rest, with one staggering exception. Atherton, his 400th victim, recalled that

> 'He wasn't as quick by 2000 but he was still as accurate and still as miserly, probably more so. What he couldn't do by this stage was turn on that explosive spell…He lacked that extra dimension he once had, but that's a natural evolution for every fast bowler.'

Walsh was the exception to Atherton's law, he was absolutely magnificent and recorded his best series total by far. His 34 wickets at a miserly average were proof that he was as good as ever at the age of 37, still bowling into the wind or uphill or with a ragged old ball if that's what his captain required and requested.

Ambrose described the tour as 'miserable' but couldn't fail to be moved by the show of affection at the Oval, a players' guard of honour was reciprocated by thunderous applause right round the ground. 'Ambrose symbolically removed his trademark white armbands, as if to say "Enough", safe in the knowledge that his legs would have to do no more pounding.' Atherton had suffered more than any at Ambrose's hands but even he was moved. Ambrose said at the time:

> "I am going to miss my great partner and friend. We have gone through a great lot together, good and bad, ups and downs. He was so eager and happy for me to join him in the '400 club'. Man, I am going to miss him terribly."

Walsh ploughed on for two more series before bowing out at Kingston the following year, still top of the averages and the only member of the 500 club. We can be sure he missed Ambrose.

What a pair they were, probably the most 'pairlike' pair of all. Both were from the top drawer of fast bowling, they played together year in year out (only three of Ambrose's 98 Tests were without Walsh) and they were genuine mates who only ever wished the best for each other. More than that though, they were the classical combination of fire and ice. Ambrose was always the one with the greater destructive powers (although Walsh's 13-55 in New Zealand was equal to anything of Ambrose's) and Walsh was just the most wonderful servant to his captain, his country and cricket. They joined a team that won as a matter of course and left a team that only won if they took most of the wickets. West Indies cricket was a sinking ship but, with Lara, they kept it afloat for another five years.

Ambrose and Walsh

Results

	Total	Won	Drawn	Lost
Ambrose	98	44	28	26
Walsh	132	52	37	43
Ambrose and Walsh	95	42	28	25

Test Bowling Overall

	Mat	Balls	Runs	Wkts	Ave	SR	ER	5W1/10WM
Ambrose	98	22103	8501	405	20.99	54.5	2.30	22/3
Walsh	132	30019	12688	519	24.44	57.8	2.53	22/3

Test Bowling Together

	Mat	Balls	Runs	Wkts	Ave	SR	ER	5W1/10WM
Ambrose	95	21408	8215	389	21.11	55.0	2.30	21/2
Walsh	95	21381	9065	373	24.30	57.3	2.54	15/3

Test Bowling Apart

	Mat	Balls	Runs	Wkts	Ave	SR	ER	5W1/10WM
Ambrose	3	695	286	16	17.88	43.4	2.47	1/1
Walsh	37	8638	3623	146	24.82	59.2	2.52	7/0

Best Series Together - England 1997-98

	Mat	Balls	Runs	Wkts	Ave	SR	ER	5W1/10WM
Ambrose	6	1235	428	30	14.26	41.1	2.07	2/0
Walsh	6	1567	564	22	25.63	71.2	2.15	0/0

Best Test Figures - Innings/Match

Ambrose (with Walsh)	7-25 vs Australia, Perth – 1993
Ambrose (with Walsh)	11-84 vs England, Port of Spain – 1994
Ambrose (without Walsh)	8-45 vs England, Bridgetown – 1990
Ambrose (without Walsh)	10-127 vs England, Bridgetown – 1990
Walsh (with Ambrose)	7-37 vs New Zealand, Wellington – 1995
Walsh (with Ambrose)	13-55 vs New Zealand, Wellington – 1995
Walsh (without Ambrose)	6-61 vs South Africa, Port of Spain – 2001
Walsh (without Ambrose)	9-94 vs India, Bombay – 1987

YouTube Bowling Highlights

Search Phrases (sic)
Courtney Walsh 6 of his 7 Wickets vs New Zealand 1st Inning 1995
Curtly Ambrose incredible bowling vs England 2000
Courtney Walsh and Curtly Ambrose Deadly Combination picks up 4 Wickets

Donald

and

Pollock

Allan Donald

In full flight Donald was a thing of beauty, the Lamborghini of pace whose action was a natural flowering that remained essentially unaltered throughout his career. – Drew Forrest

Shaun Pollock

They likened him to a bowling machine, and certainly there was something of the mechanical about his action. If it came naturally, it was in no sense a thing of natural beauty. Too immutable, with too much strain and too many straight lines, it wanted that easy fluidity which turns cricket writers into aesthetes. But the results mirrored the method, and there can be no gainsaying its utility. It was bowling as prose, written to the standards of poetry. – Rodney Ulyate

Some bowlers have to wait a while and do their time in the ranks before being promoted and carrying the pips of a new-ball bowler. Courtney Walsh's spud-bashing lasted half a decade; not that he wasn't capable of being an incisive opening bowler, there were just a few others in front of him in the queue. For Shaun Pollock things turned out very differently.

Allan Donald had been there right from the start, for the historic Test at Bridgetown in 1992 where South Africa returned, with an all-white team, to international cricket for the first time since the exclusion of 1971. They dominated the early exchanges and then learnt the value of a great pair of fast bowlers as they were cut down by Curtly Ambrose and Courtney Walsh when cruising to victory. Donald was also there for the first home Test series against India and his 12-139 in the decisive game at Port Elizabeth was proof enough that, given good health, he would be around for a long time. Brett Schulz and Brian McMillan had been his partners and showed enough without looking like long-term new-ball prospects. Then, in late 1993, Fanie de Villiers arrived. Age was against him, already 29 years old, but he showed the advantage of experience and no little talent when knocking over Australia with 6-43 (10 in the match) in a historic five-run victory at Sydney. The two Afrikaner bowlers seemed just what South Africa needed to challenge the best in the world. When he repeated the dose against Pakistan, de Villiers was outbowling Donald with his rapid off cutters. The Devon Malcolm inspired defeat in England was a blip as a foot injury reduced Donald's effectiveness. Although the operation was a success he realised that hard work in the gym, a reduced schedule and a less full-on approach to fast bowling were required to keep himself in the best of shape.

De Villiers played only five more Tests after Pakistan as injury and his disillusion with the policy of positive discrimination and the selectors' often bizarre desire to see him as a one-day specialist opened the door for Pollock. Donald had already identified him as 'something special' after seeing him bowl in a one-day game.

Pollock didn't need much encouragement. After his rain-ruined debut, Ian Botham predicted he'd be taking the new ball for a decade. Then Mike Atherton's epic 185 dominated his second game. He took the new ball in the third and the fifth game was won, thanks largely to Donald and Pollock. South Africa had found their heart's desire.

It was certainly unusual for a boy born and bred in Bloemfontein to show enthusiasm for cricket. Afrikaner-dominated in culture and language it was a city dedicated to rugby. Traditionally this had been their sport with the Europeans favouring cricket even if the demarcations had thinned before isolation with Peter van der Merwe being the first Afrikaner to captain his country at cricket. But, in keeping with his peer group, Allan Donald's first love was rugby and only the discovery that he had natural ability as fast bowler and the backing of an enthusiastic cricket-loving family convinced him to choose the game that would bring him fame and fortune.

South African policy of fast tracking promising youngsters saw him quickly into the Free State side and playing against rebel tourists from Australia and West Indies. Within two years he had made enough of a reputation for Warwickshire to make approaches via Ali Bacher and the next stage of his education began. With South Africa an unknown quantity and still years from being accepted back into international cricket Donald; like Clive Rice, Ken McEwen and so many others; saw county cricket as a professional opportunity with the added advantage of improving his limited English and rubbing shoulders and crossing swords with some of the best players, of all nationalities, in the world. And there were the skills to learn of bowling on traditional English pitches where bounce and pace were unusual commodities compared to South Africa. His first two seasons were quiet, alternating with Tony Merrick and playing plenty of second XI cricket. The breakthrough came in 1989 with the help of a Richard Hadlee video and the one-on-one help of Rice. The result was 86 wickets, one every 6.5 overs; county colleague Paul Smith wasn't far wrong when he said "It's just a matter of pitching it up these days, Al. You seem to have it all worked out now."

Any cockiness was quickly eradicated as Warwickshire signed Tom Moody and played him in preference to Donald as their overseas player. It looked like a move to another county was in the offing when, from out of the blue, Donald was retained over Moody at the end of the season. In the meantime Nelson Mandela had been released and suddenly South Africa was on the cusp of re-entry into international sports. Donald did not waste his opportunity as he came under the influence of Bob Woolmer at Edgbaston who refined his run-up and helped him develop a slower ball and offcutter. Eighty-three wickets at less than 20 was Warwickshire's reward. One of *Wisden's* five cricketers, a World Cup and thereafter official Test cricket. In September 1991 things looked very rosy. The World Cup ended in farce when a target of 22 from seven balls became 21 from one ball in the pre-Duckworth/Lewis days but Test cricket duly arrived the following year.

Unlike Donald, Pollock was born into the upper echelons of South African cricket. Father Peter was the country's greatest ever fast bowler and uncle Graeme her best ever batsman. He was not pushed into the game by this illustrious pair but watching his uncle bat at Kingsmead was inspirational. He had clearly inherited some of his family genes but it was the chance to work with his boyhood hero Malcolm Marshall at Natal that transformed him into a player ready for Test cricket at the age of 22. Having ditched all-out pace he developed the armoury, if not quite the ability, of Marshall; control, swing both ways and a slippery bouncer.

Right from the word go the new South African pair gelled and recognised what their complementary skills could bring to the team and as individuals. Donald enjoyed the control Pollock brought to the side, thus forcing batsmen to do more than just fend him off and score runs at the other end. For the modest Pollock it was no combination of equals:

> 'I benefitted more from Allan being at the other end rather than him being benefitted from me. He was express pace – 145 kph and then from the other side I just had to show control and the others were looking to score off me because they would have felt slightly more comfortable facing the guy at half pace from the other end.'

He certainly wasn't half the pace and the benefit was more mutual than Pollock gives it credit for. Donald was nonetheless allowed to indulge his pace and follow his attacking instincts and the results were immediate. A 1-0 home victory at home to England was sealed at Cape Town and showcased a masterpiece of fast bowling from the new pair. Reports on the game in *Wisden* and *The Cricketer* are so Anglo-centric that Pollock barely receives a mention. A contentious run-out decision that didn't affect the outcome was the main point of focus for Matthew Engel and Richard Hutton but it was the aggression of Donald in the first innings and the quiet persistence of Pollock in the second that enabled South Africa to win by 10 wickets.

The stars were aligning for Donald. His school friend and Free State team-mate Hansie Cronje was now his national team captain, Woolmer had left Warwickshire to coach South Africa and Donald had an eager, young, talented partner. Jacques Kallis had also just made his debut. Given the positives oozing out of the Proteas dressing-room and the combative nature of the team it was hardly surprising that they set themselves the target of being the world's number one in all formats by the end of the century. They were already ahead of plenty but Australia and Pakistan in particular were likely to provide much sterner opposition than a muddled, not to say shambolic, England had done.

Australia were not lacking in self confidence but neither were they lacking in respect, or at least most of them. Adam Gilchrist, however, batted without a helmet in their first one-day encounter and then on a tricky wicket at Durban pulled Donald over mid-wicket for six. Gilchrist's response did, however, indicate respect.

> 'Funnily, my first impulse was to run off the ground there and then – stuff the rest of my innings – and ring my mates at home to tell them how I hit Allan Donald for six.'

Soon afterwards the pair faced off again, at Perth. This time Gilchrist was wearing protection and Donald smashed one straight into the grille. 'For the next few balls I genuinely feared for my life. I'd never had this extreme sense of physical danger before.' Donald was clearly not a man to rile.

It wasn't that he was vindictive, he just identified the batsman that was most likely to be the head of the snake, which was often the captain. If Atherton or Steve Waugh could be brought down then the value was more than just a single wicket. In the case of Atherton this had begun with the 10-hour resistance at Johannesburg and grown through the infamous duel at Trent Bridge after Atherton had been reprieved by an umpiring error. In an instant Donald upped his pace by 10 mph and began to pepper Atherton from short of a length amid a welter of sledging. Atherton drew on all his experience of similar treatment from Courtney Walsh. He survived and recalled 'by far the most intense period of cricket I experienced in my career'. Donald recalled that this was the 'decisive phase' and the match would be 'decided by the next few overs'.

Steve Waugh received similar treatment over the years, none more so than at Centurion in 1997. One over involved two blows on the hand, one to the forearm, one in the ribs and a protector shot. 'It was Test match cricket the way I loved it – genuine one-on-one warfare, with no place to hide and everything on the line.' But Waugh felt he had mastered Donald:

> '[He] was a class act, mixing express pace and an excellent cricket brain that enabled him to plot, as well as plunder, batsmen's deficiencies. He was a genuine superstar, but when I looked into his eyes in the real, raw moments of heightened battle, I believed he wasn't as mentally strong as his reputation suggested…At least that's what I told myself.'

It's an interesting concept, the mental weakness of Allan Donald, but one that doesn't appear to have many supporters. He certainly enjoyed removing Waugh for 85 in his 100th Test a few months later. It was in the nature of Donald to have individual battles – with his heart on his sleeve and the panoply of expressions all exaggerated by daubings of sun blocker he was a photographer's dream.

Pollock's approach was considerably more understated – the quiet man as a foil for the explosive partner rather as Walsh was for Ambrose. But this should never be allowed to cloud our judgement of his ability. Graham Thorpe was just one batsman who found that 'he gave me more problems in Test cricket than any other fast bowler'. His consistent and nagging accuracy was comparable with McGrath or Walsh but that's not to say that he wasn't capable of real speed when required. When first appearing for Natal as a teenager out-and-out pace was his chief weapon before Marshall's tutelage refined his methods without forgetting the art of generating real speed – rather like the master himself.

With South Africa determined to prove themselves the best within three years the 1996 World Cup in Asia could hardly have come at a better time. Being dumped out by West Indies in the last eight showed there was a way to go yet in that department.

Donald had not returned to Warwickshire in 1996. With the shadow of Brian Lara hanging across his county career the chance to rest could scarcely have come at a more opportune moment as South Africa faced up to a busy schedule, making up for the lost decades. Pollock replaced Donald at Edgbaston and unfortunately aggravated an ankle injury during a season that was low on results but high on learning and when a double-header against India came around at the end of 1996 he was not fully recovered for the away first leg. Donald bowled superbly in the first game reviving memories of Marshall's approach on pre-prepared spinning pitches back in 1983-84, but then he too succumbed to injury. South Africa won one game courtesy of an explosive debut from Lance Klusener but the series was an eye opener; winning in Asia, the Caribbean and Australasia would require a variety of skills. Back on home turf they were a different proposition, particularly with Donald and Pollock back together.

If the Indians could be accused of producing pitches to suit for the first leg then the Kingsmead surface to open the second was repayment in kind. Donald and Pollock were not about to waste a golden opportunity to lay waste to the much vaunted Indian batting line up. Rahul Dravid, Sourav Ganguly, Mohammad Azharuddin and Sachin Tendulkar were beaten all ends up. When the little master had the temerity to drive Donald twice to the boundary the response was two curving outswingers followed by a lightening-fast off cutter that smashed into the stumps. Tendulkar deserved the best and he got it.

Having shared 14 wickets in the opener the going was a bit tougher at Newlands on a batting track but again Donald and Pollock headed the charge to victory despite a partnership from Tendulkar and Azharuddin that transfixed all those lucky enough to see it. The political and social significance of the 'safari series' was perhaps greater than that of the cricket, home advantage had proved too influential in both series. But the clash between Donald and Tendulkar had been riveting and with Pollock fit again he and his partner would test out the very best over the next few years.

One month later the very best duly arrived in the form of Australia. They were tested but not found wanting. From the first morning of the first Test South Africa were on the back foot as Glenn McGrath took three quick wickets and they subsided to a crushing defeat. Even if Cronje's decision to bat was faulty it was a result to dampen the country's enthusiasm. Two quick wickets from Pollock in the second Test put the boot on the other foot but a hamstring injury took him out of the game and Mark Waugh's finest hour in scoring 116 took his side home by two wickets. Winning the third match was some validation but South Africa knew they had been beaten by a better team, not much better maybe but better anyway. Donald took eight in that final Test as if motivated by the sight of McGrath stealing his thunder and lightning.

Rest and recuperation were required because later in the same year South Africa would travel south for a return series after visiting the one country which seemed able to challenge Australia, Pakistan. Unbeaten at home for 15 years before an unaccountable defeat by Sri Lanka in 1995, they had proved redoubtable opponents even before collecting their finest ever bowling attack of Wasim, Waqar, Mushtaq Ahmed and Saqlain Mushtaq. Even the great West Indian sides had twice failed to win; in context there was little to choose between Pakistan and Australia as unlikely venues for an away win.

Two rain-affected draws meant that Faisalabad would decide the series. It's rare in any country to come back from collapsing to 98-7 on the first afternoon but on a sporting pitch Gary Kirsten and Pat Symcox kept the game alive, just, and Pakistan required 146 runs to win. In the words of ZH Syed 'What followed next was beyond the wildest dreams of even their most optimistic supporters.' Cronje opened the bowling with two spinners, Symcox

.

and Paul Adams (yes, really) and when they failed to take a wicket he reverted to Donald and Pollock – 23-0 became 31-5 as Pollock ripped out four top-line batsmen in seven balls. 'The batsmen played like rabbits but Pollock became the headlights which paralysed them' was the *Wisden* verdict. Then it was back to the spinners (it was, after all, their pitch) and a famous victory was won. All of which set up the series in Australia very nicely – the two countries had informally decided that this was to decide which was the best Test team in the world.

The Australian public bought into the hype – 73,812 arrived at the MCG on Boxing Day as the South African coach, Woolmer, tried to douse the fires that were burning too violently in the bellies of his players. South Africa had the upper hand in pace despite McGrath and Australia had the upper hand in batting despite Kallis and Kirsten. Australia also had Warne, a trump card if ever there was one.

The early stages were slow and steady, two heavyweights circling and looking for an opening, but gradually Australia began to make their jabs count. Despite a salvo of genuinely fast bowling from Donald, which brought him six second-innings wickets, a draw was the only possible South African saviour on day five. Kallis and Cronje saw them home and two days later the gloves were back on at Sydney. This time Australia pressed home their first-innings advantage as Warne decimated the middle order to complete an innings victory. Pollock had been below form but Donald had tested the Waugh twins with bowling faster than anything seen at the SCG since Lillee and Thomson 23 years earlier. His efforts left him injured for the final Test but the balance was restored when McGrath was also forced to miss the match. Pollock emerged from his slump to lead the attack as a man transformed. With South Africa safe after scoring 519, Pollock bowled 41 overs of controlled fast-medium aggression with barely a loose ball. His reward was seven wickets and but for Mark Taylor carrying his bat the follow-on would have made victory almost a formality. It was breathtaking in its effort, control and penetration – pushing and pushing, offering no relief, just classic Pollock. The nominal target for Australia was 361 in 109 overs; at 54-3 Australia were on the ropes until South Africa started dropping catches, four alone from centurion Mark Waugh. Amid mounting frustration and disputed decisions, the game was drawn.

It had been a close call, perhaps Donald's presence might have tipped the balance. The certainty was that there were, for the first time, three top-class fast-bowling pairs operating in world cricket and it was hard to say which was best at the beginning of 1998. In the world rankings Donald was rated equal to

Warne but behind McGrath with Pollock eighth. Ambrose and Walsh were each one position behind their South African counterparts with 'Amby' slightly in decline and 'Cuddy' still awaiting his best days at the age of 35. Wasim was still a force to be reckoned with but Waqar was down to twelfth. The South African pair could make fair claim to the top spot. That didn't mean their team was the best though. Only one batsman in the top 20 was the problem where Pakistan had three and Australia four, not including Ricky Ponting who was fast heading upwards.

They weren't carrying the team in the way Ambrose and Walsh were but neither did they have a Brian Lara to see through their work.

The year of 1998 was to be a busy one for South Africa. Fifteen Tests in all and a chance for the young players such as Kallis, Herschelle Gibbs and Mark Boucher to show they could add some much needed steel to the batting. The main priority would, however, be keeping Donald and Pollock fit. From that point of view, and most others, it was an annus mirabilis for the pair – they missed only one game each and collected 149 wickets, Donald leading by 21. No great mathematics is required to establish that this amounts to more than 10 in each match they played. Only twice has this year of plenty been trumped. Twenty-eight combined Tests in 2005 brought Warne and McGrath 158 wickets; Marshall and Joel Garner took 150 in 1984 in the same number of games.

Pakistan, Sri Lanka and West Indies at home, England away was the whirligig itinerary. Pakistan managed to draw thanks to two astonishing centuries in one game by Azhar Mahmood and Saeed Anwar, Sri Lanka were brushed aside and an internally divided West Indies whitewashed. The choker was to lose the last two Tests and the series in England after dominating the first three matches.

The Pakistan series was played out against a backdrop of controversy. Questions surrounding the racial make up of the South African side led Ali Bacher to say:

> "We can never again field an all-white team. Our constituencies will not allow it. They are pressing for change and they want to see it at the top. South Africa is not a normal country at the moment."

Then there were issues of discipline against Symcox and de Villiers and a failed attempt to use floodlights at the Wanderers. Despite these distractions and after a wet first game there was enough excitement in the other two with both sides winning one. Shoaib Akhtar announced himself on the world stage after five wickets from Donald had given South Africa the early advantage. Then, when Donald broke down with a thigh injury, Pollock led the attack with a magnificent six in the second innings to add to his invaluable 70 not out. The target of 255 was always going to be tough for the home side but somehow everyone knew that the Australian team would have got it. South Africa didn't. Pollock couldn't sustain his form in the final game but eight wickets from Donald was an ample substitute. After rain a draw seemed likely but a furious spell from 'White Lightning' knocked over the top four in 13 balls and de Villiers mopped up the rest in his farewell match. This was Donald at his absolute best, doing the kind of thing that had been the preserve of Ambrose, Lillee or Roberts; raising his game at a crucial time to turn around the match in 20 minutes. He was more restrained second time around but 4-27 from 15 overs wasn't a bad effort.

The batsmen were still the weak link and that situation continued through two victories over Sri Lanka. An inability to cope with Muttiah Muralitharan, a common complaint, made both games hard work. Makhaya Ntini made his historic debut as the first black South African to represent his country but it was, again, the senior pace bowlers who dominated. They shared 12 wickets in the first game and then, in the second when Pollock's groin went, Donald seized the tiller and brought the ship to port. His 5-54 took him to 200 Test wickets and was achieved despite considerable discomfort. The man was becoming a true phenomenon and with his partner now scoring regular runs, supporting and stepping up when Donald was down, they made a wonderful partnership.

Little wonder that when Steve Waugh offered England some advice on how to beat South Africa in May 1998 the focus of his attention was the opening bowlers.

> 'Undoubtedly, blunting their spearhead is a major factor in one's quest for victory and it is here that Allan Donald holds the key. He is the one the South Africans use for inspiration and motivation, although Shaun Pollock continues to grow in stature with each outing and is also a danger man.'

Waugh's tip was to catch South Africa early because they come on strong at the end of the series. He was right about Donald and Pollock but 'Tugga' was completely wrong about the rest. South Africa largely dominated the first three games and then lost the last two and with them the series. If that wasn't bad enough, the fact that South Africa were rated number two and England seven going into the last games puts the cherry on the cake. Maybe it wasn't a 500-1 moment but 50-1 against an England series win before Trent Bridge would have seemed realistic.

Donald was, again, a phenomenon. Through five Tests he hurled himself into the fray for 33 wickets. He'd started the series feeling tired and heavy but a few sessions with Woolmer's innovative video analysis and a Test at Lord's with its 'stuffy conventions' were enough to invigorate. Five in England's first innings at headquarters was a match winner with Pollock bowling 'a series of 85-mile-per-hour leg breaks' in support. At Old Trafford, with Pollock missing, Donald produced 40 overs of pace and his 6-88 took his side to a hair's breadth of a second win. If he thought this was cruel there was much worse to come. Umpires Kitchen and Dunne will never be on Donald's Christmas card list after compounding a number of earlier errors by allowing Atherton to stay when out, caught behind.

Seething, he bellowed down to Atherton "You'd better be ready for what's coming, because there'll be nothing in your half." With England chasing 247 to win this might well have been the inspiration required but the result was a mass of violent short-pitched balls which endangered Atherton's health rather than his wicket. A dropped catch by Boucher compounded the misery. When the initial burst was survived on the final morning the storm blew out and the pain of an injured ankle rose above the effects of cortisone and adrenaline. It had been a bad-tempered match as rival captains Cronje and Alec Stewart both refused to blink first. Donald criticised the umpires to the press and could have been suspended for the final Test although by autobiography time he was saying that blaming events on the umpires was 'a red herring'. Ian Wooldridge wrote in the *Daily Mail*: 'Some decisions were so arbitrary that it was more like watching Russian Roulette.' It had been wonderful theatre but many thought it had crossed the lines of what was cricket.

At the forefront of the confrontation, swearing and sledging, was the warrior Donald, like a painted henchman for Mel Gibson's *Braveheart*. Pollock was an altogether different kettle of fish, a cold fish even. Despite his shock of red hair his temperament was cool and calm. The tearaway youngster who wanted to bowl faster than his dad had become the responsible young cricketer who wanted his country to win. Where Donald was all action, Pollock was, well, normal. His approach to the wicket, his action, his method were all those of a pragmatist in the manner of McGrath. But there was nothing dull in the batsmen's response or the results.

Persistence and accuracy were his great assets and a brain that he used to great effect. Sometimes it seemed as if he had been bowling all day, had taken a wicket every hour, on the hour and had barely conceded a run. If there was a criticism it could be that he sometimes went into his shell when Donald was rampaging, but that's like feeding the strike to an inspired Gilchrist or Virender Sehwag – why not? But he could step up when the responsibility fell on his shoulders and he could increasingly do it with the bat as well as ball. He was never going to be Kallis but it's a slight disappointment that he finished his career with a Test batting average of 'only' 32.3. He was a better batsman than that but bowling and, later, captaincy responsibilities could weigh heavily, not to mention his pivotal role in the one-day side.

Despite Pollock taking plenty of responsibility in the series' decider at Headingley the result was South Africa in the late nineties in microcosm. Having knocked over England in the first innings for 230 they failed to build a big lead. Again England were pushed down, this time for 240, leaving an eminently gettable 219 to win. Pollock had led the attack first time round and was unfortunate to take only three, in the second he equally shared all 10 with Donald. In a game of few runs his 5-53 from 35 overs, including four specialist batsmen, was his best of the tour when the pressure was its most intense and with his partner still feeling his ankle. Then South Africa lost five quick wickets and on the last day needed 34 to win with Donald and Pollock now batting. Darren Gough was too strong and Pollock was left stranded. If the extra half hour had been claimed the previous evening it could have been very different, Stewart had very cleverly hoodwinked the umpires who should have known better.

The level of sledging had reached new heights, Boucher and Dominic Cork being particularly witless culprits and it was left to Gary Kirsten to sum it all up to Donald:

> "I'm sorry, Al, after the efforts of you and Shaun this morning that was unacceptable. It's been a poor effort from us all series, we've let you down."

It was a heartbreaking last Test appearance in England for Donald. He had, like many of the team, set his heart on returning to the home of cricket and showing who was now boss. Pollock would get another crack.

No such trouble with West Indies – a divided and depressed team were whitewashed, Donald and Pollock picking up 52 cheap wickets. It was statistically their most prolific series together but they took no great joy in beating a team in dire straits. For Donald there was the worry of further injury; after remedial work on his ankle, his hamstring limited his effectiveness in the last two matches. Pollock had a breeze, five-wicket hauls in the first three games and far-and-away the best bowler on either side.

Over the next three years South Africa were very hard to beat in Test cricket. A total of 30 Tests in 10 series resulted in 16 games and nine series won. India, New Zealand and Zimbabwe were beaten home and away, England at home, West Indies away and Sri Lanka at home with just a drawn away series in Sri Lanka spoiling the sequence. Pollock played every game and assumed the captaincy midway as the depth of Cronje's duplicity was revealed. He took 133 wickets at 18.3 and ascended to a rating of 900 and the position of number-one bowler in the world. For three years he never dropped lower than second. Six five-wicket hauls failed to inspire writers outside South Africa, and even many in South Africa. A 10-wicket bag against India was 'accurate and incisive' but, as ever, he was damned with faint praise. Against New Zealand his 5-33 was lost behind praise for Steve Elworthy; 5-28 against West Indies was hidden behind the plaudits for Walsh in his last Test. It seemed that Pollock was fated to remain unappreciated even when driving his country forward with ball, bat and tactics.

Allan Donald was still firing, but not on all cylinders. Injuries increasingly were eating into his appearances (just 17 in those 30 Tests) although he could still be very effective, his 65 wickets costing 21.6 each. In his frequent absences Pollock rose to the challenge. Against Sri Lanka Donald took four quick wickets in the first hour and largely settled the game. When accused of losing his 'zip' he immediately took 5-40 against India.

The pair did have one great game together, against England at the Wanderers at the beginning of the 1999-00 series which finished with the ugly farce of Cronje's one-innings fix. The new-look and optimistic England side met with men on a mission who had not forgotten how things had been the previous year. Within half an hour the visitor's best-laid plans lay in tatters as they were reduced to 2-4. The pitch was helpful but Donald and Pollock were unstoppable as South Africa cruised to an innings' victory in just over three days. Nineteen wickets were shared by the 'peerless new-ball pairing of Donald and Pollock'; narrowly missing out on becoming only the seventh pair to bag the full haul. In the words of Mike Selvey 'It was chilling, clinical, merciless and utterly irresistible.'

But if the South Africans thought they were a world-beating

juggernaut the proof would only come by beating Australia. Three-Test back-to-back series commencing on Boxing Day 2001 would be the ultimate examination and maybe provide a fitting end to the career of Donald. It was most definitely not to be; there was no magical swansong as South Africa were torn apart by an Australian side bent on punishing a team having the temerity to challenge their superiority. Neither South Africa nor their opening bowlers went down fighting.

Without Donald the first Test was lost by 234 runs, with Donald the second was lost by nine wickets and the third by 10. It was a shellacking of the highest order. South Africa had made great strides but the gap to the top was enormous. Donald and Pollock had 12 wickets between them; McGrath had 14 on his own although this was partly an indication of the relative batting strengths of the two teams.

Just six weeks later the two teams reconvened at the Wanderers and things got worse for the home side, the second heaviest Test defeat in history. Pollock missed the game and Donald broke down with a hamstring injury and promptly announced his retirement. His body had let him down once again and with Australia way out in front the need to try and chase had disappeared. Pollock's response was immediate.

> "He was an awesome performer for us over the years, leading the South African attack for the best part of a decade. He was a remarkable athlete, a brilliant bowler and it was a privilege to play with him. I enjoyed a good partnership with Allan and our different styles complemented each other well."

A full seven years and many wickets later the time came for Pollock to retire too after enjoying a successful partnership with Ntini. Damien Fleming wrote shortly afterwards:

> 'As with Hadlee, Pollock stalked batsmen. The keys to his bowling were accuracy and ability to always make the batsman play. He gained steep bounce from his 12 o'clock release, which helped the ball hit the bat high on the splice, and he could seam the ball awkwardly both ways. Steely determination and an unwavering self confidence were the keys to his consistency.'

Their partnership had been a thrilling ride and largely through their work South Africa rose steadily in the rankings. In 1999 Pollock described his relationship with Donald and it provides one of the best insights into combined work:

> "I can't overrate the benefit of having a strike bowler like Allan at the other end. We work in tandem, we discuss how we might bowl differently at different batsmen. I'm not at liberty to disclose what it is we do or how we make plans but we do discuss our pairing and how to go about getting batsmen out all the time."

A recording of this great pair plotting the imminent demise of Lara, Atherton, Tendulkar or Waugh would deserve a place in any museum of cricket history.

Donald and Pollock

Results

	Total	Won	Drawn	Lost
Donald	72	33	24	15
Pollock	108	49	32	27
Donald and Pollock	47	23	15	9

Test Bowling Overall

	Mat	Balls	Runs	Wkts	Ave	SR	ER	5W1/10WM
Donald	72	15519	7344	330	22.25	47.0	2.83	20/3
Pollock	108	24353	9733	421	23.31	57.8	2.39	16/1

Test Bowling Together

	Mat	Balls	Runs	Wkts	Ave	SR	ER	5W1/10WM
Donald	47	9763	4580	208	22.01	46.9	2.81	13/1
Pollock	47	10624	4093	189	21.65	556.2	2.31	9/0

Test Bowling Apart

	Mat	Balls	Runs	Wkts	Ave	SR	ER	5W1/10WM
Donald	25	5756	2764	122	22.66	47.2	2.81	13/1
Pollock	61	13729	5640	232	24.31	59.2	2.31	9/0

Best Series Together - West Indies 98-99

	Mat	Balls	Runs	Wkts	Ave	SR	ER	5W1/10WM
Donald	5	704	395	23	17.17	30.6	3.36	2/0
Pollock	5	1184	483	29	16.65	40.8	2.44	3/0

Best Test Figures - Innings/Match

Donald (with Pollock)	6-53 vs England, Johannesburg – 1999
Donald (with Pollock)	11-127 vs England, Johannesburg – 1999
Donald (without Pollock)	8-71 vs Zimbabwe, Harare – 1992
Donald (without Pollock)	12-139 vs India, Port Elizabeth – 1992
Pollock (with Donald)	6-50 vs Pakistan, Durban – 1998
Pollock (with Donald)	9-94 vs West Indies, Kingston – 2001
Pollock (without Donald)	7-87 vs Australia, Adelaide – 1998
Pollock (without Donald)	10-147 vs India, Bloemfontein – 2001

YouTube Bowling Highlights

Search Phrases (sic)
Allan Donald hostile spell to the Waugh brothers, 2nd test SCG 1997/98
Shaun Pollock 7/87 vs Australia 1997/98 3rd test Adelaide
Allan Donald 5/40 vs India - 1st test, 1st innings Durban 1996

The Modern World

If the spin masters of the late-20th century had reinvigorated an interest in the art of the finger or the wrist then bringing this into the new century was helped by the continuing brilliance of Warne and Muralitharan. Both men comfortably top the wicket-taking tables of their respective countries since 2000.

As the interchangeable threesome of McGrath with either Brett Lee or Jason Gillespie began to falter, Australia were able to call on a variety of more than able replacements. No long-term partner was ever found for Mitchell Johnson whose career itself suffered from a number of fallow spells mixed in with performances worthy of the very best fast bowlers the country had ever produced. The situation facing Sri Lanka was more complex. For so long reliant on the skills of Murali, in the way New Zealand had been on Hadlee 20 years before, there was a yawning gap which Rangana Herath manfully tried to fill but with predictably-partial success.

The other Asian countries relied heavily on spin. Perhaps Pakistan might have found another potent left-right combination without the absurd and obscene Lord's no-ball and all that lay behind it. As it was three of their four most successful bowlers were spinners. The same figures applied to India with only Zaheer Khan and Ishant Sharma breaking the dominance of the slow men. Part of the problem for any quick bowler in India has been breaking into a team that has two spinners of such class that they are virtually undroppable, leaving little room to experiment with pace.

The increasing influence, not to say dominance, of limited-overs cricket has also ironically led to rejuvenation in slow bowling. Where once it seemed that new forms of cricket might kill the spinner, it's now clear that taking pace off the ball is a valid form of economical bowling, particularly with stringent rules governing wides and no-balls. Both quick and slow bowlers rely more on variation than any other skill and the idea of straightforward fast bowling in T20 cricket has vanished into the ether. A snick, a ramp or a deflection means a boundary.

Daniel Vettori was another spinner to top his country's table although there were certainly times when Tim Southee and Trent Boult have looked as good as any new-ball pair New Zealand have possessed barring Hadlee and any one of Danny Morrison, Ewen Chatfield or Lance Cairns.

Three countries, however, have failed to find the real spin deal and have relied primarily on quick bowlers. England have been the least guilty, boasting Graeme Swann and Monty Panesar, but for nine years Jimmy Anderson and

Stuart Broad have been a redoubtable pair in the best tradition of great quick bowlers. Perhaps neither of them ever had that furious burst of pace but Broad has proved time and again his ability to win Tests from nowhere while Anderson remained the constant reliable, except at Trent Bridge for Broad's career-defining 8-15. Once retired they will certainly deserve their place amongst those in this book.

In the almost complete absence of spin, South Africa have been the most prolific fast-bowling nation over the last 30 years. Shaun Pollock and Dale Steyn have stood at the centre but Allan Donald was the first and Makhaya Ntini, Jacques Kallis, Morne Morkel and Vernon Philander have provided support that was the envy of the world. Like Anderson and Broad, Steyn and Morkel would be a pair worth close consideration once the dust settles on their joint career. West Indies would have given anything for just one of these bowlers but with their cricket in a frightening decline over the last two decades nothing would be more welcome in world cricket than a pair of worthy successors to Marshall, Roberts and Ambrose.

The last named of these three was interviewed by the BBC just prior to England's first day/night Test in August 2017 and bemoaned the current lack of high-class fast bowling. With low slow pitches, big bats and short boundaries where is the temptation for any aspiring young man to bend his back said Sir Curtly, sadly.

Comparisons And Contrasts

Over the course of studying some of the leading pairs of fast bowlers in cricket history the question of 'hunting in pairs' being a reality or a worn cliché reinforced by erroneous received wisdom was not an easy one to answer.

It's a wonderful idea; two mates, full of respect and affection for one another, spend the evening before the game swapping tips before going out to share the new ball and the lion's share of the wickets. It does happen, only slightly less often than we would like to believe.

The increasing reliance on speed (and resurgence of spin) over the course of cricket history can be seen below by looking at the top 15 Test wickets-takers in each of the six eras used in this book.

	Spin	Medium	Fast Medium	Fast
Before the Lights Went Out:	7	6	1	1
Between the Wars:	7	3	3	2
Fifties and Sixties:	5	2	3	4 (plus Sobers)
Snow to Babylon	3	1	4	7
End of Century:	3	0	7	5
The Modern World:	7	0	4	4

It was surprising when digging into the records of the selected pairs to find grounds to doubt their status as a two-man attack for posterity. Gregory and McDonald played together for less than a year, Hall had passed his best when joined by Griffith and Statham and Holding played as many games without Trueman and Roberts as they did with them. It's also noticeable that many of the 22 bowlers featured saved their best performances for the games in which their partners were absent. This is not to make any claim that they were better apart but in reality there are only 10 wickets to go round, something Walsh found frustrating in his early career.

What would really seal the argument in favour of pair-power would be some kind of rapport that enabled the two bowlers to transcend their individual abilities when working as team and thus making the whole greater than the parts. A number of possible working methods would, inevitably, lead to this scenario.

Sharing knowledge of the batsman's weakness.
Driving batsmen to despair with a relentless attack from both ends.
Offering contrasting and complimentary methods.
Setting up a batsman for the partner.
Friendship inspiring confidence.
Rivalry inspiring greater effort.
Off-the-field rapport.

There is plenty of evidence that many of the above points relate closely to the 11 pairs under study but not all and not every time. While the choice of pairs is not made on the basis of statistics it would be foolish to ignore them and for this the inevitable home is a 2011 article for *Cricinfo* by S Rajesh.

Firstly he lists the top 15 new-ball pairs by average that took at least 100 wickets each. On top are Malcolm Marshall and Joel Garner; the simple reason for excluding them here is that they only managed just over 100 wickets apiece when paired in this way – less than a third of Marshall's total haul and half of Garner's. They were always more a part of a four-man attack than the leading pair with moderate support. Rajesh's list also includes Glenn McGrath with both Jason Gillespie and Brett Lee. The fact that McGrath was equally linked with both and his pairing with Shane Warne was the *real* deal diminishes his claims to a place here. Makhaya Ntini appears twice, with Dale Steyn and Shaun Pollock, but the latter's pairing with Donald discounts that one and Steyn is still playing and anyway his partnership with Morne Morkel carries more weight.

Rajesh then looks at pairs just outside the above restriction and then tweaks all his figures to accommodate averages during different eras. This doesn't throw up any major changes. While all these figures are of great interest none were convincing enough to alter the initial list of 11 pairs.

Gregory and McDonald

They can hardly be seen as one of the greatest pairs simply because they played so little together and their joint reputation rests on just one series. But they were the first and as such their names, along with that of the architect Warwick

Armstrong, will always be significant.

Lindwall and Miller

In some ways a carbon copy of Gregory and McDonald but their careers lasted 10 years longer and their influence and reputation carried to everywhere they played. Possibly Miller's lack of constant commitment and his preference for batting were a negative but their names are always linked, one the ever reliable and the other a brilliant man of moods.

Trueman and Statham

It is surprising that they only played 35 times together in nine years and that Trueman's average without Statham was eight runs better and that their best individual performances came when the other was missing. Injury and other issues also meant they were only the natural selection towards the end of those nine years.

Adcock and Heine

Individually neither was really from the top draw of fast bowling but they lacked nothing in aggression either individually or together. They gave their country something it had never had before and paved the way for an illustrious line of successors.

Hall and Griffith

The chucking reputation will always cloud the career of Griffith. Hall may well have been the most magnificent visual epitomy of fast bowling and at his best was very, very good. But their most famous series together, in England in 1963, did show that Hall was already in decline. He took 16 wickets at 33 while Griffith took 32 at 16.

Lillee and Thomson

The effect of these two on and off the field cannot be overestimated. The excitement of watching them in action drew crowds into the ground and lit a spark under Kerry Packer. Both were thrilling in their own ways and when they fired together there were none better. But Packer split them and both averaged better in games played apart.

Roberts and Holding

They led the way for the phalanx of Caribbean speedsters to follow and

Roberts, in particular, was a huge influence on the later generations. They led their country's bowling attack from the dark days of the 5-1 humiliation in Australia through 'grovel' into the age of domination largely before the four-pronged attack muddied the waters for later partnerships.

Imran and Sarfraz

A slightly unbalanced pairing as Imran was so clearly his partner's superior. With a bit more speed Sarfraz would have been an even better bowler but his stoic supporting work and the knowledge he imparted to Imran, which then trickled further down the line, gives him an equal share in the validity of this partnership.

Wasim and Waqar

An almost ideal pairing even if their personal relationship was sometimes fraught. They brought a newish method to fast bowling and polished and perfected it to a point that has often been copied but never, ever bettered. The left-right combination just adds to the mystique and added to the problems they caused for all batsmen.

Ambrose and Walsh

In some ways the perfect partnership. Close friends, they spent much of their careers fighting the decline in West Indies' fortunes. Resilient and almost injury free, they partnered one another 95 times, encompassing almost the whole career of Ambrose. Supportive and offering contrasting methods it is hard to imagine a better pair, especially as they were individually amongst the greats.

Donald and Pollock

In some ways they remain a frustrating pair. While Donald was at his thrilling best Pollock was establishing himself and by the time Pollock had moved to the top of the tree Donald was in decline. But they did put in some mighty joint efforts even if they could never disturb Australia's position of superiority.

Jimmy Anderson and Stuart Broad must in due course be added to the above 11 pairs. Barring injury they seem certain to complete 100 Tests together during England's tour of Australia in 2017-18 with their wicket count climbing towards 800. Mike Atherton would have them as Broad and Anderson for the sound and rhythm of the thing but it should be the other way round. In most cases the better bowler is named first, where it's hard to be sure then the senior partner should win out as in Roberts and Holding or Gregory and McDonald.

Anderson and Broad seem to have all the attributes of a great pair far beyond their statistics. Mates who help one another with a healthy rivalry that drives each on. When one is bowling the other is invariably at mid-on or mid-off offering advice and encouragement. Off the field the talk continues. This is as it should be, it's called teamwork.

Acknowledgements

James Mettyear for read-throughs, general encouragement and endless chit-chats.

Stephen Chalke for politely dissing the first draft of the first completed chapter and waking me up.

David Frith for looking over drafts and providing many pictures.

Dave Wilson for proofing, fact checking and his love of the game.

Rebecca Ferriday for support and patience above and beyond realistic expectations.

Lena Ferriday for sending me her undergraduate essays so I can see how a real historian writes.

Romy Ferriday for 'top banter' and showing refreshingly little interest in my writing.

All the authors whose books and articles I've consulted.

All the cricket nuts who put amazing things on the internet.

My co-authors on *Masterly Batting* and *Supreme Bowling* who taught me so much about so much.

Above all, to 22 special bowlers who expended so much energy so that I could wonder at, and write about, them.

Picture Credits

Gregory, McDonald, Lindwall, Adcock, Heine, Griffith, Lillee, Thomson, Sarfraz, Walsh – David Frith Archive

Miller, Trueman, Wasim, Waqar, Ambrose, Donald, Pollock – TopFoto

Hall, Holding, Imran – PA Images

Statham, Roberts – VK Images

Index

A

C

I

J